D0299269

# Teaching Skills in Further & Adult Education

# City & Guilds Co-publishing Series

City & Guilds has a long history of providing assessments and certification to those who have undertaken education and training in a wide variety of technical subjects or occupational areas. Its business is essentially to provide an assurance that pre-determined standards have been met. That activity has grown in importance over the past few years as government and national bodies strive to create the right conditions for the steady growth of a skilled and flexible workforce.

Both teachers and learners need materials to support them as they work towards the attainment of qualifications, and City & Guilds is pleased to be working with several distinguished publishers towards meeting that need. It has been closely involved in planning, author selection and text appraisal, although the opinions expressed in the publications are those of the individual authors.

City & Guilds is fully committed to these publications and is pleased to commend them to teaching staff, students and their advisers.

### City & Guilds/Macmillan titles

Ann Castling, *Competence-based Teaching and Training*
Chris Cook, *Assessor Workbook*
Harriet Harper and Ann Meadows, *Advanced GNVQ Information Technology*
Jim Kelly, *Intermediate GNVQ Manufacturing*
David Minton, *Teaching Skills in Further & Adult Education*
Graham Morris and Lesley Reveler, *Retail Certificate Workbook* (Levels 1 and 2)
Peter Riley (consultant editor), *Computer-aided Engineering*, and associated Workbooks: *CNC Setting and Operation; CNC Part Programming; Computer-aided Draughting; Robot Technology; Programmable Logic Control; Drawing Standards for CAE*
Caroline Wilkinson, *Information Technology in the Office*
Barbara Wilson, *Information Technology: the Basics*

For full details of these and other Macmillan titles, please contact Customer Services, Macmillan Press, Houndmills, Basingstoke, Hampshire RG21 6XS.

# Teaching Skills in Further & Adult Education

David Minton

City&
Guilds MACMILLAN

First published 1991
Reprinted five times
Revised edition 1997
Published by
MACMILLAN PRESS LTD
Houndmills, Basingstoke, Hampshire RG21 6XS
and London
Companies and representatives
throughout the world

ISBN 0–333–69587–9

A catalogue record for this book is available
from the British Library.

This book is printed on paper suitable for recycling and
made from fully managed and sustained forest sources.

10   9   8   7   6   5   4   3
06  05  04  03  02  01  00  99

Printed and bound in Great Britain by
Antony Rowe Ltd, Chippenham, Wiltshire

# Contents

# Part 2 Developing the Learning Programme 99

# Preface

Many people who come in to teaching in adult and further education may be entering an unfamiliar world, since not only is teaching very different from being a student but also the context in which teaching occurs has been subject to great change and development in recent years. This new edition takes due account of developments since the book was originally written. The emphasis, however, remains the same: it sets out to provide effective guidance and support for new teachers whatever the context they may be working in.

Teachers are responsible for the learning programmes of their students and should also be concerned for their personal development. In defining competence in the design and implementation of learning programmes, I set out what I believe to be good practice. To implement good practice need not be difficult, but it does require commitment.

Most new teachers receive support and guidance when they join a team in an institution, but there may be those who are less fortunate. Colleges also offer effective programmes of teacher training such as the City & Guilds Further and Adult Education Teachers' Certificate with support from tutors, mentors and peer-group colleagues. This book is intended to supplement such programmes, but may be used independently as a valuable resource by teachers working on their own, as well as by those who can benefit from shared learning and group activities.

Whatever the content of the teaching programme and wherever the context of the teaching, I trust the book will prove an exciting and reliable companion and guide as you explore your new role as a teacher.

DAVID MINTON

# Acknowledgements

I gratefully acknowledge the help, insights and guidance I received from Anne Castling during the preparation of this new edition. Her comments, suggestions and overall contribution have been invaluable, particularly for the chapter dealing with Assessment and Testing where so much has changed in recent years. Nor would the book have been possible without the expertise and good humoured persistence of my editor, Anne Webster.

Geoff Jones and John Temple formed a tutoring team for the City & Guilds Further and Adult Education Teachers' Certificate with me. Their creativity and critical judgements focused my thinking while I was writing the first edition. I was privileged to work with a remarkably able group of moderators during the rapid changes that occurred in further education during my years with City & Guilds; and I am also grateful for the support of City & Guilds officers.

Indeed, most of what is contained in this book I learned from students and colleagues with whom I worked for more than thirty years in the UK, and also in Africa, America and Asia. Some of them appear fleetingly in the case studies. Their willingness to share their experiences with new teachers through the pages of this book will undoubtedly encourage those teachers greatly.

The author and publishers wish to thank the following for permission to use copyright material:

Geoff Croxon, for the cartoon on page 3.

Fran Chard, for her description of the 'Sculpting' activity.

The table on page 160 is derived from a paper presented in 1989 to the Industrial Society by ECA of London.

Tony Buzan for material from *Use Your Head*, BBC Books, 4th edn, 1995.

Federal Publications (S) Pte Ltd for two cartoons from *Fun With Chinese Characters* by T. H. Peng, 1980.

Every effort has been made to trace all the copyright holders, but if any have been inadvertently overlooked the publishers will be pleased to make the necessary arrangements at the first opportunity.

# Part 1

# *Effective Class Teaching*

# Introduction: The Teacher's Role

*EJ and Spot*

We can almost feel EJ's frustration.

Few come to teaching without any experience, although they may not consciously be aware of having had a go at it. People do enjoy teaching others: children, friends, parents, adults, subordinates, dogs, cats, lions. They 'get a kick out of it'.

They feel they have knowledge or skills, something to share. Often they have an enthusiasm for something, or experience to communicate. Usually it is in an ordinary social context, such as wishing to make others feel jealous, perhaps about the great place they've been to on holiday: 'if you go, you must see . . .'. Or in role-modelling: children copying their parents' household tasks or leisure pursuits.

EJ's attitude is typical. 'I can whistle, you can too. You simply do this!'

How many teachers are satisfied with just having got through what they set out to teach without finding out if the students learned anything at all? What's wrong here?

Spot didn't learn to whistle; why? Was it the way EJ set about teaching him? Would EJ have been more successful if he had used a different technique? Does the dog have a problem EJ does not understand, or does not want to understand?

Who says Spot should whistle anyway? Is it for EJ or for Spot? Is EJ concerned with Spot's achievement or only with his own? Is Spot motivated to learn? How could EJ motivate him? Would it help if he whipped the dog, or fed him chocolate? Is EJ expecting Spot to do something he is incapable of doing, or sees no point in doing?

We could ask so many similar questions. Teaching can be the most fulfilling and the most frustrating of human activities. But we should always ask: who is it for?

3

*REMEMBER!*
*... A teacher's prime task is to engage the student in the learning process. What the student does to learn is more important than what the teacher does to teach.*

# Observing

Have you watched parents with a small child? Perhaps you have brought up children of your own. Parents watch and guide their child constantly. They shape its growth. They inhibit antisocial and dangerous behaviour. They encourage the child to achieve skills and understanding, and to develop certain attitudes. They surround the child with actions, words and objects that stimulate responses from the child. And they learn themselves by experience how to get the 'right' response. In fact, they are creating, usually quite unknowingly, a learning environment for themselves and their child. They are learning the job, and growing with it both as people and as parents.

Watch a very young child explore its environment. Then observe older children and adults, and make some comparisons.

*REMEMBER!*
*... The first important skill a teacher needs to develop is the ability to observe behaviour in a learning environment.*

# Exploring

What do you do when you go into a new place? meet new people? arrive in a new town or country? shop in a new store? **You explore.**

Watch the people who come into your class for the first time. What do they do? **They explore the environment.**

They will probably look for clues as to how to behave there, who the other people are, where to sit, what to wear, and so on. The classroom environment is full of such information: the way the furniture is arranged, what it is like, the equipment in the room, the dress of the teacher and the other students, information on the walls and in books – or lack of it.

Why do they look for such clues? Perhaps so that they can modify their own behaviour to fit, avoid being 'out of place'. They want to feel comfortable there.

You can watch them explore their learning environment and gradually adjust to it. And you can take control of what happens if you want to.

*REMEMBER!*
*... The basic learning activity is exploring: finding out.*

# Teaching and learning

As the teacher, what is your part in the learning activity?

This book is primarily concerned with exploring the role of teacher. Teaching is a learning experience for the teacher as much as for the students. You need to use every teaching session as an opportunity to learn: to watch student behaviour and assess the learning that occurred so that you can improve the learning experiences for them. We call this process **evaluating**.

The book is intended to act as your guide: to provide signposts and suggested itineraries, things to do and things to look out for, to help you establish good practice.

In undertaking the teaching of adults you are embarking on a most exciting journey of discovery, of yourself and others, that will last as long as you continue teaching. There will be no point at which you can say confidently, 'That's it! I've got it! I'm now a fully competent teacher.' But if you learn from the experience of teaching you will achieve confidence and skill. You will understand more about how people learn.

The more you understand people, dealing with them, involving them in the excitement of their own self-discovery and learning, the more they will surprise and fascinate you. There is no limit to the fascination of people. That is the great joy of teaching.

# Questions

The book is about questions.

Questions alert the brain: look out! new information is coming. A child is full of questions. In order to learn our brains must be alert, searching, looking for answers to questions.

Many textbooks are only about answers – and frequently the reader is not told the questions to which these are the supposed answers. They set out to provide short cuts, to eliminate the necessity of thinking.

Teaching is a journey of discovery – discovery about yourself and other people. You have come for the journey, for the challenge of thinking things through and of problem-solving, for the satisfaction of being effective as a teacher, and doing a good job.

If the book closes down your curiosity and your eagerness to learn more, it will have failed in its purpose.

# Cycles

The establishment of good practice means a repeated cycle of preparation, teaching and review. The questions become more searching and more interesting as you come back to them.

When you have observed what people do, you will want to know why they do it. If you set about asking them, you will receive quite complicated answers. You will want to get behind these answers to underlying motivation, to 'real' reasons, and so to value systems, fears, anxieties and social pressures.

---

**CASE STUDY 1**

---

Carol had a Saturday morning class of people who wanted to learn wordprocessing, databases and spreadsheets. The group included both men and women, aged between their middle twenties and late forties. A few were experienced typists; some were parents with children in local schools; some worked in offices or in retailing; two were self-employed. They were all motivated by the need to get to grips with the introduction of computer technology into their home or working lives. Some were afraid that they would not be able to cope at work or help their children.

They showed a great deal of anxiety.

Think about these questions:

1  What do you think they were anxious about?
2  How would that affect what they did and their learning?
3  What would you do to help them if you found yourself in the same position as Carol?

---

# Comment

It is important to know what it feels like to be in the situation of the students in the class. If you understand how they feel, and the barriers and anxieties they bring with them, you will be able to help them overcome the barriers and learn successfully.

We each have a perception of ourselves, our status, our potential or lack of it: our self-image. American education, for instance, values a good self-image highly; a great deal of effort goes into improving it.

If you cut down a mature tree, you can count the growth rings year by year. You can distinguish the good years for growing from the bad years. Although the tree is largely what was determined by its genes at conception, it was shaped by accident and weather, by where its roots have sought nourishment, by the nutrients or poisons that it found, by disease or by competition with other trees.

People are far more complex than trees, but each is the result of how far environment and experience have promoted or inhibited growth, realised or stunted potential, and shaped his or her self-image.

For many, formal education has failed to stimulate their creativity and damaged their self-confidence. It has convinced them that, compared with others, they are stupid or at least not clever, and so engendered mental blockages. Many adults have a fear of formal education, teachers and exams. They have developed complexes and barriers to learning. One of the great delights of adult education is to see students make quite startling discoveries about themselves.

You will probably learn as much about yourself as about anything else as you reflect on the experiences of teaching that you will undertake, and work through the activities and tasks in this book.

# Models

Learning is unstoppable.

You learn all the time – otherwise you could not cope with new situations as they arise. If you did not learn, you could not deal with the world. You would constantly stub your toe on the same step or burn your fingers, miss the chair when you go to sit down, press the wrong button on the television set. Learning is also cumulative. Once you have dealt successfully with an experience you find it easier the next time you encounter a similar situation.

When we walk into a room or encounter, say, a new machine for the first time, we look for clues to help us to categorise it. We have 'models in the head' about most things. They enable us to learn quickly how to deal effectively with the new place or machine or people.

Where do our models come from, including our models of ourselves? We are constantly creating them and modifying those that we already have from our experiences.

We hardly have to think about it usually. We instantly recognise a room as, for instance, a sitting room or a kitchen. Equipment and layout tell us how we are to behave there. We do this by transferring learning from one experience and context to another.

It is not true, however, that when we consciously set out to learn something, we can always do it easily. Why the difference? Why is it often apparently hard to learn things? There must be special factors at work preventing learning from happening.

One reason is the way, already mentioned, that the past experience of many people has unfortunately convinced them that they will not be able to deal with it very easily, if at all. They have formed a poor self-image and created barriers that stop them from learning.

As teachers we can improve learning by bringing the process to the surface so that we can look at it. We can try to understand what is going on for the students and for us. We must try to see it, and feel it, from the students' point of view.

Reflecting on our own learning experiences will help us to do that – for example, how we felt on our first day at work: what happened for us, and how we changed as we learned.

# Growth through experience

We talk about growing with the job. Learning is growth through experience. We need to grow as teachers and stimulate growth in our students. There is no short cut. Of course, some grow and flourish more quickly than others do. This is not simply a matter of luck. It is more a readiness to learn – to reflect on experience and to explore alternative methods and approaches. It may depend on creative problem-solving, ability to adapt and willingness to take risks.

It depends crucially on our belief in ourselves.

## *REMEMBER!*
*. . . Maturation is an important part of learning processes that cannot be hurried.*

# 1 How to Use the Book: Learning Through Activity

*REMEMBER!*
*... Learning is most effective at a point of need.*

Learning requires activity on the part of the learner. You have to do something in order to learn. Reading is one such activity. But when we read, our concentration span is often quite short and so we soon stop taking things in. We need to pause frequently and review what we have read – to try to process it for ourselves in some way. There has to be time for it to become part of our own perception.

You will find learning activity in every section of the book. Some learning activities require simply a change of approach, variety in what you are doing; some ask you to do something – to get up and do it – such as rearranging furniture to improve the environment where you or students are attempting to learn.

It is important to do these things. It is the way to learn, and the way to develop competence.

There is a pattern in the learning programme in the book. The learning activities are integrated into that programme. Undertake them as soon as you can after you have read the appropriate section. They relate to two aspects of learning.

1 The first, described as **Activities**, concerns your own needs and self-discovery. They will enable you to explore your strengths and to build up confidence, skill and understanding, and will help you get yourself properly organised and working in methodical and efficient ways. Activity 1, below is an example.

2 The **Tasks** focus on your preparation for teaching: these will help you develop the good practice to be effective.

3 In addition, **Case studies** are set out with questions to draw out the lessons that may be learned. Merely reading the case studies will not extract the benefit that may be had from using the experience of others. You must think about what happened and why, and compare that experience with your own. It is even better if you can share your thinking in a peer group discussion.

## ACTIVITY 1

# Your model of teaching

You come to teaching with your own 'model in the head' of what teachers do and why, and of how learning happens for the students.

You will also have feelings about what you want to learn from any book on teaching or from training sessions you may attend.

Learning is change of many things including knowledge and ideas, beliefs and attitudes, insights, skills, habits, approaches that we make to our work and to other people, our self-image. We need to monitor these changes in ourselves and our students.

To observe change we have to know what the initial state is that is to grow and change. We also need to bring to the surface what we think and how we behave in order to have a view of it.

So it is important to work through the following questions **now** before you read on.

1   What do you consider to be the role of the teacher of adults?
2   Analyse and explain your 'model in the head' of teaching and learning and how they relate to each other. (It may help if you describe students in a context that is familiar to you: how the class works, and what are the expectations of both students and teacher.)
3   Write down what you feel you need to learn in order to be an effective teacher of adults. Decide what your priorities will be, with your reasons.
4   If you have the opportunity, try to explain your model to a group of others and respond to their questions. You may also have the chance to listen to accounts by others of their 'models of teaching'. You may be surprised at what different ideas there are; and different expectations from a book or a course of training.

## TASK 1:   Building up teaching materials

You will need to keep materials in order and develop a system to file your work. This can be done using ring binders or boxes.

It is a good idea to have a file for your own learning materials, such as completed tasks in this book and other materials you will want to gather. These should be filed in date order so that you can later reflect on your own learning by reviewing your work.

You will need another file for lesson plans and teaching/learning materials.

You should also have a box-file for the audio-visual aids (AVA) and other resource materials you use or gather together for your classes.

# Learning paths and maps

You must tackle learning a bit at a time, in digestible amounts. But these will only make sense if they link in successfully to what you have already learned and to your perception of things – your world as a whole. Your perceptions will change with time.

You will find in any case that you and your students select, quite unconsciously, from whatever learning experiences you provide. You (and they) select those bits you can make sense of and can link with present knowledge and understanding. The rest will probably be ignored, at least for the present.

For example, you can easily overwhelm your brain with information about the assessment of student learning. You will find that when you actually need to assess what your students have learned in a particular context, you will search for an appropriate method. By using that method, even if you do it quite badly, you will come to some understanding of how it works; you are then ready to try to explore assessment processes in more detail.

This book has been designed to plot a learning path and to guide you through it. But all individuals have specific needs, and each will modify the design and use it in a way that suits them. That is inevitable.

Consider again exploring an unfamiliar town or building or store. You may start by looking at a map. The map is an abstraction. It made perfect sense to the person who drew it. But it may only really make sense to you *after* the experience of visiting the place. We can use a map to help us explore physically and so come to understand both the town and the map.

A design–plan is understood thoroughly only if you make something following the instructions in the plan, whether it is a dress pattern, a recipe for a pudding or a drawing of a machine part.

The same is true of a book of this kind. To undertake any task in teaching – or in anything else – you must define the task. This involves asking appropriate questions and seeking information. If we ask the wrong questions, or the wrong kind of questions, our perceptions of what we are about are likely to be distorted.

The book should enable you to identify questions in relation to the tasks that teaching requires. These become more searching as experience increases and you encounter new contexts and different groups of students.

# Growth cycles

Learning and growth are cyclical. We constantly revisit areas of experience, redo the same tasks, practise the same skills. We grow to be a whole person through this experience.

The learning programme in the book reflects cyclical reality. Learning will be more successful if you undertake the Activities and Tasks in the order set out in the book. There is an order of precedence in which we need to accomplish things. But nothing is once for all. Every group and every class you teach should be approached through repetition of the Tasks: it is by repetition that we embed good practice.

To learn, we need to know what it is we are setting out to learn. Afterwards we need to revisit the learning to fix clearly in our minds what has been learned, and so link it to other learning.

*REMEMBER!*
*... A teacher's prime task is to engage the student in the learning process. The student must take an active role in order for learning to occur.*

# The structure of the book

The book is in three parts, related to increasing responsibility.

Part 1 assumes that you will be responsible for ensuring effective learning for a learning group, whether it be a class, a workshop or a ward. It is concerned to establish the way of setting about the job, the good practice. To do that you have to understand certain principles and you must develop confidence and other positive attitudes. You need to take control of your own learning and of the conditions under which your students will learn.

To help you, there is advice on 'micro-lessons'[1] with a peer group, as part of a course programme perhaps, to gain insight and confidence. You are then guided through the various aspects of what is involved in dealing with your own students: preparation, running the class, controlling what happens and the environment, communication and the use of feedback and assessment. Good practice is defined through performance criteria – to provide a model in the head of what you are trying to achieve. There is considerable emphasis on evaluating your teaching and on what happens for you and your students.

Part 2 builds on the learning in Part 1, but requires greater depth and breadth. It develops as a case study of your own learning as you design and plan a learning programme for your students. The programme will develop over a defined time span, with a series of teaching sessions. By reflecting on what happens you build up your insight into your role. The purpose is constantly to refine and improve what happens.

The expected performance will be to more demanding standards than in Part 1, since there is growth and increasing maturity. There is much more advice in Part 2 on methods and approaches to help you.

Part 3 provides a survey of educational psychology and theories of learning as they have developed this century. The model of practice set out in the book is based on an understanding of these. I have chosen to present the theory after you have had enough experience to enable you to read it critically, and to compare it with what happens for you and your students. For this reason emphasis is placed also on developing your study skills. But the book is yours. You may wish to explore various parts in an order that meets your perception of what your needs are.

---

[1] A lesson is a structured and organised learning experience designed to achieve agreed learning goals: usually it is one of a sequence. In this book, the term micro-lesson is used to mean a simulated lesson with a peer group of student teachers, lasting between fifteen and thirty minutes. Its purpose is to promote development of the necessary behaviours of teachers set out here and in Chapter 4. Emphasis is placed on transferability of the learning to some 'real' context.

ASSUMPTIONS

The following assumptions are made about you as student and teacher.

1 You will be functioning in a teaching context where you can undertake tasks in relation to a real teaching situation.

2 You will have some responsibility for a learning group and for designing a learning programme/sessions for them.

3 You will have the opportunity to undertake teaching assignments, in order to develop your competences in the various aspects of the teaching process, and to match your ability against performance criteria.

4 You will have some opportunity to share with others in team and/or group work, so that you will get critical but supportive feedback on what you are doing.

5 You will be able to find a mentor who will support you.

6 You will be able to reflect on the learning and gradually build up a picture of good practice.

# 2 Learning to Learn: Developing Study Skills

*REMEMBER!*
*. . . Study skills are essential.*

To study successfully, you need to decide what you need to know or what it would help you to find out, where you can best and most easily find the information, and how to make the best use of it.

Teachers need to establish rules and a work-orientated environment for students in order to create positive working behaviour. What is true of students is true of our own behaviour.

No two people are the same, nor are the contexts of their work. And every learner must take responsibility for creating the conditions under which he or she will work and study. Major factors are:

- space-management
- time-management
- self-management.

## Space-management

You need personal territory for study, just as you need a kitchen for cooking. Make it easy. Like a carpenter, work with the grain of the wood. Get to know yourself and how you work best. Set out a territory, adopt a system that suits you and establish rules and a pattern to follow.

Not everyone is tidy. Some work better with clutter around them, and still seem to know where everything is. That is what matters. Don't waste energy and time looking for things when a need arises. A good idea or good thinking may disappear while you look. Many do find it easier to have a 'proper system' of shelves and files.

## ACTIVITY 2 | Preparation for study

Write down the things you will need to do where you study. How easy will it be to do them? You could be systematic about it, and make a table:

| Things to happen here | How easy? (ring your score) | | | | What I need to do |
|---|---|---|---|---|---|
| Reading | a | b | c | d | Have a reading lamp |
| Making notes | a | b | c | d | |
| Writing | a | b | c | d | |
| Wordprocessing | a | b | c | d | |

And so on.

Is there enough light to read by? What kind of light do you need? Poor light leads to eyestrain and tiredness. Will the chair be an upright hard chair? and if so, will it give back support if you use a wordprocessor? Or will it be an easy chair? Is there space to establish your territory, to spread out what you need? Will you need extra space on shelves, or room for a machine? Are things to hand when you need them? No carpenter would work without a bench and a tool rack.

# Distraction

You need to pay attention to what you are doing. Some people find 'wallpaper' music helps. Some work better in silence. Some prefer to look out on to a busy road, others choose a blank wall. Some find that looking at a wall makes them feel shut in; they will work better sitting on the other side of the desk with space in front of them. Colour has a strong effect on some people, pictures on others. Try things out; experiment to find what improves your sense of well-being. Things distract us, maybe irritating little things. Set aside specific time for yourself, so you can say 'this is my study time'.

# Goals or people: time-management

Brain behaviour appears to show pattern-making and rule-making. How goal-orientated are you? Can you shut out distraction and get things done? Or are you easily diverted?

Are you more person-centred or more goal-centred in the way in which you think and behave? If so, you may place greater value on human transactions than on tasks you need to do, and will find it hard to concentrate on what needs doing. How will you handle that?

Some people appear to be sequential in their behaviour, dealing with one thing at a time. Others are happier to have many things on the go at once. The table below compares the two kinds.

15

| Sequential people | Multi-task people |
|---|---|
| Try/do one thing at a time: time is tangible and divisible | Try/do many things at once: time is intangible and elastic |
| Concentrate on the job | Easily distracted; like interruptions |
| Take time commitment seriously, emphasise keeping to schedule | Think time commitment good, but put much more emphasis on human transactions |
| Emphasise promptness/timing: but only make casual, short-term relationships | Timing is flexible related to assessment of who it is: prefer long-term relationships |
| Strong preference for keeping to plans and getting the job done | Change plans/details easily and often: commitment is to people not to jobs |

Sequential people tend to plan by hours, set priorities and list actions: things to do and when. They do not find it hard to set targets and goals, and to concentrate on the job. In social affairs they tend to be punctual; they regard keeping to time as important, and they establish a schedule and stick to it. They have a strong preference for order and promptness, and are strongly goal-orientated. In social affairs, they make judgements about individuals in regard to time-keeping, promptness and punctuality. They find long-term relationships hard and suffer fools badly.

Multi-task people have an elastic view of time. Their goals are imprecise and confused by all the different tasks they have in hand. They tend to be distracted easily and invite interruptions – they may even create them themselves. They acknowledge system, schedules, agendas and deadlines as desirable but not pressingly important. They constantly change their decisions, plans and arrangements. They are interested in people, not the job, and in maintaining relationships: that is, they are strongly people-orientated.

You will no doubt recognise people you know of both these types. They tend to be intolerant each of the other. People, however, are tall or short – or any size in between. Honestly assess your own characteristics to help you get yourself organised.

Teachers need to be strongly people-orientated. They need to be able to establish relationships and commitment – to inspire trust and liking in their students. But to be a good manager you must get things done. Find a rhythm that will suit your personality.

**Time-management and stress-management are related.** Imposing schedules on yourself that are impossible for you, maybe because they do not fit with your personality or your style of working, can lead to stress. Equally, disorganisation is very stressful for the person who likes order. In the end it is much better to set targets and keep to schedules if you can, since stress increases with failing to do things that need doing. You must somehow develop goal-seeking behaviour.

Time is precious. Set yourself short-term goals. Plan ahead, but not more than three weeks ahead. Plan regularly, and revise your plan every day. Check where you are and what you need to do *now*.

## ACTIVITY 3 | Reflective diary

You cannot reflect on learning experiences you cannot remember.

Teachers need to be keenly aware of how learning happens for them if they are to help their students learn. As you explore the role of teacher, you need to monitor change as it occurs for you.

I once read in an examination script: 'The village school consisted of one teacher and seven other children.' There is real truth here! As a teacher you will be learning all the time:

- from decisions you make: what goes well and what goes badly
- what takes you by surprise
- what you find you can do easily or what proves hard
- what students do: what they find difficult or master easily
- what you observe and what you learn about yourself
- how people behave as individuals and groups
- sudden insights when your perception of something changes.

1  At the time these things happen, you need to make a note for yourself with the salient facts. Note too what you feel.
2  Keep a diary in which you record later reflections on your notes, while they are still fresh in your memory.
3  Later still, look back and see if your view has changed. See if it now forms part of a pattern that begins to make sense.
4  Later again, try to organise your learning experiences into some structures or patterns such as:

   student behaviour
   learning activities and teaching techniques
   important insights.

## The purpose of the diary

The principal purpose is to encourage you to reflect on learning experiences: what it felt like, what you observed, how it may have looked to others, and what you intend to do after you have thought about it.

What the diary is for is much more important than what it looks like. It must make sense to you when you come back to any entry. It can be in any form as long as it makes sense to you. You can write it or record it – on a pocket cassette recorder perhaps. It may be in a book or card index file or on a wordprocessor.

Date each entry so that you can monitor changes in the way you perceive things, so that you can see how your ideas develop with experience.

17

To see what this means try to recall a few occasions when you were acutely aware of having learned something – when your learning was accelerated. You might have said: 'Oh! I see it now', as something that was puzzling you fell suddenly into place, giving you a new way of perceiving it. This often happens. It is like the moment when we see the picture as we assemble a jigsaw puzzle. Perhaps you realised why someone you knew was behaving oddly, or you found out the purpose of the unlabelled button on the television set. Or you might have discovered something about yourself, an ability you did not know you had. You might have surprised yourself by tackling a problem: 'I didn't know I had it in me'.

---

## CASE STUDY 2

Once I was looking for a residential adult centre in an unfamiliar town. I had a map, which I had misinterpreted. I was sure the place was a large house approached up a drive behind a gate on to the road. That was my 'model in the head' of what I was looking for – what I expected to see. Two people I asked gave me directions, and I still walked straight past the place. Why? In fact it was part of a terrace of houses along the road. I did not see what I expected to see: I walked past it.

Consider occasions when you failed to see something. Why was that? What were you expecting to see?

---

# 3 Observing Other Teachers

## Class visit

1 Find a colleague or a teacher in a context you are familiar with: the more experienced the teacher, the better.

2 Negotiate with the teacher an opportunity to visit one class he or she is teaching. Students and teacher will need to know why you want to come and what you will be doing. Even experienced teachers may be a little reluctant to have an observer in the class. This is because any intruder into a class may be disruptive, even someone who just sits at the back and does nothing. Once groups form and gel, any visitor remains an outsider and affects group behaviour.

3 Find out as much as you can from the teacher, so that you have a view of the class before you visit it. Make a record along the following lines:

Date of visit:

Class and teacher:

The students:     male/female, numbers, ages, employment status, married/unmarried, and so on
any specific groupings (for example, motor vehicle trainees, playgroup leaders)
any other factors the teacher thinks important

The purpose:     relationship to any course, intended outcomes, qualifications aimed at, job prospects, who pays

The place:     what environment, special features/equipment

The time:     time of day, frequency of meeting, and so on

Learning goals for this class:

## The visit: building a picture

Armed with the above information, you can prepare for the visit.

When you visit someone's class, you need to make it clear to the teacher and students that you are going to avoid making value judgements as far as possible.

Your purpose is to share an experience with teacher and students: **to observe as accurately as you can what actually happens – what is going on in the class.**

Inevitably you, the teacher and the students will all have your own feelings about the experience. Quite often these strongly influence what happens.

**You are extending your experience by sharing that of others.** In order to do that, you have to be receptive and alert. You must arrive at the experience with a questioning attitude. You cannot simply be passive and 'let things happen'.

The information you have will help you to make sense of what you observe. It will help you to recognise what is happening in the class if you have a preliminary picture of it to take with you. Without it, you may miss important aspects of what is happening or be puzzled by what you observe.

Go armed with questions.

Set out below is a structure to enable you to get the most out of the experience. Discuss this beforehand with the teacher, who may point out things in relation to a particular context that may have been omitted from this set of questions, designed as they are for general application.

BUILDING UP A PICTURE

Make notes for yourself along these lines, but invent the questions you think are important.

| | |
|---|---|
| **Environment:** | room: size, condition, age, lighting, heating, etc. |
| | furniture/equipment: what is present, layout, desks or tables |
| | purpose: what is it designed for? what style of teaching/ learning? |
| | constraints: problems for learning activity |
| **Students:** | dress, groupings, age |
| | any things that surprise you |
| | relationships with the teacher/within and between the groups |
| **Activity:** | teacher activity |
| | student activity |
| | how they relate |
| | note timings and change of activity: movement, breaks and so on |

**Other:**

[Leave some space for post-experience comment.]

# Sharing perceptions

What you should take away from the experience is a picture that you can reflect on in private. This will arise partly from what the teacher tells you beforehand and partly from what you see. It is important, of course, to keep an open mind.

You need factual statements, rather than judgements. Avoid making notes such as: 'the students were bored' or 'were excited', or 'the teacher explained the topic very well'. You cannot know how the students felt or how they saw what the teacher did.

How far the environment, equipment, learning/teaching material and behaviour help or inhibit intended learning are judgements. Don't try to guess *why* the students or the teacher behaved as they did. Just note carefully *what* they did.

Factual statements concern such things as the environment, the dress of students and teacher, the equipment and resources used, and the behaviour of students and teacher – what they did, their level of activity, the sequence of events and so on: how learning was achieved, and what the students did in order to learn.

You want to observe what actually happens, rather than what you may go expecting to see. Just as I missed the adult centre because I was expecting to see a different kind of building, you may fail to see important things because you are looking for and expecting to see something else. This problem is worse if the context is very familiar.

But no two people will perceive the same experience in the same way. Each comes to it with an individual mind-set and questions. Clearly, we all select from what we hear, smell, touch and so on. It is just impossible to take it all in.

In discussion with the teacher after the experience, you can share and compare your perceptions of what took place. You can ask the questions that have occurred to you as you watched – about why certain things happened, maybe, and especially about student learning activity.

# Reflecting on the experience: consolidation

Avoid sharing your feelings with the teacher. You can explore your own feelings in your reflective diary, and later with a group of your peers if you have an opportunity.

To discover what you have learned you will have to wait a while, thinking about what happened, and getting it into perspective. *Then* try to set down what you have discovered. This will help to consolidate the learning. What does this mean?

We have to revisit an experience, we have to rehearse it again, in order to consolidate it in our memories. But we cannot do that unless we shape it some way – in pictures and in words. We may have visual memories and sounds, but usually we frame things and thoughts about them in words.

**Consolidation is this revisiting.** One of the most effective ways of revisiting an experience is to share it with someone else, tell them about it, and probably then respond to questions. Tell them what happened and how you felt about it. This is normal human behaviour.

# Using the peer group

It is very helpful to share the experience of observing a class with a group of your peers, and especially if they had similar experiences to tell you about. The effort you make to explain what you saw, heard and felt will concentrate and focus the experience for you.

## REMEMBER!
*... You will probably discover that you do not know what you think until you hear what you say.*

# Later reflection

Your views of what happened when observing that class will change with time and you should try to be aware of any changes in your perception. Telling the peer group and listening to their comments will help to bring these into focus.

Look at your previous comments in your diary. What has changed?

# 4 Micro-lessons or Peer Group Teaching

What are micro-lessons? What are they for? How should they work?

Once, in a restaurant in Villefranche in the Beaujolais, I had a dish of the most delicious garlic mushrooms. Madame ran the restaurant, Monsieur did the cooking. Foolishly, I asked Madame for the recipe.

'Monsieur, it is not what, it is who,' she said.

The difference between one dish of garlic mushrooms and another depends on who has cooked it. I had asked the wrong question. Asking wrong questions is what people do most of the time. They get unhelpful answers. **First find the questions.**

There are no foolproof recipes for a good lesson. There are only teachers. So we must concentrate on 'who'.

Teaching behaviour depends critically on teaching experience. Teacher educators have little control over real classes that teachers teach, so they choose to use simulations: here they can control what happens, what teachers are asked to do, and the conditions and pressures that they face.

It has become standard practice to set up simulations in training for anything. You probably know that airline pilots are trained on a simulator: a highly sophisticated, expensive piece of technological wizardry that puts the trainee through an experience that feels like the real thing. All the senses – sight, hearing, balance, movement – are used to create a grand illusion. The pilot is then put under stress. From normal take-off and landing, the pilot is made to deal with emergencies, engine failure and so on, to ensure that he or she will be able to cope whatever happens. Whenever a pilot changes from a familiar aircraft to another, from flying fighter aircraft maybe to civilian passenger planes, a simulator is used. A minimum number of flying hours must be clocked up before a certificate to fly is awarded, and it is much cheaper and more effective to do it on a simulator. (Of course, the trainees must also fly.)

With the realisation that present training and testing for car drivers do not prepare people at all adequately for real driving – indeed avoid putting them into situations that require rapid response and ability to cope under stress – there is a move to using technological simulators in this field too. If you have ever been on rides in theme parks such as Disney World, you will be aware of what it feels like to be in one of these things. I use the words 'feels like' because these methods are experiential; the trainee/participant goes through a learning experience. The simulation experiences are intended to change people's behaviour.

It is recognised that changing behaviour means changing not only what people do, but the way they think about it – their attitudes to themselves and the things they are asked to do. To take an extreme example: if I propose to walk across a plank suspended far above the ground between two high buildings, I must know that I can do it – I must have a belief in my ability. How do I get the knowledge or the belief unless I actually do it?

People learning to walk the tightrope start close to the ground and go on to using a safety net until they are confident enough to do without it. Someone who is frightened of water can't be taught to swim by being thrown into the deep end of a swimming pool; even if the victim survives, the fear is likely to remain.

The astonishing thing is that most people do cope with such an experience. People do survive their first terrifying drive on the motorway, where they have to react much faster, deal with so much more baffling information and suffer from so much more aggression than their training set out to prepare them for.

One effect can be that they learn bad behaviour, become equally aggressive say, or discover techniques to defend themselves from the dangers they perceive. These then inhibit good practice. We should think about that in relation to learning to teach.

As a way of learning, immersion has certain advantages. We do not usually make tiny steps in learning – we make leaps from one state of being to another. If we try to use a gradual approach, the learner usually gets way ahead of us and is likely to become bored. So long as my motivation to succeed is high enough, I can go through hell and high water. From the point of view of my self-image, succeeding against the odds, overcoming fear and solving problems is very effective. In the end I have to risk drowning in order to swim.

But there are bound to be casualties, since there is a level of risk. Who calculates the risk? What is an acceptable casualty rate? We reduce the risks as far as possible with airline pilots since the costs of failure are very high. But we accept a scandalous rate of failure and casualties on our roads. And what about our classrooms?

Air crashes are still put down to pilot error. However experienced pilots or brain surgeons are, they still have to take risks, and they make mistakes in their professional judgements.

We rely on professional judgements in pilots, doctors and teachers. The judgements they make are based on their knowledge and experience. They depend critically on the depth of that experience and the learning that has occurred as a result.

# Simulation in teaching

The simulations that teacher educators use vary widely. Their choice may well depend on their 'model in the head' of what teachers do – on assumptions they make about how learning happens or how it is transferred from one context to another.

There was a fashion in teacher education to analyse teaching into an array of teacher skills, which could be developed and perfected in isolation and then somehow brought back together into a 'global performance'. Micro-training is a better description of this training. Sophisticated set-ups were built at great expense to allow this to happen. A commonly used method was to use modelling: that is, allowing students to watch a teacher in a micro-session using the skills and then video-recording them practising the skill so that they could evaluate their performance against that of the model and so improve it.

But the problem of transfer to a real situation remained. Since the use of skills is only one part of what makes it possible for me to be effective in a given situation, I must integrate my skills with all the other things I need. In teaching, it is what the students do in order to learn that matters. A skilful performance by the teacher, impressive as it may be, will be of no value unless it also engages the students actively in learning.

Early arguments for 'competency training programmes' were based on the assumptions that underlie this approach to training. Since it is impossible, they say, to practise all the skills a teacher needs at once, let us develop them individually. There is, I believe, a misconception here of how changes in behaviour occur. If I practised for ever the individual skills needed to walk my plank between my two buildings (whatever I analysed them to be), when it came to setting off across the plank my fear of falling would drive my skills away. After all, I could walk across the plank easily without training if it were on the floor.

There is no doubt, however, that there are important skills that teachers need to acquire and practise. I believe they are best practised at a point of need – that is, with your own students. What then should we do in micro-lessons?

# Planning micro-lessons

The micro-lessons described here occur within a teacher peer group who are attempting to achieve agreed learning goals in a training programme.

## Purpose

What are micro-lessons for? There are many answers:

- to provide enrichment of the learning through sharing ideas
- to provide the opportunity to experiment and take risks
- to provide feedback by evaluating the effectiveness of what occurs
- to learn experientially as both student and teacher
- to challenge assumptions about how learning can be promoted
- to develop confidence and insight
- to encourage a creative, student-centred approach.

Each micro-lesson should be approached as a simulation of a real class but with constraints of time. It would not be sensible to ask your peers to role-play your students as they are in reality. Your peers have to be themselves. The 'teacher' must deal with the learning needs that they have, not those that some others might be supposed to have.

The constraints of time and place are real. They provide the same challenges as

25

in any other teaching situation: the production of teaching/learning material, the need to think through what is to happen, and the response and ability to adapt to feedback. But there is also a chance for formal feedback and evaluation from the 'students', to let you know how it felt for them, what worked and what didn't, what they learned and what they failed to learn.

You must learn from the experience as a whole. The intention is to create a class experience not dissimilar from the real thing. This is most important, since in a simulation what matters is to be able to transfer learning from the simulated experience to the real one. One should illuminate the other.

**One thing you might well learn is that learning can be fun.**

All this is easier to understand from examples. I am grateful to those students who have allowed me to use their ideas and to report on their micro-lessons.

---

## CASE STUDY 3

---

Sandra, a teacher of students with learning difficulties, thought about what she wanted her peer group to learn. This group was made up mostly of part-time teachers from a wide variety of backgrounds: nursing, hairdressing, motor vehicle work, catering, plumbing, engineering, computing and work with students like her own with learning difficulties and disabilities. Indeed, the advantages of groupwork of this kind derive from the richness of experience and challenge in the group.

It was clear to her that most of them had no experience of working with students like hers for whom learning is a much slower process. Sandra decided that if they were to find themselves working with such students they needed to know what it felt like to be unable to learn – and that she would put them through the experience.

She produced work-cards for each 'student' which gave simple instructions as to what each had to do – written in letters of the Greek alphabet. She also provided paper, patterns, scissors and so on, since they had to try to make something.

The class had fifteen minutes to complete the task on the work-cards: this was the time allowed for the micro-lesson. Sandra had thought carefully about the time constraint. She said nothing to them except that they should read what was on the cards and get on. Of course, they could not read the cards. Here is an example:

ΤΗΚ θε σκισσορς ιν θε λεφτ ανδ.

The class asked her to explain it to them.

'Why? can't you read it? It's in English.' Sandra then read it.

'Oh! is that what it says?'

The instructions deliberately made them clumsy by setting them to do things backwards or upside down, using the left hand if they were right-handed and so on. They made a mess of it. They laughed at their own clumsiness and what others were doing. It was fun.

But it was serious learning too. At the end, Sandra asked them what they had learned. They said they knew now what it was like to have a learning difficulty, what it felt like to be clumsy and unable to cope.

One engineer said, 'But you haven't taught us anything.' You may imagine what a good discussion arose from that remark.

What can we learn from a case study like this? Here are some questions to think about.

1  What would you have said to the engineer at the end?
2  What model of teaching did he have that made him say that?
3  What model of teaching was Sandra using?
4  Do you sympathise with the engineer's point of view? if so, why?
5  Why did this class of adults laugh so much when they could not do what they were trying to do? What can we learn from this about adult learners?
6  Can you think of ways of exploiting an idea like Sandra's in your own classes?
7  Could you plan a micro-lesson along these lines?
8  Make a note of ideas you could use: come back later to them.

# Comment

Sandra was new to teaching, but she had had years of experience in helping Scouts and other people. She started with a simple question and a simple idea.

## REMEMBER!
*... Try to be straightforward: avoid being complicated and 'clever'.*

Sandra thought through what she wanted the group to learn, how they should learn it and what they had to do in order to learn. She set up a learning experience for them to go through. It involved them in attempting to do something and so discover things about themselves that they did not know.

There were clear learning goals. Sandra knew what they were. She could have made it clear to the group what they were to learn, but she felt it would affect the process of discovery. They were able to say afterwards, and confirm, what they had learned. Usually, it is better to share the learning goals at the beginning. Sandra was right, of course.

The method she chose involved her in considerable preparation of the cards and materials. But during the session she had little to do, and could concentrate on watching the learners and giving a hand when asked. The students were very busy; it was entirely learning activity, mostly discovery learning, on their part. There was a lot of variety too in what happened in the class in fifteen minutes. The students could say what they had learned at the end to consolidate.

## REMEMBER!
*... Preparation pays off. Thinking through and preparing properly matter even more than enthusiasm and giving a good performance.*

Sandra came into her own mainly during the final session when she made them consolidate what they had learned by getting them to tell her about it.

Finally, she was able to exploit the comment made by one of the group to tie up the principles on which she was working and to make them clear.

The students went away from the experience changed in important ways. It had made them think. They had found out things about themselves and others that were important. It almost certainly affected the way they thought about student learning difficulties.

All this stemmed from just fifteen minutes of learning experience. This was learning by leaps: a great deal of important learning is of this kind.

## CASE STUDY 4

Tony, who was in the same group, taught plumbing. He decided not to follow the easy option of giving a mini-introduction to pipework but to share an enthusiasm of his, a working hobby that he pursued with his wife on market days. He went round the markets dealing in antique pottery. He was very knowledgeable about pottery, and had a good collection.

The room was set out with comfortable chairs and some tables. Tony set up on the tables a representative sample of plates. He had made photocopies from a catalogue of the makers' marks that are usually stamped or printed on to the bottoms of plates and show the manufacturer and the year of manufacture.

Armed with these, groups of two or three students were asked to identify and date sets of plates. They moved around the tables to do this, picking up the plates and examining them closely, looking for and comparing the makers' marks.

At the end, Tony marked the groups' scores and helped them to understand where they had gone wrong. He revisited the learning with them and consolidated it. He communicated his own enthusiasm, and talked about the feel and look of the glazes, the patterns and so on.

In the evaluation afterwards, there were expressions of genuine enthusiasm and excitement about what they had found out. It had opened their eyes to a whole new area of interest they had not known existed. Some brought their own plates the next week to be identified and dated. And so did I. I was particularly fascinated by a Toby jug I had which turned out to be French, not English as I supposed. I have continued to learn. So have they.

Consider the following questions.

1 What preparation did Tony have to do?
2 Tony's input of information came after the students had had the opportunity to discover about the marks for themselves. What do you think was the advantage of that? Would they have learned better or worse if he had given a lecture first?
3 What was the advantage of doing it in small groups?
4 What was the point of marking the scores?
5 What lessons can you learn that you can apply in your class?
6 Make a note to yourself about these things. Review it later.

# Comment

Most teachers rely heavily on only one of their students' senses: hearing. Usually they do so without any idea how to develop the listening skills such reliance requires.

It is a great pity, since for most people hearing is a poorly developed and inaccurate faculty. We are even worse at listening: our concentration span is about fifteen minutes. We are much better at seeing than we are at hearing things, particularly since television has replaced radio as our main leisure activity. Seventy per cent of what we learn we learn through seeing. It was probably because our ancestors relied so much on their eyes that they took to walking on their hind legs, to give themselves a better view of the world. And most teachers ignore the importance of touch, of handling things.

If you really want to know about something, you try to explore it with all your faculties. You look at it closely, you pick it up, feel it, weigh it in your hand, smell it, even taste it maybe. A baby does all these things as it explores its world. This is what the students did with these plates.

Tony loved pottery, the feel of it, the look, the different glaze mixes that were used, and how the different makers produced the tell-tale characteristics. He communicated its sensuousness to us. His plates were the products of loving craftsmanship.

Most real-life learning is of this kind. People explore, walk through their environment, handle objects, smell, touch, feel. Most adult classes are about hands-on activities, 'doing it' learning. Teachers and textbooks tend to make it academic. Why do we so often take the fun, the exploring, the doing out of it?

There was a great deal of cognitive learning in the class. I now know something about china marks. I can recognise the differences in plates and glazes which I certainly did not know before. I wanted to know more. My interest had been aroused. I had been shown how to set about learning more also.

Tony's class ran over its allotted time. When something so good was happening, it would have been stupid of me as the tutor to stop it too soon – and that is another lesson. The ability to adapt is most important. Often teachers are trapped by their own rigidity and determination to get through what they had planned, and stop student learning just as it was about to take off, to everybody's annoyance.

## CASE STUDY 5

A small group of students wanted to try an experiment in learning with their peer group. They had learned about the difference made to learning by using structure.

They used two low tables set in different parts of a large room. On each of the tables a collection of the same things was displayed. On one table, the many objects were set out in random order, deliberately jumbled up with no possible logic to connect them. But on the other, they were grouped so that a learner could easily recognise the category to which each object belonged. For example, ink, pen, paper, a book and paper-clips were placed together; so were a screwdriver, screws, a tape-measure and a hammer.

The students were selected randomly in groups. Each group was then allocated one area of the room and not allowed to see the other. Members of the two teams were to complete in trying to memorise the contents of the table in front of them. The contents were covered with a cloth. The cloth was removed and they were asked to look at the table and its contents for two minutes. The cloth was put back and they were then individually to write down as many of the objects as they could remember.

The scores were then added up and people were invited to talk about the difficulty they had in memorising the objects. The team who tried to memorise objects that were randomly distributed on the table had had great difficulty, but the other group, with objects set out in categories, found it not too hard. Neither team, of course, knew that the thing had been rigged. They were amazed that one team had done so much better than the other.

Of course, the real learning came when each team was shown what the other had to learn. 'Oh well! If I'd had that . . .'.

Again, in this case the learning goals were known to the persons who devised the game, but were only divulged to the students at the end when they had perceived them for themselves.

1 What do you think was the advantage of having a small group plan a microlesson together?
2 This was a game set up as a competition between teams. What do you think might be the advantage of that approach?
3 How do you think the losing team felt when they saw the arrangement on the table for the other team?
4 How effective do you think this approach might be in getting students to learn some important principle?

## Comment

Games are very powerful learning tools. The competitive element, if used well and properly controlled, can create a strong motivation towards achieving group or individual goals and can improve the level of achievement overall. Used badly, however, games can be disruptive of co-operative, friendly relationships.

The peer group here had come together well by the time this game was devised, so that everyone in the group was able to relate well to the others. Even so, the losing team felt they had been cheated. This probably had something to do with self-image.

What is important is that the learning was highly experiential. In fact, it was much more powerful for the losing team than for the students who found it quite easy. We often learn a great deal more from working hard to do something than from a task that is easily accomplished, and if we have to come back from failure.

## CASE STUDY 6

Fran taught personal relationships and coping skills with various groups, including adult students with moderate learning difficulties. She wanted to show her peer group how she set about getting people to understand how relationships develop – for instance, what might go wrong within a marriage and why. Here is her description of the activity, given to the students at the end of the experience as a handout.

SCULPTING

Begin with two willing volunteers. Choose any situation you like. You could choose the family, because it is a common experience. If you want to explore conflicts and relationships at work, you could choose that instead. In the descriptions that follow I assume you are looking at family relationships.

1 Place your volunteers in positions which you feel convey the relationship that would exist between a couple in a newly formed relationship. Ask the group to tell you what the postures suggest – affection, closeness, protective, absorption and so on.

2 Now move the time scale on – two years perhaps – and introduce the first child (another member of the group).

You can do the rest of the exercise in one of two ways: *either* continue to position additions to the group and explore feelings, *or* allow additions to stand where they feel most natural. If you are working in a real situation with a group it is best to use the second method because you can explore why they have stood in that position – for example, closer to one person than another.

3 Continue to add 'family members'. They need not all be children; some can be elderly relatives, for instance. Either use volunteers, or choose people if you know them well. You can also remove members – perhaps a sister who has married, a brother who has moved away to take a job, a partner who leaves home and then comes back, one member who has died.

4 At each new addition/subtraction, explore with the group their feelings about the changed situation and how they would prefer the relationship to develop. Let them adjust their postures and then talk with the other group members to see how they now feel.

5 At intervals, encourage the group members who are observers rather than participators to say what the groupings suggest to them. See if 'family members' agree with their viewpoints/impressions.

6 Finally, ask the first couple to stand exactly where they are while the others return to their seats. Explore with the whole group how the original body postures of the 'parents' have changed and what this might indicate about the changed nature of the relationship. Why has it changed? How could this be avoided.

Fran conducted the exercise above for about fifteen minutes. The peer group found it entertaining. At the end, comment was hardly necessary, but it led to a fascinating discussion.

1 What advantage do you think there might be in getting people to 'be' someone else and to try to express their feelings about it? (This was *not* role play, which would require the students to play out a scene of some kind, but a wordless 'sculpting' of postures to express feelings/relationships.)

2 Fran was using examples of 'body language' here. What do you think is meant by that phrase? Why is it so important?

3 Was the teacher able to predict what would happen? How far should she have tried to control and shape what people chose to do? What effect would that have had on the learning?

4 How well would you need to know your students in order to use this kind of technique successfully?

5 What effect do you think the experience had on the learners?

6 Can you think of other ways to use an idea of this kind?

7 Make a note of any ideas/thoughts you could use.

## Comment

Such complex ideas as the relationships between people and how they change with time and different pressures are very difficult to deal with. Usually they become abstractions, or get bogged down in anecdotes and discussions of people's personal problems.

This method was marvellously powerful in creating an abstraction and at the same time allowing individuals to explore relationships in their own way. It produced striking visual images and made people walk through the experience. It was as fascinating for the observers as for the participants.

People were encouraged to draw their own conclusions: there was no ready-made moral, no advice from Fran. My own conclusion was that you have to work hard to hold a relationship together if so much is going on to force people apart.

What we discover for ourselves may be much more creative learning than what other people tell us.

This was another example of a simple but powerful idea well used.

### CASE STUDY 7

John needed to explain a particular concept to his class of modern apprentice plumbers. He wanted his students not only to be able to apply a formula but to understand how to calculate heat loss from a building, and hence how much heat you needed to put into it. They had to visualise the problem: the rooms were in three dimensions and heat loss in six directions – through the four walls, the ceiling and the floor – and they needed also to take into account the number of rooms inside a house.

He felt it would be a good idea to try to explain the principle to people who knew very little about plumbing in a micro-lesson: to experiment with them first before doing it with his students. He and I agreed that it could be done by using a doll's house. So he managed to get hold of a large doll's house and brought it to the class.

The students were asked to examine the house in small groups and then to work out in their groups what factors had to be taken into consideration in designing heating input into the house, and in particular to discover the problems of heat loss. Each group was asked to come up with a solution to the problem.

It took them very little time to analyse that heat loss problem, and their solutions were quite fascinating. They saw the insulation was as important as heat input and the reasons why.

So the students told the teacher what the problem was, and jumped way ahead in understanding other principles as well.

1 What was the advantage of using a physical object?
2 Why do we find it so hard to deal with abstract ideas?
3 Would it have helped if the students had known formulae for calculating heat loss/heat input?
4 What was the advantage of setting them the task in teams?
5 What do you understand by a 'principle'? Why are they so important to grasp? Why are they sometimes so hard to grasp?
6 Can you think of ways of using this idea?
7 What principles do you need to get across? Write them down and think of ways of achieving that.

## Comment

It is usual to present principles to students as abstractions, but a principle is much better understood in a concrete situation. When you explore something physically in the round, you are using all your faculties rather than just that part of the brain that deals with language and concepts. Equally, you will create your own abstraction in language that makes sense to you. There are marked differences in the ability of groups of students to deal with abstractions. We need to observe carefully how hard it is for any particular group: their difficulties will depend critically on their experience, and also on their ability to visualise something as a mental model. Many people find this extremely hard.

## Creative use of micro-lessons

Micro-lessons allow us to rehearse teaching techniques on a small scale and get the feel of how they work, without the fear of the consequences of failure.

It is important to take risks – to try, and maybe to fail. We can learn a great deal from such experience. For instance, if the students had become really angry when they found they had been tricked in the game with the objects on the tables (unlikely, but possible), the teacher could have explored with them why they felt like that, and think of ways of dealing with it.

The only way you will find out what tremendously good things can happen in micro-lessons is by taking part in them. However many examples I might give, they will lack the excitement and challenge of being there as either student or teacher, sharing the learning of others and matching your experiences with theirs.

Micro-lessons do not have to be confined entirely in time or space. It is perfectly acceptable to set the group things to do before your micro-lesson, perhaps as a game.

For instance, if you want to interest them in local history, it is good to get them to do some simple research first. You could ask them during the week, whenever they are about the district, to look out for things of interest, anything that catches their eye and that might have a history to it. At the lesson, get the class to tell you what they spotted and then show them how and where they could find out about their observations. You will no doubt be able to explain many of them, but if there are gaps in your knowledge, you can use them to advantage too.

All this focuses their attention – they arrive with questions to alert the brain. A catalogue history lecture on the town might evoke nothing but yawns. They also develop the ability to observe and to research for information. The questions are theirs, not yours or those of a history book. It's all much more fun.

Another approach is to give them a list of places to discover, or questions that can only be answered by searching through the town. 'What is on the weather-vane on the Town Hall' 'What colour is the lion on the White Lion?' It is possible to make it competitive too: you could even award prizes!

**Take risks. Be inventive. And, whatever you do, prepare thoroughly.**

# Effectiveness

There are numerous examples of successful and inventive lessons. Peer group work can bring about a startling release of creative energy once people stop worrying about their own performance and concentrate instead on student learning.

Many micro-lessons involve demonstrating techniques. A lesson is about learning; it is not a challenge to the teacher to prove something. Most of the many demonstrations I have seen were adequately done, but a fair number were so 'clever' that all they did was convince the students that this was a kind of magic they could never learn. Others encouraged the students to believe just the opposite.

It is hard for teachers to remember what it was like when something they now do easily was difficult for them to do at all. Their present skill has come naturally without their having to think about it. All skill learning is like this. With sufficient practice it is a matter of habit, 'memory in the muscles', so that the concentration of the skilled person can be given to other things such as the design of the object that is being created, while the skill takes care of itself. Skills, after all, are not an end in themselves; their purpose is to enable us to create something, maybe a meal or a table or a document.

It is also hard to slow down: to demonstrate a skill at a pace that the students can 'see'. At the same time you have to ensure that all the students can see what you are doing and this can be hard if you have to demonstrate on a flat surface to twenty people, or if you have to have your back to them – working at a lathe, say, or with a 'patient' on the floor or on a bed.

To be effective, demonstrations must provide opportunity for the students to have a go. So the students must be able to learn the skill/techniques quickly. For example, catering students can learn to make quite reasonable 'roses' by peeling tomatoes thickly with a sharp knife, well within the fifteen minutes allowed. Students can learn to do a fireman's lift or simple resuscitation, or how to find someone's pulse and measure the heart rate, or how to bandage an arm – or almost anything that is simple, easy to follow, and achievable by the students within time constraints. There are many things you cannot learn in fifteen minutes: how to use a typewriter or a computer or how to write a poem. But I did once learn a Cantonese children's song that taught me Chinese numbers.

Obviously, you have to decide where your lesson is to happen, and what equipment or resources you will need. You cannot plaster a wall or lay bricks in classrooms designed for ordinary teaching, any more than you can reasonably ask students to dice a macedoine of vegetables on a desk. I have seen wet clay presented on large trays with desks protected by polythene so that people could experiment with it. But if you want to throw a pot on a wheel you have to go to the wheel; you cannot bring it to the class.

You do not have to be trapped in the normal classroom. But if you are going to ask students to meet in a specialist environment, they need to know where it is, and it may be important that they wear the 'right' clothes: they must know in advance and come prepared. All this requires thinking through, planning and organising.

## Evaluating micro-lessons

Ask before:

- What are the students setting out to learn?
- What are you going to get them to do in order to learn that? What preparation do you need to do, and by what time?
- How will they know what they have to learn and whether they have succeeded or not?
- How will you know whether they have learned what you intend? How will you consolidate the learning?

Ask after:

- Did it go as intended?
- What actually happened?
- Why?

**Evaluation must be seen as entirely concerned with consolidating the learning.** We are trying to learn about learning, and what the teacher's behaviour and thinking has to do with it.

A micro-lesson is always about learning, not the performance of the teacher. Evaluation must be concerned with how effective the learning was, not with scoring the various teacher skills. So let us be clear what micro-lessons are for. They are not part of the assessment of competence as a teacher. If they are used for this purpose most of the excitement and fun will disappear, and so will much of the potential for learning.

Evaluation is an opportunity to revisit a learning experience, so that the group can take a reasoned view of what actually happened and why, and draw some conclusions from it.

First, you must establish the facts – this is where sharing the perceptions of the group is valuable. Consider again the advice on observing a class on page 19. You can compare the teacher's idea of what happened, what she or he noticed and felt, with those of the students. If they are different, so much the better.

How did the students feel when trying to learn using the method chosen? Did they feel threatened? confused? stimulated? Was it easy or hard? challenging? infuriating? Were they amazed at their ability or depressed by their failure? If some succeeded and others did not, what was the difference? Why so?

Perhaps there was some sex stereotyping. In some exercises women generally seem to do better than men, and in others not so well. If that does not happen, it could lead to asking why that might be so: does it relate to self-image? to experience? to conditioning?

I am not going to suggest all the possible questions. But that in the end is what it is for: to discover the questions. It is no help to learn theories about how people learn if you have no practical experience against which to test them, and to judge their validity.

You need to look consciously at how you learn, how you feel about what is happening to you, if you are to understand how it is for your own students. The more experience of teacher–student interactions you have, the more fascinating the questions become.

Task 2 sets out some structured ideas for planning a micro-lesson. In Task 3 you will evaluate one by reflecting on the experience.

## TASK 2:   Preparing a micro-lesson (checklist)

LEARNING GOALS
1 Clarify for yourself what you want the students to learn.
2 Set these out as statements of learning goals. For example:

The students will

- locate a fracture in a limb
- make a sling
- make the patient comfortable.

Make the statements simple.

3 Try to ensure that what you describe can be done in the time, and can be easily observed happening.

METHOD
1 Think about how the students are going to learn.
2 Try to ensure they will learn, as far as possible, by being required to do something actively.
3 Think about what they might enjoy attempting to do.
4 Are they going to work individually or in groups?
5 Will there be any element of competition?
6 How practicable is it? Where can it be done?
7 What are the things they and you will need?
8 How much organisation time will you need for room/equipment?
9 Will you need a specialist room? How do you organise that?
10 What information will the students need beforehand? Map? What clothes to wear? Ingredients? Anything else?

INPUT
1 What do you have to provide as input to get it going?
2 Will this be you talking, or will there be instructions?
3 Will you need to demonstrate something?
4 What time will you need to do your bit?
5 How much time do they need? What is to be the balance?
6 How much can be prepared beforehand – handouts? overhead projector transparencies?
7 Will they need anything a week before, or to do anything in advance?
8 How will you grab their attention? How will you make them want to learn?

PREPARATION
1 Make clear for yourself what you need to make or prepare.
2 Give yourself deadlines – 'do this by' such and such a day. Have a checklist.
3 Have it all together and ready. Make sure everything works!
4 Have a cue-sheet, showing teacher activity, student activity and timings.

CONSOLIDATION
Ensure there is time to focus on what they have learned.

## TASK 3: Evaluating micro-lessons (checklist)

FACTS
1 What did you expect to happen? Did it happen that way?
2 What actually happened? Can you describe it?
3 Did the students understand what they had to do? and do it?
4 How well did they do it? Did anything surprise you?
5 What would you do differently next time?

LEARNING GOALS
1 Restate for yourself what you wanted them to learn.

2 Do you think your view of that has changed? Why?
3 Did they achieve the goals? Did they know? How did you?
4 What else did they and you learn?
5 Did anything about the learning surprise you?

METHOD
  1 Was the method you chose appropriate for the learning?
  2 How active or passive were the students?
  3 Did you get the balance right, do you think?
  4 Did they enjoy what they did? Why, or why not?
  5 Were there any problems? Could you have foreseen them?
  6 How well did you cope with making it all happen?
  7 Did they co-operate, or was there any tension?
  8 Did you get the practicalities right?
  9 Did they have the right things to learn with? Was the place right?
10 How could you have improved what happened?

INPUT
1 What about your preparation and what you actually did?
2 Did it take too long? Was it clear?
3 Was there too much information to absorb? Was it confusing?
4 Was everything ready? Did it work? What else did you need?
5 Did the environment support the learning or cause problems?
6 If you did it again, how would you change it?

CONSOLIDATION
1 What did they learn?
2 What did you learn?

# 5 Teams

*REMEMBER!*
*... The ability to work as part of a team is an essential skill in all walks of life.*

Why is it so important to practise working as part of a team?

Part-time teachers in particular often feel isolated from other teachers, left to cope largely on their own without adequate support from the institution they work in. It is not a happy situation to find oneself in. We all need support even if it amounts to no more than a listening ear. In most institutions these days, there is a strong movement towards the creation of teams of teachers with identified team leaders. But teams will only work well if the members develop the appropriate skills and attitudes.

Humans are social animals. It is normal human behaviour to work together in a social group. History records a number of solitary geniuses who had a profound effect on their society. But human beings would have achieved little if each had worked alone. We should have no great cities or even village communities. We live in a technological age that is the outcome of competitive co-operation in which individuals with specialised skills and knowledge work together. Our students need to function well within this kind of society and to do so they need to develop not only those specialised skills that will give them employment in specific roles but interpersonal skills and positive attitudes to others, especially in regard to problem-solving activity. Employers will always value good team members above those who just want to do their own thing.

How do we develop these skills and attitudes? Mainly through the experience of trying to solve problems together with others. This is a cumulative learning experience for us as individuals as we build up confidence to tackle problems in a creative way. For example, suppose you are driving a car at night down a completely dark road. You see lights coming towards you. From experience you can make a reasonable (we might say an 'educated') guess as to what those lights are. You predict how the 'oncoming car', not 'the lights', will behave – that it will keep to the side of the road away from you and safely pass by. On the basis of this prediction, you are able to decide what you should do. Well, of course, you could be wrong! We all need to be able to predict what is going to happen in most situations we meet. We learn to do this by experience of similar things happening in the past. We cannot deal with people or things that happen unless we have some hypotheses, guesses, to guide us.

When we are faced with new and challenging circumstances, with problems we may not have met before, or where our theories are not in fact working very well, we are puzzled as to what to do; we are forced to try out new ideas or new tactics. If 'the lights' coming towards you present a totally unfamiliar pattern that makes no sense to you, and you cannot make an educated guess as to what they are, you cannot make any predictions or take action. You might be best advised just to stop and wait to see what happens.

If there are other people in the car, you can consult them. Perhaps, if you put your heads together, you will come up with a workable hypothesis and an action plan.

This is normal human behaviour. As social animals, we work most effectively in groups rather than alone. The only way we can explain how an animal as physically weak as *Homo sapiens* came to dominate much stronger animals is in terms of this combining of strength and talent. After all, the most terrifying 'animal' in the jungle is a column of ants on the move. Here, truly, the whole is much greater than the sum of the parts. The same is true of good teams.

Individuals alone are less likely to solve problems than are groups. We have seen that management is essentially the harnessing of the energies of groups of people that have agreed goals that they are committed to achieving together. Those countries that value the group more than individuals have achieved technological dominance in the last few decades.

If we want our students to be able to become adept at problem-solving and developing the insight, skills and confidence needed, we have to encourage them to work in teams, to share and to support each other. One thing an employer will always value highly is a good team member. What is true of students is true of teachers. A team is any number of people who are working together to achieve agreed goals, as in a football match! It is not unusual to specify roles within a team.

Apart from any other consideration, it is much more fun. It is also very satisfying to achieve particular goals together with a group of colleagues. We learn so much from each other. This also provides a point of challenge, testing our ability fully.

# Setting up a team exercise

First, there must be a context in which the team exercise will occur. It is much easier to practise the skills as an extension of the micro-teaching. It needs a whole day to do it properly.

Identify teams of three or four teachers and invite them to plan a learning activity to last about 30–45 minutes. Of course, planning and preparation must take place well ahead of the day.

All the same considerations apply as for micro-lessons (or, indeed, for planning learning of any kind). What is special is the greater potential for creative thinking and design of the learning. Again, the model is:

- explore ideas
- choose one and shape it

- design a session
- implement the learning
- evaluate it with the group.

## CASE STUDY 8

Karen, Christine and Frances formed one of several teams, set up from among a class of teachers, who were given the task of planning team-teaching exercises for a day's programme of micro-teaching. They thought of a simple task like answering the telephone and how difficult people find it to do it well.

They set up a large room with telephone sets, putting them into six different contexts in different parts of the room. They wrote instruction cards, each defining a different situation and a problem using telephones. The situations included:

asking a difficult bank manager for a loan
answering the phone in a busy shop with one insistent customer on the phone and
    another in the shop
dealing with an answering machine
having a one-sided conversation
taking down instructions by telephone

The teachers started proceedings with a role play of a secretary who committed every possible error in dealing with the phone. It alerted the students to problems they might encounter and was fun to watch. It created a good atmosphere.

Students then went round in pairs to experience all the situations. The team positioned an observer at each station to note what students did as they followed the instructions.

At the end the students reported what they had discovered and the observers what they had observed. The learning was then agreed in relation to certain principles.

# Comment

The team exercise was fun. Students explored a range of different but perfectly realistic situations, and discovered quite a lot of important principles about communicating by telephone.

Having observers meant that there was an opportunity to take different views of the same experience. The observers were able to compare different people doing the same tasks. The participants could explore their own feelings. And sharing the experience with a partner allowed the students to extract maximum benefit from the whole exercise.

The teachers learned a great deal also about generating ideas and about making students work together as a team.

## TASK 4: Planning a team exercise

Plan a team exercise as a micro-lesson, or a class with some of your colleagues working as far as possible as a team – to gain the experience.
    Implement and evaluate the plan.

What have you learned?

# 6 Getting Started

What are the students going to do in order to learn?

## Teaching

There is a great deal more to running effective learning sessions than the ability to maintain control of the class or to deliver your material clearly, or even to manage the learning activity you have devised. All these skills are required and no class is likely to be successful without them. But these are all about what *you* are going to do.

In developing your skills and competence as a teacher, you must constantly keep in mind that **you are there principally to engage the students in a learning process**. Whatever you do, however well you do it, their learning depends critically upon what *they* do in order to learn.

This must be your starting-point for planning learning sessions. If you are anxious about your own ability to manage, how well you are performing, what the students think of you – or how critical your head of department or tutor is going to be of your performance – it may prove very difficult to avoid concentrating largely on what you do and ignoring what the students are doing.

In observing other classes, therefore, concentrate your attention on the students: how they are responding to what the teacher is doing, on the balance of activity – that is, who is doing all the work in the class.

Think about the role of a doctor with a patient. The doctor has to deal with needs of individuals, listening carefully to what the patient says, asking questions in order to elicit helpful information, and then making a professional judgement about the patient's needs in order to prescribe a course of therapy.

The responsibility for getting well lies with the patient as much as with the doctor, however. The doctor may prescribe a regime, advise a change of life-style, perhaps, or of eating habits or work patterns, but it is what the patient chooses to do that affects progress. If he or she goes on over-eating, refuses to take the pills and muddles and/or abuses their use, it is the patient who is to blame (though, of course, the doctor must ensure that the patient understands what the instructions mean).

I remember a surgeon saying to me: 'A surgeon can only do damage. It is the body that must do the healing.' The body's capacity to heal itself amazed him. He set me thinking about teaching.

It requires effort on the part of students to learn, and a commitment to doing it. A teacher must create the right conditions for learning to happen and find ways to motivate the students. A teacher should be able to generate lively excitement about the subject and communicate enthusiasm.

Often enough, you will feel the need to do much more. You will want to be certain the students get it right. But in doing so you may well take away the excitement that comes from intellectual or physical challenge. You may do all the thinking and all the work, only requiring the students to sit quietly and listen.

# Learning

## REMEMBER!
*... Unless the student makes the effort to learn, learning is unlikely to happen.*

What makes someone want to learn, to move on from where they are now, when it obviously requires a lot of effort? Who will want to change unless they are somehow discontented with the way things are now? Perhaps the teacher should be like the grit that gets into the shell of an oyster. How does it feel for the oyster? an itch? an irritation? a pain? The result, whatever it is, is a pearl which may be very beautiful.

A learner has to worry at the thing. Many teachers will provide the pearls ready-made. Students are asked to value them highly for what they are, and to store them in their bags. But they are only borrowed, put into the bank. It is the pearls the students make themselves that they really value, that matter for them, and that will have a significant effect on their thinking, behaviour and self-esteem.

# 7 Lesson Preparation

In the next few chapters we are going to consider separately each part of the process involved in preparing for and teaching a class, beginning here with the preparation of a lesson.

Any new experience is difficult to grasp as a whole because there is such an enormous amount of information, so many different and confusing things to try to take in all at once. Initially we explore and deal with the bits as they arise. Only later can we try to make sense of it all, when we have an opportunity to look back over our experiences and try to get them into perspective.

You will have had this happen to you many times. With anything new, whether it is trying to read a book, to make some new thing that you have never tried to make before, or to visit an unfamiliar town or a supermarket, there has to be a learning period.

We can, however, try to adopt a strategy that will enable us to deal with the new experience more effectively. With a book, for instance, we could decide first of all what information we want and then search the book for it, rather than just plough through what the author thought we should be told. We can approach a film or television programme with the same questioning attitude; all too often, we are completely passive in the cinema or in front of the television set.

Think about starting a new job. What happens when you arrive? You can wait to be told by your new employers whatever it is they feel is necessary or important for you to know. Of course, this will be important information. But the trouble is they cannot start from what you already know and what you don't know, nor can they address their remarks to what *you* feel is important for you to find out (or in a sequence that will suit you), unless you tell them. They cannot know what difficulties you find as you try to come to terms with the job. You must say what is worrying you.

From past experience, we can identify for ourselves what we feel it is important for us to find out. And we can then set out to discover these things, and so make sense much more quickly of the experience.

Think about that from the point of view of your students as they join a new class. If you look at things not only from the point of view of the teacher taking on the new class, but also as the students coming to the class may see it, you will recognise what needs to happen early in the proceedings.

You need to share with the students your perception and theirs of what the class is about, find out where they are starting and what they perceive as their learning needs. I asked you to do this for yourself early in this book.

So we need to ask ourselves certain kinds of question when we start thinking about teaching a class – and to go on questioning as we gain experience by teaching the class. What questions? They are of the kind: who? what? where? why? how? when?

---

## TASK 5:   Finding the questions

**Preparation pays off:** thinking it through, having things ready.
  In preparing to teach we need to ask questions such as these:

WHO?
Who am I going to teach?
What age are they? What is their background?
Why are they in this class?
What do they want, or what do they need to learn?
Why do they need to learn it?
What are they going to learn?
What do they know, or what can they do already?
What are they expecting from me?

WHAT?
What are they going to learn?
What do they have to do in order to learn that?
What do they need in order to do that?
What are they going to learn with?
What do I have to do in order to provide that?
What do I have to do to help them learn?

WHERE?
Where are they going to learn, or where am I going to teach?
What kind of support and help will they find there?
What kind of difficulties are they likely to find there?
What equipment can they and I use?
How do I get hold of it, set it up, find out how to use it?
What reorganisation and preparation must I do?

WHEN?
How much time have I or they got for each class? and for the programme?
What time of day will it happen?
How often will they meet?
What might be the effects of time of day or frequency?

HOW?
Where are they starting from? Where should I start?
How are they going to learn?
How am I going to teach? What pace of learning?
How will we agree our learning goals?

How will I get them working and committed?
Can I assume they will want to learn what I teach?
How do I engage them in the learning?
How far can I trust them to be responsible for learning?
What kind of problems are they likely to have in learning?
What can I do to make what they have to do easier to do?
How can I anticipate these problems and make it easier?
How shall I know whether they are learning – and what?
How shall I get feedback, and how shall I use it?
How should I adapt what I do to what they need?
How flexible should my learning/teaching programme be?

How will you answer the questions? Initially, by asking your employer. When you meet your class, in discussion with them.

In discussion of micro-lessons I focused on 'how' and 'where' questions in relation to planning learning for the student group. In planning for your own class, you have to consider so many other factors, such as motivation and purpose, needs and expectations, effects of the teaching environment, time of day and group dynamics. **The context of the teaching has to be clearly understood.**

Questions must still be simple and direct. They must lead to useful, clear answers, and so to action you can take. There is no real point in trying to discover information you cannot use when planning your teaching programme.

# Who?

In very many contexts, students are not used to teachers showing interest in discovering their views, or being concerned to draw them into discussion about the learning process. Many may resist if you ask questions about them personally. They may take the view that you are the expert and they expect you to make the course interesting for them: how can they contribute if they don't know about the subject?

But they do know about themselves, which you do not. Most people will in fact welcome the chance to talk about themselves and what they feel they need. Teachers often report that their students were grateful and welcomed the opportunity to talk to a teacher who 'wanted to know about me'. This is the critical starting-point of a process of **building up a spirit of trust between students and teacher.**

If it goes wrong or is handled badly, it may make things harder. It is perfectly possible to find out most of what you need to know without asking the students at all. If your class is part of a larger programme, the other teachers, or the head of department, will know what you want to ask. Of course, they may not have asked the students their views either. And it is valuable to compare what the teachers think with the students' own views.

Consider ways in which you might find out about your students.
Write down the options and think about what you have to do.

# What?

**Learning goals** should be set out clearly. 'What are the students going to learn?' is the important question. 'What am I going to teach?' can only be answered after that.

Your students will expect you as the person with knowledge and experience to have a clear idea of what they are supposed to be about, what they have to learn. That is the starting-point.

It does mean that they should know what they are trying to learn. They should also know what you are trying to teach. And these must be the same. Frequently and unfortunately, they do not appear to be the same. So many classes fail simply because the students did not know what it was the teacher was trying to teach them. It is not unusual for students to come to class with a fixed expectation of what they will learn and how – and for the teacher and students to have a mismatch of expectation. This is why it is so important that all agree what they are about.

This is a process of sharing. Telling them is not enough. You do have to ensure that they understand what is intended, and that they agree that it is what they are ready to set about learning.

In preparing a teaching programme, you have to make assumptions. Make clear to yourself what the assumptions are that you use. Look carefully at them again once you have met the students and worked with them to check where the assumptions might be wrong. It is easy to continue with a lesson style and structure based on the wrong assumptions. Be ready to admit when it is necessary to change; that depends on readiness to observe what actually happens in your classes.

Clarify for yourself what you want the students to learn. It will be best to have a general statement of overall learning first for a programme, with more detailed statements for lesson plans within the programme. They and you need to know where they are going and how they are going to get there: and what they need to learn along the way. This will help you to sequence learning and activity in a helpful way; and to provide the essential links to make the learning easier to perceive and assess.

Once the learning goals are agreed, type them up and ensure that each student has a copy.

Learning goals for a lesson should be given to the students at the start of the lesson so that they know what they are to learn, and you and they can assess the effectiveness of the learning at the end of the lesson. They can also link learning in one lesson to learning in the next lesson, and so build up a structure. With no idea of the structure, students find it hard to learn.

Learning goals are always a compromise between what the students feel they want to learn, and the teacher's perception of needs – of what they have to do to pass the assessment, for instance. Of course, the assessment should arise from the learning and not be imposed on it.

There must be a working match between the two pressures. **You and your**

**students must share and agree the learning goals.** This is not the same as arriving at the first session or lessons with a blank page and asking them what they want to learn. Even a negotiated programme must start by declaring the options.

---

### TASK 6: Learning goals

Set out the learning goals for your class. Make the statements simple. You might say:

The students will

understand the various methods and techniques for making $x$
develop skills necessary for using the techniques
use the techniques successfully to produce examples of $x$
use the equipment and materials efficiently/effectively
be able to evaluate the quality of the product.

How will you make sure the learning goals are reasonable and make sense?

Who needs to look at them or agree them? your tutor? your head of department? your students? When should that happen?

Ensure that you and the students are committed to achieving the learning goals.

---

# How?

Think about how the students are going to achieve the learning. With the learning goals set out, it is clear the students must use techniques in order to understand them, and use equipment to develop skills in its use. They must produce examples of whatever the thing is they are to make in order to evaluate them.

Consider carefully which learning methods are likely to be the most successful. Why is that likely to be so? What should you do as the teacher? What is your part in the learning process?

There is little value in their seeing a demonstration, however excellent it may be, if they do not have the chance to 'do it themselves'. It is useful to watch someone turn metal on a lathe, for instance, or carve a piece of wood or ice a cake; but to learn how to do these things we have to do them. Our eye–hand co-ordination, our clumsiness, the weight of an object we handle, the speed at which things can happen, can only be known when they happen to us and by our reactions.

Are the students going to learn individually or in groups? Students themselves bring tremendous resources to a class, in the richness of their experience. What is to be learned in your class must link into and arise out of their experience. How are you going to exploit that experience? How are they going to make sense of it, starting from where they are?

Consider how to promote group sharing through group activities. They can learn so much more together and from each other than on their own. To do this, you have first to establish a group identity that is supportive of each member of the group. You will need to think about how to get people sharing. And whatever you decide, it must be practicable and possible within the time available.

> Make a list of all the possible ways in which you might teach the class and the ways in which they might learn what you have set as learning goals above.
> Choose one way. Try to say why that one.
> Sketch an outline of what is to happen in your class. Think about who is going to do what, and when. What will they, and you, need?
> What preparation is needed to have things ready?

## Your role

There has to be energy in a system for anything to happen. Where does it come from? How much of the energy in the class has to come from you? How can you get the students to work in order to learn? If you do all the work, will they actually learn anything? What will be the balance between what you do and what they do?

In the preparation for the class, it is important to decide how much you will need to talk and for how long, how you will get them working and how quickly. What will you need to prepare for them to do that? Time spent preparing teaching and learning materials will be well rewarded by the energy and excitement that it will facilitate in the learning.

Once you have decided what they are going to do, you can think about how much time they will need to do it. Then you can work out how much time you will need to make the input that will get them going.

How much do you need to do? Remember that students can only deal with a limited amount of information at any one time. Trying to cram a whole mass of facts or words or symbols or ideas into them all at once is very ineffective. We need to absorb a few things at a time and do something with them. It is better to have variety of activity in the class.

Even if you want to get through a large amount of information, you will need to present it in sections of no more than fifteen minutes at a time, and then make them do something to learn and assimilate what you have presented. Often a teacher will assume that the students have understood what has been presented and hurry on. Even if they have, by the time they have attempted to grasp the next package the first one is gone.

Try to see it from their point of view. Ask: what is hard here? what is it that a student will find it difficult to understand or do? You can then approach it by tackling that difficulty.

## Getting ready

How much can you prepare beforehand, and in what form? What would best help the students to learn, get them active? Would it be better on paper as a handout, or on an overhead projector (OHP) transparency? Do they need to have something in their hands that they can use?

What teaching aids do you need? What do you have to get ready? Where are they? Do you have to make anything or carry it to the room? Are there ready-made materials somewhere? if so, where?

Can you get the room set up before the students arrive? This matters! How much time do you need beforehand to set things up and make sure that they work? There is nothing more frustrating than to have to wrestle in a class with something that won't work: an OHP with a dud lamp, say, or a video machine that doesn't function. It is a good idea always to carry a small screwdriver to repair the plug that has a loose wire. And your own supply of whiteboard and OHP pens and chalk. Be prepared.

# Lesson plans

Your lesson plan is essentially a cue-sheet. The plan of the lesson should be clearly in your mind, related to the use of teaching and learning materials that you have produced. It is helpful to have a paper that you can refer to from time to time to check where a lesson is going: whether it has got lost or is basically still on the right programme. It is not unusual for teachers to lose their way in a class – nor for them to adhere too strictly to a plan and not respond to student needs.

A lesson plan should state the learning goals for the lesson and give some indication of how you will check if the students have achieved those goals.

It should identify both teacher activity and student activity, with a clear relationship between the two and some indication of the use of time, and also of what both teacher and students will need to use.

Remember that student learning activity is itself an assessment of their ability to cope with the tasks and so of the learning. A reasonable test of someone's ability to produce something, or of skill in using a technique or piece of equipment, is doing it. The students can assess their own performance also.

## Examples of lesson plans

This section includes examples of lesson plans. Their style suits me, but you should try to develop your own.

There are different approaches. What matters is not the plan itself, but what it is about. The plan is a tool that will enable something to happen. It must be flexible and usable: it should alert you to what needs to be done, and when, and by whom.

The learning process you set up depends on what you may think the whole thing is about – what it is for.

Many lesson plans tell only what the teacher is going to do: what aids the teacher is going to use, the content the teacher is going to cover. They are rather like the micro-lessons in which a video camera points only at the teacher and records what the teacher does. In my view, any video camera should point at the students. What are they doing while the teacher is teaching? After all, what

51

matters is that the teacher observes carefully what the students do – or don't do. Many video recordings made on that basis would be very dull to watch.

---

**LESSON PLAN 1**

---

**Class:**     Evening class in local history, one evening a week for ten weeks
Duration: two and a half hours, Thursday 6.30–9 pm
Location: Adult Centre; classroom with tables and chairs
Equipment: whiteboard, OHP. Photocopying available
Facilities: central 'coffee-break' area with easy chairs
Students: age range 35–55, four men, twelve women
Main purpose: personal interest, no examination.

**Session 1:**  First evening session: 'Getting Started'.

**Purposes:**   To get to know each other
To share interest and motivation: what do we bring?
To agree learning goals and programme to achieve them
To establish working procedure – set targets.

**Learning goals for Session 1**

The students will

● share their reasons/expectations in joining class
● agree what we are all setting out to learn
● establish good working relationships as a group
● identify a learning programme and responsibilities.

**Evening programme**

A:  Teacher Activity A (10 minutes at most!)

Welcome students and introduce myself: who, why I'm here
Set up and explain 'ice-breaking' activity
Divide students into pairs (mix up men and women if they have separated themselves out); they may have to move
Provide an 'interview brief' (very short, some cues).          *Paper A*

B:  Student Activity B (10 minutes)

Each one of pair to interview the other and change over (5 minutes)
Make brief notes – use my cues as starting-point.

C:  Student Activity C (30 minutes)

Each student introduces his/her partner to the class.
(Note: must ensure it's light-hearted and fun. Spot a 'jolly' character to start it off – set the tone.)

D:  Teacher Activity D (5 minutes at most)

Tell them what we are going to do after the break.

**Coffee break** (Ask them to be back in 10 minutes)

E:  Teacher Activity E (20 minutes)

Set out my own interest and background in local history
Outline:    how to find information
            what to look for: clues, evidence, gathering information and
            ideas.
(Note: make it interesting! photos, old newspapers, artefacts on a table to
handle: hand around.)

F:  Student Activity F (15 minutes)

Students, in pairs again, examine the articles and try to see what can be
learned from the ones they look at. They make notes.

G:  Student Activity G (30 minutes)

Each pair comes to the front to explain what they discovered.

H:  Teacher Activity H (5 minutes)

Consolidation of the learning: what we have learned.
Use students' ideas as far as possible.
Learned about:
how to go about local history
what interest can be found in ordinary things
each other, the group.

I:  Teacher Activity I (5 minutes)

Setting up the programme for the 10 weeks
Tell them my learning goals                                          *Paper B*
Learning approach to be used:
individuals or groups to agree the topics to tackle
they share the tasks – agree who will research what
they will prepare and present a paper to the class.
Present my own outline: what I think important and why               *Paper C*
Get them to take papers B and C away and think about them
Make their own programme around mine:    what to add
                                         special interests
                                         research each to do.

J:  Teacher Activity J (5 minutes)

Agree with them    what we will do next week
                   what they will do before then.

Complete the register

Thank them for coming – what a pleasure and so on.

### Note to myself: Preparation

| | | |
|---|---|---|
| 1 | Set out learning goals | Paper B |
| 2 | Design my own outline programme | Paper C |
| 3 | Design my cues paper | Paper A |

### Before the class

Arrive early.

Find the caretaker and make friends.

Make sure the room is comfortable: check heating, windows.

Check on fire drill and evacuation procedures.

Set up tables and chairs as I want them – committee style.

Set the 'articles' table.

Make sure there are copies of the lesson plan, Papers A, B, C.

Ensure OHP etc is in place and working, in case I need it.

Ensure there is chalk and other things I need.

Find out the drill for coffee, paying etc: when, how, who.

Get the register and make sure I know how to complete it!

---

### LESSON PLAN 2

**Class:** Full-time course in catering

Subject: communication skills

Duration: one hour, twice a week

Location: drama studio with some tables and chairs

Equipment: lighting, whiteboard, OHP

Facilities: central refectory and student areas

Students: 20 men and women, ages around 17+

Main purpose: to improve interpersonal skills

**Purposes:** To improve communication skills and confidence in dealing with clients

To integrate work in accounts with writing skills

To improve team-working

To stimulate good working practice

**Methodology:** An extended simulation for a term

Class divided into teams: a management game

Each team to 'set up' a catering company for weddings.

### Learning goals for course

The students will

- improve their interpersonal and communication skills
- have increased confidence in dealing with clients
- establish good working relationships in teams
- use accounts to improve understanding of need
- understand, have insight into managing a small business.

**Programme for sessions**

| | |
|---|---|
| Session 1 | Setting up teams and agreeing learning goals<br>Setting competitive goals and targets<br>Establishing working practice – team behaviour<br>Roles and responsibilities |
| Sessions 2–8 | While teams are working, practise skills team by team<br>Use feedback opportunities: tackle problems. |
| Sessions 9–10 | Presentation by each team of what they have done. |

**Lesson plan for Session 3**

Face to face with the customer – how to handle it
Learning goals (enabling overall learning goals 1–2)
The students will

- be able to establish a welcoming, helpful manner
- explore with the 'customer' what he/she wants
- guide the customer carefully: advise, be helpful
- clarify what is required and agree to cost it.

(Note: in a subsequent session the students will prepare a firm proposal/estimate to meet the customer's requirements and cost it. The customer will receive different estimates and choose one, taking into account the whole package. The 'bottom line' is whether they can make a profit on a sufficient scale to keep going.)

**Programme**

| | | |
|---|---|---|
| Teacher activity: | Make sure teams know what they have to do<br>Check on progress so far and understanding of activity and goals<br>Set up the role play, explaining it<br>Provide a cue-sheet for the role play<br>Evaluate what happened with the teams. | *Paper 1* |
| Student activity: | Take roles and work them out<br>Observe carefully and note what happens<br>Reflect on what happens, evaluate performance | |
| Teacher activity: | Explain what each team has to do now. | *Paper 2* |

Time allowed for each team: 30 minutes.

**Note to myself: Preparation**

Design role play guidelines, cue-sheet and guidance Papers 1 and 2.
Set out room to facilitate role play.

---

To understand the nature of the questions let us consider a few examples of actual classes. The examples are drawn from different countries: contexts change but learning and teaching present similar questions everywhere.

## CASE STUDY 9

Karen was to teach wordprocessing in the School of Business Administration in a college in the United Kingdom. She was new to teaching. Her class was a full-time business administration group of sixteen-year-olds. They had no experience of producing real documents in a working environment, although they had some basic keyboarding skills. She tried to discover from the other teachers about the students but felt safe in assuming they were like she had been at that age. So she felt reasonably happy about understanding their needs.

As a new teacher, Karen played safe using the model of teaching/learning that she knew best. She had been taught wordprocessing using a textbook. The textbook had worked for her; why not for these students? What she had not thought about was how many students the method had *not* worked for. She had been highly motivated and able to learn her skills whatever method was used by the teacher. Many students learn from what appears to be very poor teaching.

The textbook provided a 'lock-step' approach. It assumed every student needed to learn exactly the same thing at the same time, in the same way and at the same pace. Clearly, this cannot possibly be true. Individuals have personal learning patterns and learn at a pace that suits them.

Rote-learning has a place. And skills like keyboarding certainly do need repetitive practice. Learning to be a secretary or a keyboard operator in the real world requires a very different approach, however. The skills are a means to an end; what matters is the ability to create letters and other documents of a quality an employer needs. And that requires all sorts of other skills.

Karen quickly discovered that some of the students who chose to sit at the front of the class did the exercises in the book at a pace she felt happy with, and at the same pace. Most of the class got left behind, and some who chose to sit at the back did very little work. The room was clearly set up to encourage the approach Karen had adopted. The workstations stood in rows facing down a long room to the teacher's desk and a whiteboard at the front. Karen could not supervise the students misbehaving at the back.

The teaching/learning strategy was clearly unsuccessful for most of the students. Karen decided to redefine her learning goals.

What the students needed was not just to learn the orthodox methods of paragraphing and so on from the book as some kind of abstraction, but to have tasks that simulated real world demands and which gave a point to what they tried to do. She decided on a new strategy.

She prepared packages for all the students to enable them to adopt the role of a keyboard operator in an estate agent's office. They had to use the computer to complete all the tasks which an employee in this role would undertake in the selling of a house: the advertisements, the house details, design of a brochure with a photograph, a window display, the letters to buyer, seller, solicitor and other agents, and so on. Each had a worksheet identifying what they had to do, as well as other resources.

The pressure and excitement of the simulation radically changed the behaviour of the students. Karen spent a great deal of time in the preparation of the sets of materials, and found herself in the class with little to do except to encourage the students and respond to requests for help from individuals. This happened only occasionally. She was anxious, but as tutor I encouraged her to do nothing and just watch. The 'naughty' students at the back got on as quickly as the ones at the front. One girl noticed a mistake in her letter as she took it from the printer, looked at her neighbour and said, 'I'll still beat you', and quickly edited the text.

1　What were the assumptions Karen made about the class?
2　Why did she choose to use the model of teaching/learning she had experienced as a student? Why was it unsuccessful?
3　Try to explain the differences between her first strategy and her second.
4　Why was it more successful in involving all the students?
5　What do you think she had to do to use this method well?

## A LESSON PLAN FOR KAREN'S CLASS

It is possible to design a *pro forma* to help teachers in *planning classes where these conform to a well-established pattern as on a college timetable*. What is essential is that you do not allow use of a pro forma to limit your own inventiveness. Here is an example of a pro forma that I hope allows sufficient flexibility for planning a wide variety of learning activities. (It is in a shortened format; to use it you will need wider spaces for your information.)

*Lesson Plan Pro Forma*

Class:
Room:
Equipment available:
Constraints:
Time available:

Important notes:
Students – who are they?
How many? Ages?
Why are they in this class?
Learning strategy:
Learning method:
Learning goals:
Preparation:

*Class* (1, 2, 3 . . .)
Date and time:
Learning goals:

ACTIVITY Who? How long? Doing what?

A:

B:

C:

D:

E:

(or more)

Consolidation. What to do before next class.

Notes on preparation and setting up.

---

**Karen's Lesson Plan**

How might Karen's Lesson Plan fit into this pro forma?

*Lesson Plan Pro Forma*

| | |
|---|---|
| Class: | Business Administration Wordprocessing 2C |
| Room: | Computer Room 3B |
| Equipment available: | Workstations with computers and printers, OHP, whiteboard<br>Range of cupboards and filing cabinets |
| Constraints: | Workstations in rows in a long room facing the whiteboard |
| Time available: | 2 hours a week (could plan over several weeks or a term) |

**Important notes:**

| | |
|---|---|
| Students – who are they? | Full-time college students. Must have GCSE English, grades A–C |
| How many? Ages? | 35, all 16, all female. |
| Why are they in this class? | Business course – want clerical jobs. Not very ambitious. |
| Learning strategy: | Tried class programme with the textbook. Not so good.<br>It was boring – they can already do a lot of what's in it.<br>**Simulation of an office.** *They work in an estate agent's.*<br>Suggest they go and talk to agents: look for good ideas. |
| Learning method: | Set them up to complete a task in a folder of materials. They have to prepare letters, adverts, etc. to sell a house. |

| Learning goals: | To take responsibility for a real piece of work. |
| | To use their own initiative and take pride in presentation. |
| | To set out letters and advertisements properly. |
| | To use correct and appropriate language. |
| | To use the right style in business letters. |
| | To complete everything by a deadline. |
| Preparation: | Make up a folder for each student (could work in pairs?). |
| | Find the materials – get them from an estate agent. Maybe better if a different property for each student? |
| | Plan and photo of each property – outline information; |
| |     name, address of owner, valuation and so on. |
| | Instruction sheet (Sheet A): what to do – order/sequence: |
| |     letters to clients, newspaper, (solicitors later?); |
| |     advert for the paper – a Display for the window; |
| |     a brochure with 'details' of the property. |

## Class 1. Setting up the simulation

| Date and time: | Wednesday 12th January 3–5 pm |
| Learning goals: | To understand exactly what they have to do. |
| | To clear up any misunderstanding: questions – answers. |
| | To examine the folder of materials, find out what's what. |
| | To plan: what to do, when, what is needed and so on. |
| | To plan: who to see – what to look for, questions to ask. |
| | To decide on the right format and style of business letter; |
| |     a good style for display and newspaper advert. |

ACTIVITY Who? How long? Doing what?

| A: Myself (15–20 mins) | Hand out folders. Explain what is in them and what we are going to do – a project for 6 weeks till half-term. |
| B: Students (10 mins) | Examine contents of folder. Make sure they understand what is in it and what they have to do. Read Sheet A. Any questions? Are they quite clear about everything? |

| C: Myself (20 mins) | Question and answer round the class. Tell them they have to go and visit an estate agent – what questions will they need to ask? what will they look for? bring back? *Get their ideas. Build up ideas on the board/OHP* Where? who? what to ask? What to look for? What will they take away? What models can they use? |
|---|---|
| D: Students (30 mins) | Planning, sorting out, making notes about what to do. Create a programme for themselves. |
| E: Myself (10 mins) | A business letter to an estate agent asking for help: set up a visit, what they want and why? |
| F: Students (20 mins) | A letter to an estate agent asking for information with an explanation of what they are trying to do. |
| G: Myself (5 mins) | Consolidation. What to do before next week. *Make sure they bring their folders with them each week!!* |
| Notes on preparation: | Prepare Sheet A and folders. |

## CASE STUDY 10

John was appointed as an education officer to Northern Nigeria. He found himself in an isolated town south of the Sahara desert. The people were Muslim with a strong tradition. English was the language of education and government, but the main language there was Kanuri and many people also spoke Hausa. He was teaching in a government secondary school preparing students to take English overseas examinations.

The young men had passed local examinations in English and felt they were privileged to be at the school. They were keen to do well, since getting the examination passes would open up good jobs for them in the future. But there were strong cultural barriers that affected their learning and John's understanding of them.

He was to teach English, history and health science. History was concerned with the expansion of Europe and the Industrial Revolution. Europe was no more than a word for the students, and at that time an industrial revolution had not happened in that part of Africa. How do you create a feeling for industrial towns or factory life for people who have only known an agricultural society?

Health science was a more promising subject. This required some basic knowledge of the human body: where various organs were, how they worked, what their function was, and especially what part they played in the health of the person – what could go wrong.

Africans tended at that time to be afflicted by most of the diseases that affected people in Europe, plus a profusion of illnesses that were specific to Africa, or which had largely been controlled elsewhere. Many were insect-borne and most were preventable; this was the point of his students learning health science, although they also needed to pass the examination.

John thought about them. What were their needs? Why was it thought they needed to know about the Industrial Revolution? It was hard for him to convince himself of the necessity, let alone the students.

But they certainly needed to understand health science. John felt he had a high level of motivation on his side. People are fascinated by themselves and their own bodies more than by almost anything else, and these young men had a strong desire to be fit and well. They all had the experience of being ill; most had relatives who had suffered from a whole range of ailments. All had had malaria and knew what many of the diseases felt like when you contracted them. This was not an abstraction, but very real. They also had their own bodies to relate experience to. John decided to use this experience.

The main obstacle to learning health science was the large amount of special vocabulary they had to learn, a 'naming of parts' and medical terms and conditions. And John had no access to organs in bottles or laboratory equipment.

What they needed, he felt, was some way of visualising what the body was like inside. They needed to be able to see how the body worked, how the various parts fitted together as a whole, how the organs and their functions related to the whole 'machine', what a malfunction could do and its likely effect.

His solution lay in a plastic construction kit of the human body that he discovered advertised in a magazine. He sent for the kit. As a group, they had all the bits and a diagram to help them assemble them.

This allowed them not only to see things in the round, but to handle them and try to fit them together in the places they belonged. 'You have the diagram: you have to build it.' They had a great time and they learned the parts very quickly. They were also able then to understand the diagrams in the textbook and draw diagrams themselves to show how the parts worked. They learned technical terms quickly, and passed the examination.

Most importantly, however, they learned health science as 'real' and relevant to them, as practical knowledge related to their own life and well-being. It was not simply something to swot up to pass an exam and then forget.

1   What was the essential difference between what John was asked to teach as history and as health science?
2   Why should this make so big a difference in learning?
3   What factors did John feel he could exploit with them? Why were these so helpful in relation to the learning goals?
4   What was it in the method he chose that made it successful? Would it work with any students in any context?

# Using prior learning

One clear advantage of using the energies and resources within the student group is that they will start from where they are and not attempt to start from where the teacher believes them to be – or, as usually happens, from where the teacher is. A teacher can only make assumptions about a group: it is even harder to be clear as to individual learning needs.

To use and integrate prior learning – that is, what they bring with them to the class from experience – the students must use their new information and skills to create new perceptions and behaviour. It is actually not possible to ignore prior learning, because it determines what students select from what is presented to them.

New ideas and new thinking have to link to those that are already there. Skills can only build on previous skill levels. What teachers provide is information and opportunity: to acquire knowledge and skills and to gain insights. Information is usually presented neatly packed as a parcel to take away. Unfortunately, that is all it remains unless the students process it in some way to make it part of their own knowledge structure. Packages remain as useless lumber in the memory if they are simply stored to be repeated as answers to tests, and dumped afterwards. This information only becomes knowledge when they do something with it. Knowledge is a process, a constant change in perception, not just an accumulation of packages. The same is true of skills.

## Pace

Students usually do not know what they know, where they have got to in their learning or where they are going. They have to learn to use experience, to reflect on it and integrate the parts. We have to find some way for them to explore their own resources and experience while matching it against new challenges. Equally, we have to help them remove the barriers to learning that previous learning has probably created for them. How fast can the process go?

Pace in learning is a major concern. How quickly can we expect an individual to learn something? Some methods promote learning more quickly than others. Many students in Karen's class in Case Study 9 would hardly have learned anything if she hadn't changed her teaching strategy. Nor will simply learning names for a test change perception of ourselves or our world, as John discovered (Case Study 10).

The methods both chose accelerated the learning dramatically. No doubt Karen's students would eventually have learned how to work properly, perhaps when they were employed in an office somewhere. Karen by using a simulation hastened the process. She also ensured that each one progressed at his or her level of readiness and commitment to learning. It gave them something to do that they found interesting. They all progressed faster and gained insight into the 'why' as well as the 'what' they had to do.

## Learning/teaching materials

Most new teachers, and many established teachers, rely heavily on textbooks. The trouble is that this allows the author to decide what students are going to learn and how they are going to learn it. A book is a resource to be used wisely. It is not intended to dictate what happens in class. A crutch can eventually prove a handicap and should then be thrown away.

New teachers frequently lack the courage to take charge, and to take risks. They look for what appears safe. Some adopt a pattern of defensive behaviour. One of the results of relying on a book, of course, is that it takes away the need to think things through.

Similarly, new teachers can find it difficult to challenge what seems to be established patterns in the classroom or workshop. Often a caretaker seems to dictate how a class will run. Some teachers lack the nous or the courage to move the furniture to promote the activity they want to happen, however hard that actually makes it to do.

It is not necessary to try to produce 'professional' teaching or learning materials and aids. Some searching in resource areas in colleges and schools may produce useful stuff. It may be that what you need is available, but in the wrong place. Whatever you make or get, make sure it really is helpful to students. I have seen astonishing effort made by new teachers in producing teaching aids that are far too elaborate for their purpose.

The test is: will it help them learn? Anything can be an aid in the right context. Tony's plates were effective learning aids; so were Sandra's instructions written out in letters of the Greek alphabet. If there is something available which is real, it is better than any simulation of it. The main criterion is: how useful is it?

Usually, you can follow the principle of 'the simpler, the better'. Instructions on a worksheet need to be clear and simple to understand. The less an OHP transparency has on it, the easier it will be to grasp, and the more effective it will be. Look at the cartoon at the beginning of the book. It could hardly be simpler or more effective.

# 8 Tasks and Performance Criteria

The language used in education, as in all other disciplines, changes with time. Indeed, education more than most other human activities is subject to cycles of fashion. The current emphasis is on 'competence'.

You will certainly wish to become a competent teacher. It is one of the purposes of this book to help you define the competence you should have in particular aspects of teaching. I hope in fact you will want to raise your level of understanding and skills well beyond simple competence. Teaching is about decision-making, about creative interaction with students to promote learning.

A teacher is to be judged at least as much by what the students do and what they achieve as by any demonstration of competence in particular aspects of the role. Indeed, there is a danger that too great an emphasis on the teacher's performance will tend to divert attention from the effort to improve student learning. But a teacher who lacks competence in particular important areas cannot do even an adequate job for the students.

## REMEMBER!
*. . . What is important is that you are effective in the role.*

A teacher cannot exist in a vacuum. Every teacher must teach in a context of a specific learning programme with specific students. This is where we must develop skills and understanding to an acceptable level. But we must also ensure that the skills and insight that are achieved in one context are transferable to any new context.

In attempting to define competence in terms of performance criteria, we must bear in mind that their achievement is part of the process of becoming effective in a particular context. Many factors will determine how effective a person is in any role. Some are definable as performance criteria, while others relate to environmental and contextual pressures, or to interpersonal skills and relationships, to working in teams, to confidence and adaptability. This is where growth in the job is most marked as a teacher gains experience.

## Mentor and tasks

Overall, a person's learning and perception of learning is achieved by reflection on the experiences which enable him or her to learn. Teaching is just such a learning experience. *The first part of this book outlines a process*, a learning path, by which any new teacher in any context may gain insights and confidence. Yet you cannot reflect on experiences, learning or teaching, unless you can first observe what happens. This is actually quite hard to do, since the closer we are to something, the less of it we can see. It is much easier to observe what others do than what we ourselves do. To see ourselves we need a mirror. Some other person can act as that mirror for us (even our students if we are ready to listen to them!). To be really helpful the other person should be someone we can feel has experience of the problems and experiences we are dealing with and is sympathetic to our needs, but who is prepared to be open and honest. An over-indulgent tutor or mentor is not that. But we must have something to share, some structure that will help our interchange. It cannot just be statements about what each of us 'feels'. We need to define clearly the things we are looking for, what we are hoping to see, what 'good practice' may look like.

We need to know, *before we do something*, what it is we have to do in order to do it well, how to set about it properly. We also need to know how what we do will be judged or assessed. Finding out afterwards that we have failed is demoralising, worse if we have no idea what we did wrong or failed to do at all. Stating performance criteria should enable teachers and mentors to know clearly what patterns of activity they are both looking for; and it will give them objective 'out there' things to concentrate on and discuss rather than 'in here' subjective feelings. So, performance criteria relate to both setting out to do the Task and to observing what happens with our students in order to reflect on it afterwards: to have common ground to share with our mentor.

Set out below are Tasks. They define the learning path, the process; things to do in a logical sequence in relation to the job of teaching. The Tasks are 'generic': they are essential elements of teaching in any context, wherever it occurs. Each Task may be tackled in a rather different way according to the context (what normally happens there, what others do), but there are patterns of behaviour which will make for more effective teaching in any context. Since the context of teaching will be whatever it turns out to be, we cannot be over-precise in stating performance criteria. Achievement of criteria in any one context must be transferable to another context, too.

I have used the idea of performance criteria throughout so that you can focus on the nature of the skills and attitudes which you need to develop. These are not taken from actual NVQ programmes, but do convey the essential aspects of your role.

The term 'performance' is used here to mean 'behaviour as a teacher that can be observed and assessed', preferably in a real teaching situation – that is, a classroom, workshop, laboratory, ward or anywhere else that the teacher has responsibility for the learning of an identified group of students. The 'criteria' are the judgements to be made. We have to rely on judgement in making our assessment. Clearly, the quality of the judgements made will depend on the level of experience of whoever is making them.

There has to be a sharing of perceptions, just as there is in the observing of a class and in micro-lessons. The teacher has principal responsibility for assessing his or her own performance against agreed and stated criteria. But it will be much more valid and constructive if an experienced mentor can be involved, not only in assessing with performance criteria, but in the whole learning process.

What is needed is that you, as teacher, should perceive clearly what is required to be effective in the role you fulfil at the level of responsibility you carry. That is partly defined by a statement of performance criteria, and partly by feedback from a mentor who can share the context in which the teaching occurs.

As you read on, you will encounter statements of performance criteria for each of the aspects of the role of teacher. They are intended to help you understand the principles that are involved in what you do as a teacher; they define 'good practice'.

Study these criteria, and match what you do against them. Where you meet with a clear lack of success in achieving any of them, ask yourself why that is so. Look carefully at what you are doing to evaluate what happens and what needs to happen. And don't ignore the effect of what you as teacher do on the learning of your students, and how it promotes their competence.

---

## TASK 7:  Lesson preparation

1 Find out what you can about the students in your class (group of students) that might be useful in planning a learning programme for them.
2 Use that information in planning learning sessions. Decide how you will go about agreeing learning goals and their learning activities with them.
3 Design at least one lesson for your group. In developing the ideas and lesson plan(s), think about what you have learned from micro–lessons and from your own experience as a student.
4 State your learning goals for the lesson(s) in simple ways the students will understand. How will you share and agree them with them? Are you prepared to be flexible at all?
5 A lesson plan is a cue-sheet. What matters is the thinking that leads to the choices you make and the way you design your plan. Develop a style that suits you and where you are, the kind of students you deal with. You should identify clearly Activity: what you will do, when for how long; and what the students will do. How do these relate?
6 Try to ensure you have thought through how the students will learn and how activities you have designed will help.
7 Make sure you think clearly about feedback: how will you find out what the students have learned?
8 Identify clearly what learning and teaching materials you will use.

---

## TASK 8:  Evaluating your preparation

Look critically at your lesson plan(s). Read through the criteria below.

1 How well do you feel you match up to these criteria?
2 Have you shared your evaluation with a mentor?
3 What do you think you should concentrate on improving?

PERFORMANCE CRITERIA

1.1 Information is obtained about the ages, educational background, motivation and past experience of the student group. Some questions were asked about personal learning goals. This information has been used in planning learning sessions.

1.2 Students and teachers have agreed learning goals for the lessons and have shared their perceptions of what they are setting out to do and to learn.

1.3 Lessons are planned to achieve the specified learning goals.

1.4 Where appropriate, the learning goals are consistent with requirements of examining bodies.

1.5 Teaching methods and learning activities are well-designed.

1.6 What the students bring with them, their prior learning is taken into account.

1.7 The lesson(s) will engage students actively in learning.

1.8 There is enough flexibility to allow for the different pace of learning of individuals.

1.9 Learning materials and teaching aids are well chosen and are likely to promote the intended learning.

1.10 Methods of obtaining feedback and assessing the learning are identified.

# Good practice

What we are about is the establishment of a pattern of good practice in your preparation for your classes. This implies repetition of the pattern in preparing for *all* your classes.

Don't be too anxious to achieve all the criteria that relate to performance in the first class you take. There is a process of maturation that cannot be hurried. It is by reflecting on your experiences that you will learn. Each time you undertake preparation of a class, you will understand more.

The criteria are not goalposts between which you can shoot the ball once and then feel 'I don't need to do that again.' They are signposts: they point a direction of travel. Every time you attempt to meet them they will show you more of the road. You will find you can always do better.

## TASK 9:   Evaluating the experience/reflection

Use your lesson plan (or series of lesson plans) in a teaching context and evaluate its effectiveness – what actually happened.

If you have the chance, share the evaluation with your mentor and agree together an evaluation statement. Match perceptions of what happens in your classes to the performance criteria below, and use them to shape what you do.

PERFORMANCE CRITERIA

2.1 The lesson has specified (and/or negotiated) learning goals that are clearly stated and shared with the students.

2.2 The structure and content of the lesson is known by students and takes account of the identified needs of individuals and of the group(s).

2.3 Teaching methods are appropriate to the specified goals.

2.4 Learning problems are identified during the lesson and the work programme (or lesson plan) adapted to take account of them.

2.5 Learning materials and teaching aids are used thoughtfully to promote the intended learning.

2.6 Individuals and groups are managed well. Control of the session is maintained. There is good linking and structure.

2.7 Learning is assessed by the students and the teacher and is consolidated at the end, with clear linking between lessons.

# Evaluating a teaching session

You will need to think about the following aspects, in relation to your initial lesson plan.

## Facts

Class: students, course, time, duration, place.

1 What did you expect to happen? Did it?
2 What actually happened? Do you and your mentor agree?
3 If there are differences, make a note of these.
4 How well did students carry out the activity? Any surprises?
5 What was really important in what happened there?

## Learning goals

1 Did your view of those change?
2 Did they achieve the goals? How well? How do you know?
3 What else did they learn? Did anything surprise you?
4 Did they/you consolidate the learning? take it away?
5 How do you expect them to use it? How will they link to next session?
6 Was the method you chose able to provide assessment?

## Method

1 Was the teaching method you chose appropriate?
2 Did the students *do* much to learn, or were they mainly passive?
3 Did they enjoy what they did? Why, or why not?

4  Did they understand what to do and why they were doing it?
5  Did they have the right things to learn with?
6  Could you have improved the organisation? room? equipment?

# Input

1  Was it right? Did it take too long? Was it effective?
2  Were the teaching aids/learning materials effective?
3  Were instructions clear? Were there enough? Was there too much information?
4  Was everything ready? Did it work?

# Communication

1  Did the students work as a group? Was that partly down to you?
2  Were there any problems for individuals or groups? What did you do about them?
3  Did you feel sufficiently skilful? Comment on that.
4  What about the students' attention, their enthusiasm, their concentration?

# Consolidation

1  What did you learn? What would you change, or rethink?
2  What do you need to work on now?

# 9 Using your Plan in Teaching

Activity 1 asked you to set down what you felt you needed to learn to be a teacher of adults. Many new teachers, when asked this question, replied; 'I need to know how to control the class.' What did they mean and why did they feel it to be a need?

Managing the learning is certainly what it is about. Any manager wants to feel in control, but what is it that you, as a teacher, can control? We shall explore the answer to that question in this chapter. Certainly, you need to control the environment and the learning materials. What about the people?

You cannot manage others if you cannot manage yourself. Self-organisation was mentioned in the discussion of study skills in Chapter 2. We have also discussed other factors in the mechanics of management, such as stating clearly what you and the students are about and preparing competently, so as to have things ready and properly structured.

But you cannot manage people in the same way that you manage a machine or an environment. I believe that the new teachers were afraid of the loss of control, that the fear of students and what they might do pressed on them – that they had little confidence in their own ability to manage them in the class.

## Rules

Teachers will adopt defensive behaviour if they feel insecure.

Your students will look to you to lead. That means, at least, that you should know where you are intending to go and how you want to get there. But it also means establishing roles and responsibilities. No groups can work successfully without rules that govern their interactions and behaviour. In establishing the group, you will need to create the framework of understandings within which it works. Usually these are well known to all from previous experience of learning groups. Most of the important rules governing behaviour of groups are unspoken but clearly understood.

Nevertheless, you need to make it clear from the beginning what is acceptable in your class and what is not. This is a matter of observing behaviour and interfering to shape it. If, for example, your class uses computers (or any other equipment) the students must know how to treat it properly, not to abuse or damage it. There are also safety considerations – wearing protective clothing and so on; we shall discuss these later.

Do you allow smoking? Who decides? Do you set deadlines? What about absence? Or being late for class? Or failing to produce work?

Making clear rules and responsibilities like these will help to create a good working environment, without disruptive actions on the part of individuals upsetting the working of the group.

The essential quality is leadership. Perhaps the teachers above had an image of the teacher as 'boss' and were not sure they had the personality or the presence for such a role. They might remember a teacher they were afraid of: 'you didn't muck about in her class.' Why not a teacher they found stimulating to be with?

# Managing

Good management, in industry and business as well as in teaching, consists largely in creating good teams of people working well together to achieve things. This is done in various ways. It helps if people know where they are going, have set targets, schedules and goals to achieve. The managers can then motivate them to accept 'ownership' of the targets, and to harness their energies to work together for a shared purpose. They need to identify strongly with the group, to see their achievement as part of the achievement of others. Will it happen if all the decisions are taken at the top? When managers want robots, they can buy them. People need motivating, guiding and supporting; it must appear to them that they, their ideas and their talents are valued and worthwhile. The leader can help to give them shape.

# Sensitivity: identifying needs and problems

Clearly, we have to work with the consent of students, especially adults. But we need more than passive acceptance: we want active participation and commitment.

If we concentrate in designing our classes on what the students have to do in order to learn, the methods we choose will be student-centred and activity-based. The teacher in the class is thus relieved of a great deal of pressure, and can concentrate on the quite different role of supporter and guide – a reference point to assist the learning. Consider Karen's class again (Case Study 9).

The teacher can also watch the students. This ability to observe and to be sensitive to what is going on is most important. Case Study 11 describes an example.

---

**CASE STUDY 11**

---

Richard taught a GCSE history syllabus to full-time British students of mainly 16–17 years. He was faced with trying to get them to understand the reasons for the partition of India after 1947. They had as much experience of the conditions in India as John's Nigerian students (Case Study 10) had of an industrial revolution – none.

Richard's principal learning goals were descriptive, but he found he needed to get over to these youngsters what it was like to be there: what religious fanaticism means, how people could feel so strongly that they would go out in mobs to massacre hundreds of people of other tribes and beliefs. History is apt to take all the emotion out of events, giving dispassionate accounts and analyses. No wonder some students find it boring. People are not like that – in 1947, Indians were driven by the wildest of emotions.

As it happened, there was a level of experience in the class that he could exploit. For some reason (which he did not know), the girls in the class appeared to 'hate' the boys. The messages were clear in their behaviour. The girls came to the class in a bunch separately from the boys and deliberately late. They challenged Richard and the boys when they came in and sat in a group as far away from the boys as they could. Richard did his best to make them take part in the discussions and to get the class working together. But what an atmosphere, and what a conflict!

The problem had to be faced, and Richard adopted a strategy to tackle it and maybe turn it to advantage. He needed to get the girls talking to him and explaining why they felt as they did. Their powerful feelings could also be used to help them understand partition, and why it was thought a necessary solution in India.

They could be helped to see that reasoning with people whose behaviour is driven by hatred and fear and strongly held beliefs just will not work. He hoped that they would find that their own emotions were trivial by comparison and that the problems could be talked out.

1  What was Richard's original approach? What were his learning goals? Why were they unsuccessful?
2  Even if the conflict had not arisen in the class, would they have been appropriate? What other major difficulties were there?
3  Had Richard really thought about what the students needed to learn and how they might learn it?
4  How would you have tackled conflict in the class?
5  What can you learn about observing carefully what is going on in your classes and using it to advantage?

# Comment

Richard revised his learning goals and his approach to achieving them, while the students by exploring their own emotions could understand those others and what drove them to behave as they did. The girls' anger could have destroyed any possibility of achieving the course learning goals. He prevented that.

However well you prepare, you cannot predict how things will go in any particular class. All experienced teachers will confirm that you can prepare exactly the same material and work for two apparently similar classes; in one class the lesson goes tremendously well, with commitment and excellent learning activity, but in the other it dies. Why? It's very difficult to say. It could be something in the chemistry of the class – the mixture of personalities, perhaps – or the time of day or week, or the way you or they are feeling; it could be something that has happened in another class or in the corridor, or the weather or some other outside factor. You need to be sensitive to what is happening and adapt, change, adopt some new tactic.

Teaching is about complex human relationships: the way groups (and groups within groups) form and feel about each other and about strangers, including perhaps the teacher. Without a relationship of mutual trust linking teacher and students, difficulties are bound to arise.

No doubt, for many people the prospect of teaching is daunting. There are memories of being in a class of difficult students who are making the teacher's life hell. For many there is almost a stereotype image of the teacher doing battle with the class. But it is easier to remember the sensational rather than the routine: of the vast number of classes that happen every day, only a very few become battlegrounds, and not necessarily with the teacher involved.

That does not mean that teachers do not frequently lose control or fail to manage the learning effectively. Some do fail to get organised, to identify clearly for themselves and the students what they are trying to teach, and to motivate or stimulate their classes. Some students do rebel – out of boredom or protest at what they see as a waste of their time. There is much pressure on the teacher to 'deliver'. It can feel as if everything rests on you.

## REMEMBER!
*. . . Preparation is all-important.*

You will find that your students respond well if you appear ready and well prepared, showing interest in them and involving them in 'ownership' of the learning goals, and if they know clearly what they are to learn and what they have to do to learn. It must be a combined effort: them and you together. They will want to co-operate with you.

# Structure and links

## REMEMBER!
*. . . It is much easier to understand the parts of a thing if you have a view of the whole of it first.*

The most obvious evidence to your students of your competence in dealing with their class is your structure. Share it with them.

It is helpful for the class to have copies of your lesson plan, so that they know what is going to happen and what they will be asked to do. They can see what you are going to do, and what that has to do with their learning.

They also need a baseline from which to start. Learning goals for the lesson should be clear to all. At the end of the session they should be invited to assess their achievement of the goals and provide you with feedback on how it was for them. They will then perhaps be able to focus on their own learning needs – what has to happen now, whether they can consolidate the learning or come to terms with it by reflection at home or by more effort.

Whatever we set out to learn has to build up into a structure. The same is true of a programme of classes. They need to build week by week, the learning from one week helping to make sense of the learning from other classes. The student has to be able to see the links. Your structure should make the links plain.

In order to make the links, the beginning and the end of each session are particularly important. At the end, students need to focus on what they have learned, partly to assess their own learning, but also to be able to do something with it: unless something is done with the learning it will quickly disappear. At the beginning of the next class, they need to revisit previous learning to ensure that it links into what they are going to learn now. The first activity of any subsequent class should be to establish this linkage.

And what of the time in between? What happens to the learning in the time between classes? The left-hand graph in Figure 1 shows the rate at which what we have learned evaporates away. Within twenty-four hours we have forgotten 75 per cent of what we learned today. And after a month there will be very little left. This explains why revision is so difficult: you are not really revising at all, but learning everything again from scratch. How then should we tackle the problem of recall?

The more often something is recalled, the easier it is to recall it. What is required is some way of regularly revisiting what you have learned, reviewing it and refreshing your memory. Of course, it will also be processed each time by the brain and become part of understanding a greater whole, linking it to other learning. This process allows students to take control of their learning.

Reviewing is simple. The more frequently we revisit learning, the more easily we will recall it; it becomes familiar. So students should be encouraged to review the learning between classes. The effects of reviewing are shown diagrammatically in the right-hand graph in Figure 1:

*Fig. 1   Learning recall curves* (derived from *Use Your Head* by Tony Buzan, BBC Books, 4th edn, 1995)

# Teaching methods and learning materials

Students must be able to deal with the learning activities and materials that you provide. Similarly with your teaching: your style, your language, your visual aids. You should assume nothing.

Whenever you write anything, come back to it and look at it again and again to try to see it as others see it. You know what you mean, it is clear to you. Will it be clear to your students?

How complicated we can make things when we try! sometimes, particularly, when we present an OHT or a handout in class. The main criterion is that any material you use should be as brief as possible. Get rid of anything that is not absolutely essential for the students to have. Give them the bones, not the flesh – you can build up the flesh in class.

When you put up an OHP transparency or write on the board, walk to the back of the class and look at it from there. Can they read it? Does it make sense? Is it easy to grasp?

Make your instructions simple, direct, easy to follow. And what of your voice? Just as visual aids are of little use if people cannot see them, so a teacher must at least be audible. Some rooms are very difficult acoustically, and some are full of distractions.

What matters is that the learning is successful, not that you as the teacher feel pleased with how it was for you. Any teaching method may be successful with a particular group under the right circumstances. You need to choose a method you feel comfortable with and can handle effectively. But watch to see how it works.

There is no point in trying to be 'clever'. But think critically about what you are doing – and particularly what they are doing. There may well be alternative ways of approaching the learning that are no more difficult than the one you have chosen, and which could be more interesting and stimulating for you as well as for them. All teachers fall easily into repetitive methods.

There has to be variety of activity in each class and between classes. No activity should go on too long, whether it is the teacher explaining something or the students reading for information or watching a video sequence. There is a curve that relates to concentration (as there is to learning and also to forgetting), and the curve drops sharply after about fifteen minutes. So you should change the activity at least as often as that. As with the revisiting curve above, changes of activity in fact will keep the learning/concentration curve rising or steady.

## ACTIVITY 5

### Concentration curves

In Figure 2, the concentration curve (a) indicates a general tendency for concentration to fall away about fifteen minutes. Curve (b) shows the effects of changes of activity every fifteen minutes or so.

75

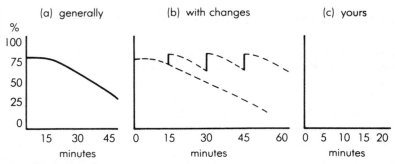

Fig. 2 *Concentration curves*

You can find out how you compare with the general pattern – discover what works for you.

1 Find a book that requires concentration. Make sure that you have suitable conditions for study. Note the time when you start reading, and the time at which you stop 'taking in' what is on the page in front of you. Sketch your concentration curve on the axes (c).
2 Now experiment with breaks or changes of activity, such as making notes, to see how your ability to maintain concentration is affected.

# 10 Communication

In Task 9 you evaluated the effectiveness of your lesson plan in a teaching context. In Task 10, we look at a particular aspect: communication.

---

**TASK 10: Communication skills**

In evaluating your teaching in Task 9:
1 Consider how effective your communication skills were.
2 Use the criteria below to assess what needs improving.
3 What do you need to do? How can you do it?
4 What difficulties are you experiencing in communication?

PERFORMANCE CRITERIA
3.1 Interactions between individuals and groups are observed.
3.2 Groups as they form are noted. There is control.
3.3 A class group identity is established that supports members of the class in their learning activity.
3.4 Learning difficulties of individuals receive help/support.
3.5 The teacher responds to student feedback.
3.6 There is sensitivity to problems students have in grasping information and instructions.
3.7 The teacher uses appropriate vocabulary and delivery.
3.8 Learning materials and aids take account of student readiness and ability in language, and are effective in promoting the intended learning.
3.9 Visual materials are well designed and distraction removed.
3.10 The teacher watches carefully and observes what happens.
3.11 The teacher makes use of feedback and evaluates honestly.

---

## Messages

Communicating is not just about transmitting messages. No amount of improvement in transmission will help if the radio receiver is switched off. How will you switch it on?

Are you, as a teacher, switched on to receive the messages from your students? You can be sure that when they arrive in your class they will come with all kinds of expectations: about you, what they will be doing, what the other students will be like, what it is all for.

As they explore the new experience, they will take messages from the room and the furniture, from the behaviour and language of the teacher and of other students. They will tend to form groups, create 'territories' and 'private space', and do things to try to feel comfortable there.

You will need to watch this behaviour carefully, alert to the messages it carries. Sometimes worrying patterns of behaviour develop, such as hostility between groups and individuals. You will need to interfere, perhaps to take control fairly early on, so as to ensure that a network of co-operative relationships develops.

You will probably notice that students choose a particular place to sit where they will establish 'my' chair or desk. They will tend to return to their own 'territory' and stay with the friends they first make. This may be defensive behaviour – they need to feel safe. Try to ensure that small groups do not become too well-established, and regularly create new groupings for groupwork. Groups and behaviour, once firmly established, will resist change. A stranger who joins an established group will find it hard to become a member. You will probably notice also how your group identifies itself as different from other classes, other groups of students.

Be alert to how it looks and feels to them. Try to manipulate the situation to the advantage of the group as a whole, rather than just let things happen. Try to think of ways in which you could get your class to talk openly to each other, remove the barriers we all have when we are in a new social group. Just talking is usually ineffective. They need to have a specific job to do, something to give it focus.

For example, Lesson plan 1 (page 52) attempts a deliberate structuring of group behaviour, in which students are asked to interview each other in pairs and then introduce their partner to the class. This works well and becomes light-hearted fun; it also allows you to be open and honest with them, telling them about you, your interests and what you have done in the past. It establishes a bridge.

Can they do that if they are sitting in rows? How will you have to organise the room so that they feel able to talk easily? This activity may not be appropriate in other situations, but you should be able to invent something that will serve the same purpose.

Once you have broken the ice, once they know each other and there are smiles, how will you maintain the momentum? It will help if they have other things to share. Perhaps they might be asked to agree in larger groups on their expectations and needs, which can lead on to agreement of learning goals. Or they might begin work on a small-scale project.

# Your messages

Look carefully at the messages in your own behaviour. As people come into a new experience they explore it: they look for the messages that tell them what kind of place it is, and what are the patterns of behaviour, dress and relationships there – what role the teacher intends to adopt, and what their role is to be. It is your behaviour rather than your language that tells them how you feel about them.

Watch your students too, and observe their behaviour. Are you creating barriers? Are you creating distance between you and them? Most of what we 'say' to people is transmitted in body language – the closeness or distance we create, the things we do, the things we get them to do or allow them to do, the way in which they see our value system. How are they reacting to what you do?

Your tone of voice matters greatly. Listen to someone dealing with a dog in a park. Notice how the dog is controlled by and responds to the tone of voice, not to the words. Unconsciously, we do that with our students too.

Look at what you do, and ask: why do I do that? Some teachers like to have a large desk between themselves and their students, or to create distance in other ways. Some teachers seem to be trapped at the front of the class and do not move to get closer to students.

## REMEMBER!
*... We have to show a genuine interest in students' needs and problems if we want them to respond well to us.*

---

### CASE STUDY 12

Gillian taught computing in a college in the United Kingdom. Most computing classes took place in a computing room, but a theory class was in another classroom. She had thought carefully about what she was going to do and how.

The room had been set out in an open square to encourage the students to interact with each other as well as with the teacher. Gillian had prepared well. She was showing them how computing techniques had developed, and had things for students to handle such as a large magnetic tape and perforated paper rolls.

The class, however, had divided itself into three distinct groups, each with its own territory. A group of girls, age 17+, sat along one arm of the square, out of direct eye-contact with Gillian. The boys, of much the same age, sat along the opposite arm (except two who made a home for themselves in a corner). In front of Gillian sat about eight mature students, women of 30–40 years.

The girls and boys took no part in the lesson. They gave the impression of disliking each other and the class. The women were eager and had got close to Gillian, who was of their own age. They held her attention and things went very well there.

Afterwards, her mentor who watched the class asked Gillian what she felt about the lesson. She was sure it had gone well, that the students were keen and interested. Her perception of what had happened and his as observer were far apart. She had been unaware that the class had divided into three groups, two of which had taken no part in the lesson.

This characteristic of student behaviour in the class was important: she needed to change her approach in order to deal with it. Her chosen method had been highly successful with the mature students. Why did it not work for the younger ones?

She needed to find some way of integrating the three groups. She had in fact been doing most of the work in the class. Most of the students had been idle, not participating and not learning. The students had to be given learning activities. She agreed to try putting them into sets of three, one from each divided group. There would no doubt be opposition because people dislike change once groups have formed so strongly. But in practice it worked quite well.

1 Why do you think the behaviour of the mature women and youngsters was so different? Have you observed this yourself?
2 What activities do you think they could do in sets of three that would help to bring the divided groups together?
3 Why might there be opposition to this happening?
4 What is the best way to take control of group behaviour?

## Comment

It is easy to fail to see what is actually happening in your own class. This is why it is important to observe other classes; micro-lessons are especially useful here. This is also why you need an educated eye, a mentor to share your class.

# Models

Your most important task is to establish a sense of belonging and co-operation within the class as a group, to include you too if possible. Help them to feel comfortable with the group and with you. They need to agree purposes and goals and a method of working together and with you. Good management is partly setting targets and then motivating people to achieve them. This is much easier if there is a good team spirit and supportive behaviour.

Getting to know one another and having social contact is essential. Lesson plan 1 deliberately includes a coffee break after they have introduced themselves. It may be helpful too if they are prepared to ring each other up when they are having difficulty with some learning task – so they need to know each other's telephone numbers.

Your approach, the way you come across matters. Your behaviour, warmth, enthusiasm, interest in them, energy, even your health and your value system, are communicated in many different ways. The clothes you wear say a great deal about you. Students will be looking to see what is acceptable. You cannot help being some kind of model. Everything about you will be studied by students, since you will be the focus of attention – but don't worry.

People will, of course, adopt a pattern of behaviour, language, style of dress or whatever that belongs to the group rather than to any one individual. It is fascinating to watch what they choose to do and to learn from it.

## CASE STUDY 13

An external examiner visited a course of teacher training in a college in the United Kingdom. There were two male tutors and twenty-four mature students from a wide range of backgrounds. The assessor wanted to find out if the tutors saw themselves as models for their student teachers.

The two tutors were rather worried by the idea of being models. They felt that teachers had to develop their own personal style: the teachers must be themselves, since they taught in so many different contexts. And this of course was true.

But when the assessor asked the student teachers the question the answer was different. 'When Ray comes to watch us teach, we do as he does. We have it all neat and tidy. We have a structured lesson plan, time things carefully, all our visual aids set out – have it all organised. When John comes, we don't bother. It's all thinking on your feet and letting it develop – jollying it along, seeing what happens.'

They reflected back to each tutor his behaviour in class, which they thought he would probably want to see.

1 Consider your own use of models. How did they affect what you do?
2 Where did your model of 'the teacher' come from?
3 What kind of role model would you consider appropriate for your students to see? Would that worry you?

# Comment

We cannot avoid using models. Sometimes they are not helpful. Many people come to teaching with models of 'the teacher' and 'what teachers and students do' that are barriers to understanding.

Don't imagine that as a teacher you can avoid being seen by the students as a model. An important aspect of teaching is to ensure that the model you present is one you would like the students to adopt. You project a pattern of behaviour. For example, if you adopt careless or even dangerous practices in a workshop or laboratory, it is no good telling the students they must do things the 'safe' way.

This makes clear the nature of communication. We want to belong, to be accepted as part of our group. To do that we have to adopt the behaviour, language, style and so on that identifies us as a member of this group. You will be able, I am sure, to think of groups that exhibit quite bizarre special clothes or language or behaviour to identify 'belonging'.

And what about the groups you belong to? since we all belong to more than one in different aspects of our lives. Do you change your language style, clothes or behaviour as you move from group to group? Think carefully about that. How do you categorise people?

The student teachers in Case Study 13 had two models to compare and took a delight in the comparison. That was no doubt good learning.

# Energy

Communicating is not one-way transmission, nor is it most of the time consciously done. Most important messages are unconscious, contained perhaps in the tone of voice or body language.

Most of the energy has to come from the receiver, who has to be actively seeking to find out. Humans are exploratory animals. Unless the brain is actively processing information, no change will occur in perception or understanding. Consider what you are doing now. These words simply sit on the page. The energy has to come from you to make them mean anything. In this book I, as author, must try to present what you, as reader, think is important for you to read, do, think about. I have to try to be interesting; I have chosen to do that partly by using case studies of real situations. But you have first to want to know.

# Convictions

There is the problem of mind-set. People come with fixed mental images and models, so that they cannot see what we want them to see – just as I walked past the Adult Centre I was looking for because my mental image of it was wrong. We tend to select what we find easy or familiar and reject the rest. This happens if a new teacher has a fixed image of teaching behaviour.

We resist challenges to our accepted images, especially if they are part of our value system or deeply held convictions. If the evidence is all against us, we just shout louder to drown it out. You must know people who do that. Some teachers do that with students who challenge them.

Many people prefer to walk away from things rather than to face a possibility of challenge to their self-image or of failure. One of the most accurate measures of motivation is the readiness to come back from failure and try again. It is most clearly seen in individual sports. I gave up trying to ice-skate since I could not deal with the damage to me and my self-image when I performed badly. But if people are determined to succeed, nothing will stop them.

# Barriers

## REMEMBER!
*... We have to be genuinely interested in problems that our students have in learning.*

Often, people bring a history of painful learning experiences of the past, like mine in the skating rink. I have known graduates of famous universities declare, 'I am hopeless at maths.' What do they mean? Why should they believe it?

Such a strong conviction about oneself is usually a result of past failure or, quite often, of poor teaching or the absence of any attempt to discover what the learning problem really was. People like this present some of the strongest barriers to learning.

If you are to succeed, you have to believe there is at least some possibility of learning. Obviously, it is even better if you think you will learn if you try hard enough. As the teacher, you will need to recognise the barriers that individual students present and help them to look at them objectively and ask: is it really so?

The things we want students to do must be do-able. I take the view that if I want students to do something, I had better do it myself to find out how hard it is. Whenever I set a task I do it too; it's the only way I can find out what is involved. It helps me to assess their level of success properly, and if necessary to provide a model. How else will I know what problems they have to solve to be successful?

It is important that students do not set about trying to learn things with the wrong idea of what kind of a thing it is. They are bound to fail if they don't know what they are trying to do. Equally, they have to know beforehand what criteria will be used to judge their success. One clear advantage of stating criteria is to give the students means of assessing their own success and what they still need to learn.

If we are all learning together, there is excitement and energy in the system. As with a map, you have to explore the area so as to understand the map fully. Group and individual learning projects are exactly like that. Everyone has to be involved in learning.

They must know what they are trying to learn and, by reflecting on the experience, focus the learning for themselves so as to make it part of their learning structure.

## ACTIVITY 6 | Your learning barriers

Look at your own learning barriers.

1  What are the things you find particularly hard to do or to learn?
2  Can you list them? Do you know what they are?
3  Why is that? Can you think of the circumstances that led to it?
4  If students turn up in your class with such barriers, what can you do to help them?

## Variety and pace

It may be that even in group activities only some are actively involved, while the others are just there. All classes should have a variety of activities that involve everyone to maintain attention. Classes need changes of pace too, including periods of high energy and periods of rest.

## Language

Do we share a common language? All groups develop shared language that helps to bind them, and separates them from other groups. It is the same with academic subjects: special vocabulary has to be learned that allows specialists to communi-cate. This is as true of pottery and flower-arranging as it is of computing, say; I have been amazed at some of the vocabulary to be learned in a class on horse-management.

If this book is too full of jargon, or perhaps if my sentences are too complex, we will not communicate. We have to think about the readiness of students to work with these words, and of how they can link them to their own experience. Without such linking the words will not make sense. It is not a matter of intelligence, it is where we are, you and I, or you and your students.

If I were talking to you, instead of writing, you could use the expressions on my face, my gestures, my tone of voice and so on to help you to share what I am say-ing. Equally, I could use how you respond to what I say, what you feed back to me, to shape what I say next. More importantly, you could question me, have me repeat things in other words, or reframe them with you into your words. We can't do these things through the printed page.

But you can and must do them with your class. **Feedback matters.**

# Attention

Questions are an important way of presenting challenges. And using questions to involve the group with you is also a valuable technique. Unfortunately, many teachers use the technique very badly.

One good way to improve its use is to name the person you want to answer. A general question fired into the air will usually not challenge most of the students directly enough to make them attend and concentrate. As the teacher, you lose control of what is happening.

The answers the students give must be treated as valuable, worth exploring and developing. Students soon know if you're playing the game of 'spot the teacher's right answer'. They have to make progress in their thinking from where they are.

If you want to talk or to engage in class discussion and you want them to listen, make sure they are ready to listen, not distracted or still absorbed in what was happening before.

An experienced teacher arranges the class so that, when necessary, eye-contact can be established with every student. The power of eye-contact is well known. Communication is not just words, but the whole behaviour pattern that the words are part of. We communicate in a multitude of ways. If a student is not looking at you, held by your gaze sometimes at least, what you want to share with him or her is lost. Listening usually depends on looking too.

A group of students staged a rather adventurous production of Christopher Marlowe's play *Doctor Faustus*, with an ambitious set and a lot of mysterious lighting. They invited a very famous actor to come and see the play and to give them some comments. His verdict was: 'Everything was going for the play, the set was really good for creating the right feeling. The main trouble was in the lighting. The curse of the theatre is inaudibility. And I find if you can't see it, you can't hear it.'

In discussions, in groupwork, when people have to work together they must be able to look at each other, establish eye-contact, get close enough to establish group space rather than individual space. They need to have a group territory in which they work.

## REMEMBER!

*... If we want people to 'hear' what we say, we have to establish contact with them first. Eye-contact is important. Physical contact may be necessary, for example grabbing someone in extreme cases to protect them from danger. Generally you would not touch your students in case your actions were misinterpreted. Sometimes it is appropriate, however, perhaps to attract the attention of a student with a degree of deafness.*

Students with special learning difficulties respond much better to touch than to words. A whole range of human relationships is determined by the level of contact that is made. Think about it.

Ask yourself at intervals:

- Have I lost them?
- What should happen now to restore their attention?
- Is this the time to change the activity or the focus?

Obviously, it is far better to change the activity, to involve them, to engage them actively in the learning process again.

# Visual aids

The major purpose of visual aids is to create a change of focus. They help to create attention. If the class has to focus on the teacher all the time, the pressure on the teacher to perform is acute. And we all have distracting mannerisms – some teachers cultivate them deliberately.

If you switch on an OHP or a slide projector (or indeed a sound source), attention switches away from your face to the screen. This is helpful in dealing with attention span and gives variety. But it becomes self-defeating if the OHP is then left on all the time. You must switch it off again when you want the students to concentrate on something else; otherwise it becomes a distraction.

Since we experience 70 per cent of what we learn by using sight, visual images and presentation are very powerful aids to learning. They are usually more effective than sound alone. Most people's seeing skills are much more highly developed than their listening skills. But this also presents a problem. What we want is attention, and so we should attempt to control the visual images to ensure that we get it. Most rooms are full of visual images. Many of these will divert attention and distract people.

Most teachers use a chalkboard at some time or other. What does it have on it?

Its purpose is the same as any other visual aid: it helps to focus attention and to present information visually. If anything on the board is irrelevant, clean it off. And try to ensure that work on the board is easy to absorb and to follow, that it has some structure. Don't use it as a jotting pad with no attempt to organise what you write.

Take control of the visual stimuli in the room, and make them work for you.

# Information

Try to present a great deal of information visually. To make it effective you need to eliminate unnecessary and possibly confusing detail. A picture is worth a thousand words, but not if it is a poor one or if it is too hard to grasp. We can only absorb and make sense of a limited amount of information.

For instance, suppose you wanted to present the ideas in our earlier discussion of competence and performance criteria (Chapter 8) in a lesson. You could use a visual form, but what you use as a visual focus would not be the same as I am using here as written material in a book, or what you would have on some handout I might use in support. The handout can carry more information and detail because a student has time to study it (although it must still have a clear structure). You could use the format of Tasks 8 and 9, with performance criteria attached.

You might try using this on an OHP transparency. But there is too much information – in the wrong form – here for it to be usable in this way. The information is too wordy. The visual aid is intended to focus attention, not present *all* the information. You are to talk about it, to amplify and explain it. So what you want is a structure of key-words the students can learn quickly and remember.

The OHP transparency might be designed to look more like this. It might even be better as several transparencies, with even less on each to talk about. It could be improved even more by the use of colour. But the important thing is not how 'clever' it is. The question is: how easy is it to read and take in as a whole? to see links between the ideas? to grasp and to understand?

| KEY-WORDS |
| :---: |
| observe – interactions<br>recognise – needs/difficulties<br>respond – feedback<br>appropriate language<br>effective teaching aids<br>skills<br>confidence – understanding – sensitivity<br>honesty – evaluating |

## TASK 11: Designing a visual aid

In designing anything to present visually, whether it is an OHP transparency or work on the chalkboard or a handout, ask critically:

How much information is there on here?
How much of that actually makes it harder to understand?
How much can I get rid of without changing what it says?
What is the least that I need to have on here?
Will one word do? and an arrow? or a simple structure?
How do I help them to see the structure? relationships?
What do I want them to take away?

# 11 Control of the Environment

In Task 9 you evaluated the effectiveness of a lesson plan in a teaching context, and in Task 10 you looked at the communication that was taking place. Let us now consider another important aspect: environmental factors.

Control of the environment is so important in enabling the intended pattern of learning (and teaching) to happen that I have chosen to deal with it separately here. Nevertheless, it must be seen as an integral part of the communication process, receiving due attention in your preparation for teaching.

### TASK 12: Control of the environment

In completing Tasks 9 and 10, were you able to meet the performance criteria below?

PERFORMANCE CRITERIA
4.1 As far as possible the environment is made suitable for the intended learning activities. It is properly equipped.
4.2 The effect of environmental factors on learning is noted.
4.3 Learning areas are set out to support the planned learning activities and are structured to facilitate them.
4.4 Effort is made to optimise the use of the environment.
4.5 A safe working environment is created.

There is nothing particularly difficult to understand here. You know how you react to colour, light, darkness, being too hot or not having enough oxygen in a room. You get depressed when it is always dull and raining – a winter of eternal grey. How cheering it is to see bulbs coming through on a lovely spring day! You've noticed children becoming excited and noisy in a high wind. You have gone to sleep in the cinema or in a lecture. You have felt the atmosphere of railway stations and airports, the pressure of tunnels and the thrill of bridges.

Our surroundings have a marked effect on our feelings and our behaviour. Some people seem to be particularly conscious of the effect of colour – some even choose a car because of its colour. These things do not happen at a conscious level normally.

But there is an extraordinary lack of apparent concern about this kind of thing when it comes to classrooms. They are painted (or not) in rather depressing colours, and workshops and other such places are even worse. They are poorly designed for the activity that is to happen there. Quite often they are badly lit and badly ventilated – they are too hot or too cold. Both have a bad effect on the students' ability to work: in airless rooms they simply go to sleep. Unfortunately, teachers fail to see the cause.

---

**CASE STUDY 14**

---

David visited a high school in Florida to talk to the students. He was asked to compare British schools with those in Florida. He started by asking them if they liked living in caves.

Every public building he visited there, he said, was built without windows. People worked in artificial light and artificial air. The reason was simple. If you have windows you suffer from solar gain: the sun makes the room uncomfortably hot and air conditioning is made even more expensive.

In the more northerly states of the USA and in Europe we try to bring the outside inside with large windows where we can. In Florida, however, they hid from it. It makes for a rather strange experience when you come to it for the first time: you feel chilled to the bone as you walk from a humid street at 90°F into the cool, dry atmosphere of a room at a temperature of only 70°.

Of course, the students had not noticed the absence of windows: they took windowless rooms for granted. Almost anything can be 'normal' if that is all we know.

1  What do you consider to be 'normal' in classrooms here? Given the opportunity to start from first principles, should they really be like that?
2  If you look closely at the environment your students have to work in, how do you think they react to it? What is it saying to your students, not only about the credibility of the teacher who is expecting them to do certain things there, but also about how they are valued as people?
3  What are the effects of the environment on what is supposed to happen there? Is it supportive? suitable?
4  What improvements should be made to make learning easier?

---

# Problems

There are many problems that may be caused by an environment that is hostile to the learning activity and attitudinal changes you wish to encourage. Look carefully at your teaching situation, and try to ensure that it provides an appropriate model of behaviour.

In a computer room there may be broken chairs or scanty work-space for the students to get themselves properly organised to work. The keyboard operator is expected to learn about the importance of posture and organisation, of having a ship-shape office.

Is a room saying 'do as I say, not as I do'? This will handicap both student and teacher. Where is credibility in the learning?

Usually, the problems are more routine. When you observe classes, ask your-self: what are the messages in this room? how is it controlling what happens here? what kind of learning or teaching behaviour does it assume? how much distraction is there? does it make it hard for students to concentrate? how noisy is it? what are the acoustics like?

Again, how much effort is required to get the things the teacher may need? an OHP or a tape-recorder or even a piece of chalk? Or to have any photocopying done? Teachers may stop trying to do more interesting things with their students if it is just too much hard work to get things ready.

# Taking control

## REMEMBER!

*... It is your responsibility to ensure that the environment supports as far as possible what students have to do in order to learn.*

When students arrive in a new environment, they explore it; they look for clues as to how to behave there, as to what is expected of them. The messages are easily, and quite unconsciously, read. They come to it with 'models in the head'.

If they see desks in a row facing a teacher's desk, they know it means: sit down, listen, be quiet. Could they reasonably be expected to engage in groupwork, or even to share ideas in discussion? They can only react with the teacher. Eye-con-tact is possible with no one else: they only see the backs of other students' heads. We need to see people's faces to talk to them, to watch their expressions, to look for the subtle ways in which we communicate: 'how did I know you intended to be funny?'

So move the furniture. Set it up to do what you want to do.

Opposite are four diagrams of possible layouts in a classroom using the same desks and chairs. There are other possibilities. It is useful to look at a few alterna-tive ideas for your own class, using plans of this kind. Think of interactions between individuals, creating groups, sharing activity, or concentrating on private work as with a computer or in language work using a machine. You need to remember that the layout of furniture in any room tells people what is expected to happen there. Think of a kitchen or a bedroom or a dining room. What advan-tages or disadvantages do you think there might be of having the students sepa-rated or grouped in the ways these different arrangements would dictate? When would you use one layout or another? Is it sensible always to use the same layout whatever you want students to do?

What if there are no desks, but comfortable chairs in a circle? What does that say? Or a large table with chairs around it – a committee meeting? What if there is gentle background music playing? What if coffee is set out ready on the table in the corner? What if there are pictures on the wall, and a carpet?

You can create your own environment with a little ingenuity. You are in charge, not the caretaker (though the caretaker is someone you should make friends with). You could plan it with a group of other teachers.

*Fig. 3   Diagrams of classroom layouts 1–4*

You may need to be quite forceful. How many teachers will have the courage or confidence to say, 'Hey! this isn't good enough for my students. If you want them to learn, help me to make it possible.' But you may be surprised how much co-operation you do get if you make enough noise – in a nice way – about it.

There are, of course, many simple things you can do. Open the windows. Make sure there is enough light. Move chairs and tables around. Put up posters and learning materials. Plan the situations you want to create. Create space and territories.

## Overcoming obstacles

Quite often teachers fail to see the potential in the environment, or what can be done with a little imagination. Students may be more inventive than you are, so enlist their thinking too. Encourage them to take control of their group territory if you want them to do certain things, so long as their suggestions are not silly or destructive. They are often less inhibited than you are.

If you know in advance what you want to get hold of and plan well ahead, it is not too hard to ensure that you have the things you want. You can find out where things are, what the system is – or isn't. You can work with the technicians and media resources personnel.

## REMEMBER!
*... Most problems arise because people do not think ahead.*

# Safety

## REMEMBER!
*... Your principal responsibility is to ensure the health and safety of your students at all times.*

Institutions and workplaces have safety rules and regulations. You *must* know what they are and ensure that your students are aware of them. You can begin by looking on the walls of practical rooms, where warning notices and procedures must be displayed – every workroom will have a fire/evacuation procedure prominently displayed, usually by the door.

There will be a member of staff designated 'Safety Officer' with responsibility to carry out checks, organise training and give you the information you need. Ask a member of your team or your section leader who this is in your workplace.

By law, your organisation has to have a safety policy and you are entitled to have a copy of this. So, again, ask your section leader who to approach. You can find copies of the legislation from the Health and Safety Commission in your workplace library, if you have one, or in any public library.

# 12 Assessment

Here, I deal with basic concepts and ideas; we shall explore the complexities of educational examining later in Part 2 of the book. Here we are concerned with feedback, and in assessing learning to facilitate it.

## TASK 13: Assessment

Use feedback and assessment in your planned lesson to promote the intended learning of your students. Evaluate your success in meeting the criteria below.

PERFORMANCE CRITERIA

5.1 The teacher notes carefully interaction between individuals, with the teacher and in groups.
5.2 Learning difficulties are noted: support and help is given.
5.3 There is clear evidence of sensitivity to the problems the students experience and willingness to use feedback.
5.4 Individuals are encouraged to take responsibility for their own learning and progress.
5.5 Assessment methods are identified in the lesson plans.
5.6 The assessment that is planned and used is appropriate for the intended learning and will provide good feedback.
5.7 Learning is assessed by students and teacher.
5.8 Learning is consolidated.
5.9 The session and outcomes are evaluated.

## Feedback

Feedback enables learning to take place. How does it work?

The simplest example of feedback in a closed system is a thermostat to control a heating system and to keep the temperature constant. It feeds back information about the temperature to the boiler. When the desired temperature is reached the thermostat cuts out the boiler. When the temperature drops it re-ignites it.

But learning is not a closed system. It is dynamic and changes with time and experience. Feedback here requires not only some way of monitoring change from inside, but additional input from outside. We need a mirror to reflect back to us an image of what we are doing, or what we are not – some means of judging how well we do whatever we are trying to achieve.

When we work with other people, they provide that mirror. To use the mirror effectively, we have to know what we are looking for, the kind of responses we want – or don't want. Then we change what we do accordingly, to get the desired response.

Everybody knows how to do that. We do it all the time in our normal daily affairs. Otherwise, social groupings and social interaction would be impossible. It is the way we learn.

In formal education and learning, however, we need to invent very complex systems of feeding back information. The learning activities we engage in are complex, so that is hardly surprising.

The learning activities themselves usually provide the feedback that we need. If I am trying to learn to skate, I know whether I am being successful or not! When we attempt sophisticated tasks, when we set up learning as a series of targets with performance criteria, we need to find more complex ways of measuring success. Usually another person's perception is then crucially important.

# Evidence

We have to have some evidence and we must decide what kind of evidence; then we have to make judgements about the evidence, and about what it demonstrates.

What really matters in assessment is the nature of the evidence. If we look for evidence, we must be sure that it is valid – that it actually relates to what we are trying to observe or to measure.

For instance, does it make sense to try to measure how much more skill I have acquired in playing tennis by having me write an essay about it? Yet there is a strongly held view that exams are what matter, and 'an exam is writing essays, isn't it?' What in fact will my ability to write such an essay demonstrate? That I can write the essay, of course, but that is not what I want to find out.

If I want to show that I can write a good essay, however, the only proper evidence I can provide is essays I have written. It is unlikely that I shall succeed in writing a good essay at the first attempt. By using feedback, my own assessment of what I have done maybe and what other people think about it, it is to be expected that my next essay will approximate more closely to a model of what a good essay is. I may also read essays that are said to be good models and try to imitate them. I have to build up a mental picture of what a good essay is like if I am to be able to create a fair approximation of one. It may take me many attempts before I am happy with it.

In education, we may provide feedback within an on-going assessment process. This is called *continuous assessment*. Assessment at the end of a learning programme is called *summative assessment* (summing up). Where assessment is intended to shape learning by feeding back into the learning process, it may be referred to as *formative assessment* since it is intended to give shape or form to the learning.

We can attempt to measure *change* or *achievement*. In both cases, we may use continuous assessment formatively in the learning process; or we may simply use it to record grades in a cumulative way. Where we are concerned principally with change as the student learns, we are likely to use assessment frequently in a formative way so as to shape the learning; and use summative assessment at the end of the course to grade students.

A practical example: as a swimmer, I want to be proficient in life-saving. How shall I achieve that? How shall I know when I am acceptably proficient? How shall I demonstrate it to others?

What I have to do to demonstrate that I am proficient is the same as what I do to learn in order to achieve it. The difference between the two lies in the judgements that are made about what I do. My standard of performance is judged against criteria.

In this case, I might actually be required at some point to save someone from drowning. Proficiency cannot simply be arbitrary judgements made by a judge: either I save someone from drowning or I don't. This is the case with most important learning that we do. The test that matters comes when we have to do it 'for real'.

All learning systems require proper feedback. We must try to see the purpose of assessment as principally to improve the learning. There is a view that assessment is the same as testing. Tests do come in many forms these days and they certainly have value. They are not restricted by any means to essay-writing. But their use in providing feedback is limited. They usually attempt to show some numerical score which may not be helpful in identifying what it is students need to improve or need still to learn.

We need to know this: what we still have to learn, in what way we must improve. In trying to find this kind of evidence we have to look at what students have to do in order to learn. There are usually skills to be learned, and quite often products that can be evaluated. The essay above is a product; so is the pot I have turned on the wheel, or a flower arrangement, or a properly presented word-processed document.

These products are tangible evidence of achievement. They can be compared with previous attempts by this student and compared with those of others, to try to identify some agreed criteria on which we can focus our attention and thinking. We can probably identify what has changed between one attempt and another, and we can try to establish criteria for excellence.

# Criteria

Clearly I will progress more quickly if I do not have to guess by what criteria my success or lack of it will be judged. In most things in life we learn by trial and error, gradually teasing out an idea of what we have to do to be successful. Often this can be a painful experience. We may ask: what are teachers for?

Unfortunately, teachers frequently fail to tell students what they have to achieve: what they must do to succeed rather than fail. What can the learner learn? Do the teachers know what the criteria are? or is it just a feeling they have?

External examinations, set and marked by examining boards, are of course designed to provide summative assessments (see Chapter 23) against which an award may or may not be made. You should seek to provide feedback to your students at every opportunity, however, and to obtain every scrap of information that will assist both you and your students to enhance your performance. Most examination boards do provide feedback; seek it out, and use it to modify and improve your teaching programme.

As we learn, we change in so many interrelated ways: knowledge and skills, perception and insight, attitudinal development. Very little of this can be measured statistically. Most of it is not accessible to the kinds of test that produce scores.

If, as many teachers are, you are required to use tests as part of your teaching programme, please look at the discussion of tests in Chapter 23.

## Progression

The kind of criteria I have devised for this book are to be viewed as signposts, pointing a direction to establish good practice. They define the roads down which to travel, rather than points of arrival beyond which we do not need to go. A teacher who is fully satisfied with a personal performance in any aspect of teaching ceases to ask important questions.

As with the professional painter or musician, each product, each performance, provides a critical evaluation so that the next one can be more mature, more fully formed and more impressive. No artist is ever satisfied: every performance is a learning experience that helps the performer to improve. Your professional judgement will change with experience, insight and knowledge. Progress depends on using experience, reflecting on it to change your perception of what you are about.

It is the same with your students. They have to be fully engaged in the process of learning, and that means also in the process of assessment. They need to reflect on their learning experiences, on what they achieve, in order to improve. So your criteria for them are also signposts rather than goalposts.

## When to assess

Surely, at the end of each learning experience. We need to know what we have learned, whether we have achieved the learning goals and how well: what we need to do *now*.

In designing learning experiences, we must have a clear idea of what students are setting out to learn and how we, and they, will know how far they have progressed towards mastery of it.

There are long-term goals and short-term goals. Each lesson has its short-term goals. They should be perceived as part of those longer-term goals towards which they contribute.

Much of the assessment must take place 'on the wing', as it is happening. The feedback must be as close as possible to the learning for it to have any useful effect. It is not much use knowing that we need to do something differently once the point of need has passed – a week later may seem a very long time. If I am to improve my golf-swing, I need help on the course. Much of the most useful help and feedback a teacher can provide is when students are coming up against difficulties in doing things.

---

**TASK 14:   Evidence and criteria**

1  In your own area of teaching, identify what evidence you would look for to measure the progress of your students.
2  How would you get your students to produce that evidence?
3  What kind of learning would you consider it would measure?
4  In relation to the learning goals, try to identify criteria that you think the activity, or the product of the activity, could achieve if it was well done. Make the criteria as simple and clear as you can.
5  Can you share these criteria with your students before they set out to undertake the activity?
6  How will you provide feedback to your students? Will it be through discussion or in a more formal way?

---

# Self-evaluation

At the end of any learning experience we need to evaluate, take stock of what has happened, where we are now, decide where we go from here. What have you discovered so far? What decisions do you need to make?

ACTIVITY 7 Try to answer the following questions as honestly as you can. There is no need to be highly self-critical. Use your reflective diary to try to see what has happened, what has changed and, perhaps, why.

Where you can, try to identify the evidence for your statement that you might show your mentor for comment or discussion.

1  Lesson planning: how have you rethought your approaches, and why?
2  Communication: what do you now understand? or what has now come into focus?
3  Environment: what do you now have the confidence to do?
4  Observation: what have you observed?
5  Teaching: look again at the performance criteria. How far do you match up to them? What still needs work?
6  Attitudes: do you feel you can relate better with students? How confident are you? Can you explore various methods? How flexible are you, and how adaptable?

## Part 2

# Developing the Learning Programme

# Introduction

While Part 1 focused on preparing and teaching individual lessons, Part 2 is concerned with designing and implementing a programme.

Relying on learning from experience for your further growth simply takes too long. To accelerate the process, you need much more information, ideas and practical advice. This is what Part 2 provides. There is a range of approaches, methods and strategies with analysis of the attendant skills and how to develop them. It is not intended, however, that you attempt to try out all the methods: you must select those that are appropriate to the learning. Select also those Activities that meet your requirements, addressing the material with your own questions related to your perception of what you need. All the Tasks are important, however, and should be undertaken in the order set out.

You will need feedback. We all do in order to learn. You also need to be able to articulate your feelings and your discovery. Ideally you will be able to use this material in a context where you can receive such support. It is feasible to do it on your own, of course, but it is so much better with a mentor and/or colleagues too.

# 13 A Case Study Approach

You have already become familiar with case studies. It is normal for us to deal with problems by reference to what happened on other occasions, usually anecdotally ('I remember when . . .').

Case studies are different in that we try to impose some discipline on them. We give them shape and form so that we can learn from them by interrogating 'the experience' with questions. We can then apply that learning to find a solution either to a present case or to future cases. Or we may compare several case studies, to look for similarities and differences.

## The case study

When you carry out the Tasks associated with Part 2 you will be making an extended case study of your own learning as you design, prepare, implement and evaluate a teaching/learning programme for a group of students in your own context. Your principal responsibility is clearly to your students, but you are also a student in the classroom or wherever it is you are teaching, and you will be exploring your own learning. The case study should enable you to focus on what occurs so as to monitor growth and change throughout the experience.

In Part 1, I adopted a linear approach to designing assignments and supporting ideas and activities. There is a sequence within which good practice in teaching must operate. You cannot plan in a vacuum; you need sufficient information of the right kind.

In designing your case study in Part 2 the same sequencing will be required, for exactly the same reasons. A case study develops over time and within a context. Tasks have to be undertaken in order. You cannot implement what you have not designed, nor evaluate it until after it has occurred.

A useful structure for any design project (a teaching programme is such a design project) is to follow the stages:

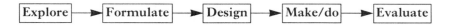

In order to design a programme you have to discover and attempt to answer questions. 'Explore' invites you to discover questions and structure them into a useful, practicable approach.

# Strategy

One area of exploration is to look at alternative strategies for the teaching/learning programme. You need to have some view of the curriculum model you wish to use. To help you, think about a design project you are familiar with – making a dress, a menu for a dinner party, a holiday programme.

There are appropriate and inappropriate ways of setting about doing these things. There is a very wide range of alternative ways of setting about learning. You must choose one that is appropriate for what you want your students to learn: far too often, students and teachers choose unhelpful methods of learning because they have not thought the matter through.

Once you have a clear overview of what you and your students are supposed to be about, you can formulate it into an action plan. You can then design the programme and all its parts.

All this has to be done before the teaching/learning can begin. The case study, however, starts with this thinking and planning, even if the bulk of it is reflection on what actually happens in your teaching. You could usefully start with:

- Who are the students, and what do they need to learn?
- What do they have to do? What do they have to know?
- How will they know what they have to learn?
- How are they going to learn? Where and when? What is the time-scale?
- How quickly can they learn?
- What do they need in order to achieve this learning?
- Are they going to do it alone or with other students?
- What support do they need?
- How will they know when they have learned it?
- How is learning to be demonstrated and tested?
- What standard should it be set at?
- Under what conditions?

Once you have made a list of questions and structured them you will know where to look for answers, and what helpful answers might look like. You can then make decisions.

The strategy chosen here is that of experiential learning. You have now considerable experience to build upon. In order to learn through experience, you have to be able to stand back from what happens to reflect upon it. It will help greatly if you share that reflection with others, if they can provide you with a mirror.

## TASK 15: Student group

The first requirement is a more detailed study of your students. If they do not form a coherent group meeting for a programme of study, it does not invalidate the exercise. You have to design and plan for students as they really are.

If at all possible, discuss various ways of setting about this with your peers and/or your mentor. Agree the form it should take, and the time by which you need to have it ready – of course, the sooner the better in relation to planning, but many teachers have to do preliminary planning work before they first meet the students.

There are many ways of setting about it. One is to create a short questionnaire for yourself or students to complete, perhaps at an enrolment or precourse meeting.

What matters is that you actually use the information. Students may not be too happy if they are asked and then ignored.

Bear in mind that the purpose of this information is to assist you in designing the learning programme. Don't overwhelm yourself with so much information that you cannot use it effectively. Decide what is relevant and useful, what you really need to know. Identify the information that, though interesting, is not particularly useful, and decide whether it is worth having.

Set down clearly for yourself what you need to know. Validate it with your mentor and your peers. Then you can decide how you are to discover the information. Again, the experience of what you did in Part 1 should help you.

# 14 Identifying Needs

Considerable emphasis has been put so far on identifying needs. It will by now be clear that this is not a simple matter. We may distinguish certain needs that arise from practical considerations and are similar for most people within the same situation:

- to create the conditions needed for study, maybe; or
- for groups to work effectively together sharing the same learning programme as in a class.

There are other needs which are less tangible or observable and therefore more difficult to analyse, such as confidence, development of a positive self-image, or the identification of our own or others' psychological barriers to learning.

Creating conditions suitable for learning and study I discuss in various chapters of this book: some may be physical, some psychological, some a matter of structure or priorities, managing time, space, oneself and so on. Here I want to look at some of the needs that affect groups of students and then the more intangible needs of individuals. Naturally, labelling a need as of this or that kind may not be particularly helpful in terms of doing something about it, since we cannot isolate one 'need' from the whole of a person's psychological make-up. But it does help in discussing such needs. Students' needs are complex and largely unknown to them; often there are feelings that are hard for them to express. Even though what they say is not a safe guide as to what is really important for them, they should always be encouraged to articulate their perception of need.

## Groups

Adults require to be consulted, to agree to what the goals are and what is to be learned, what their roles and responsibilities in the learning process are to be. Students ultimately must be responsible for what happens. This may be affected by:

- bad feelings between individuals (or with the teacher)
- a failure for the group or working groups to 'gel'
- poor working conditions that do not value them as people
- pace of work, time of day, tiredness
- lack of comprehension of the teacher or of what they are to do
- lack of commitment if the work seems boring or pointless

- demands that are too heavy or that fail to stimulate or challenge
- lack of relevance to their perception of what the learning is for.

This list is merely a guide to help to shape your thinking about what needs might look like, and most of it is, or could be, within the control of the teacher.

In identifying needs, it is necessary to carry the students with us. But it requires sensitivity on your part, as the teacher, to see it from the point of view of the students. You need to experience what it is like for them. To do that you must watch, observe carefully what happens, how students respond to what they are asked to do, and how the social context of the group develops.

When a class goes well it develops its own momentum. If it dies, you have to know and try to discover what is not going well. The students may feel under-valued or badly treated; individuals or the group may exhibit withdrawal behaviour.

You, as teacher, have to make decisions on behalf of the group. You have to win commitment to a programme, establish common goals and good working relationships to achieve them. You must create supportive conditions for learning activity. To do that you must know what it is for, what is the purpose of the whole enterprise.

Asking students what they want to learn may be ineffective: they will have come expecting you to know and to tell them. You must have your own programme to present to them. Negotiation needs a baseline. To arrive with a blank piece of paper and say, 'well, what shall we do this week, this term?' will usually cause dismay.

# Learning goals

Consolidation and assessment both require that learning goals are stated and agreed. Learning goals need to be stated simply, in terms it is easy for the students to comprehend and agree to, and which make it easy for them to assess in terms of progress and achievement.

Any negotiation of goals must begin from the teacher's statement of learning goals and a programme to achieve them. You need to have a rationale for your choice of programme. You should also make it clear how flexible you are prepared to be to meet your students' perception of what they need to learn. They will trust you so long as they see what they are asked to do as stimulating and interesting, and they feel they are making progress in the learning.

The better organised the teacher, and the easier it is for students to do the things planned as learning activities, the more success there will be within the programme as a whole.

# Personal needs

Almost all of us, as social human beings, have personal needs. Most of us are usually shy of telling people about these, although some have no such inhibitions.

Encounter groups in both the United Kingdom and America encourage people to express their anxieties and needs.

Many people come to adult/community education as a way of satisfying some of these deeply felt needs. Every student is dealing with a host of conflicting emotions and pressures. Teachers should not attempt to be counsellors or try to deal with students' personal problems, however, though the relationship with individuals may allow some of that to happen. Nevertheless, they need to be sensitive to what individuals bring to the class. Much of the behaviour relates to such feelings.

All of us need to maintain a self-image we are happy with, self-esteem and a sense of achievement. We all need success and find failure damaging. We need social contacts and friendships. Many people come to our classes looking for these things. Others feel themselves constantly under pressure from the demands of others, and are trying to identify goals or interests peculiarly their own.

There are extrinsic pressures too, such as the need for qualifications and to get or keep a job. Students may feel threatened by change in their working environment and the need to keep up with it.

It is easier to deal with personal needs as part of a learning programme through individual (or even small group) tutorials (see Chapter 17). The progress, or lack of it, in learning activities may be because of personal factors that students cannot express in front of the large group, or even in a small group they work well with.

What students (or employers) pay for in teaching sessions is time, and the effective use of time is what planning of programmes is mostly about. It is impossible to do everything in class time. Whatever programme is set up, much learning has to take place outside class time with students working on their own or in groups.

In designing teaching/learning programmes, teachers will need to cost the use of time in some way. To be effective, students must take an active part in the learning process. Setting the learning up as individual and group learning activities should release time that can be used for individual tutorial support. They require opportunities for individual feedback and support.

## Motivation: tasks

Herzberg, in *The Motivation to Work*, saw 'motivators' as largely arising from tasks: what the individual or group was expected to do. Many women, for instance, complain of the menial quality of much of what they have to do, and how this defines their role. Such feelings tend to demotivate.

Our perception of our role and the tasks we have to do can give rise to satisfaction, excitement and stimulation, or to hostility and even despair. Bear this in mind as you identify roles in group learning, and as you design tasks for your students to do.

What roles do the students perceive? How does it look to them? For example, what effect will it have on apprentices who are expected to take dictated notes in class for three hours and practise for hours in a workshop things they do every day at work, if they are then told by the boss, 'You can forget that – we don't do it that way'? Things like this do happen.

Motivation has been studied intensively. What makes people want to do things? to put in effort? to overcome pain? Most people find they do much better, keep going against the odds, if they have the support and challenge of others with them. There are so many examples. It explains the enormous growth of clubs for slimmers, cyclists, those trying to give up alcohol or people rebuilding their lives after emotional trauma. We all need others to share what we do, the pain and the thrills. It is so hard to keep going on your own. We need competition as well as support.

From this stems the importance of groupwork and group tasks. Individuals will often achieve a great deal more through peer group support. But peer group pressure may level down as well as up, so that the teacher needs to monitor carefully what actually happens.

Success breeds success, failure demotivates. Ensure that the tasks and the learning programme you set up are likely to be achievable by your students. If they are too hard (equally if they are not challenging enough) or incomprehensible or seem to have little to do with what the students feel they are actually trying to learn, little real effort will be put into them.

In designing learning programmes, designing the learning tasks will be the most important part of the preparation.

# The cost of failure

Much motivation can be calculated by the cost of failure and how well people are prepared to come back from failure.

Perception of the cost of failure to achieve goals set by oneself, by parents, by employers or by one's peer group, is vitally important in what people are prepared to do. In some societies, the cost is very great – it can lead to high suicide rates. Elsewhere it may lead to people playing very safe, and being unwilling to take risks or personal responsibility.

In other societies, individuals are encouraged to take risks when failure is tolerated or there is always a second chance to do it. When failure is over-indulged and all pressures are removed, the tendency is to drop out and take it easy.

This is why it is so important to establish clearly the rules and expectations within the learning group. Teachers can use the natural competitiveness of groups to good effect here. Peer group pressure not to let the group down is a powerful motivator. But individuals also need to know what is expected of them in regard to their personal learning programme. They need an action plan and time schedules. These should be monitored through tutorials.

# 15 Devising a Learning/Teaching Strategy

A strategy is an overview, a model in the head if you like, of the kind of course you are setting up. It enables you to know what you are trying to do, how you see it happening. Although there are many strategies that may be used in whatever you set out to do, some are much more effective than others; but what works well in one context may not be quite so effective in another. You have to choose the one that is right for you and your students and for the kind of learning you hope they will achieve.

Strategy is a word used originally in a military context and comes from Greek, that may be translated 'military leader'. It describes an overall plan for winning – anything from a war to a game of hockey, or a successful business venture. You will have to win the co-operation of 'your team', but yours is the responsibility for the overall plan: where you are going, how you will succeed *together*.

Clearly, it is 'the team' who must make the plan work. What the leader does on his or her own is not likely to achieve much. It is not enough for teachers to adopt a teaching strategy; it must link clearly with the learning strategies devised for their students, which should be the ones most likely to succeed. It is irresponsible to send students off to do things if they have not been thought through in terms of where they will lead them. In most cases, too, there will be added benefit in working with colleagues in groups or as teams, especially if the tasks involve problem-solving.

Learning, as we have seen, is change in many things. Teachers should have an overview of changes in students that the teaching/learning programme they are designing seeks to promote, of how those changes will occur, and how they will be managed and assessed.

Any course or programme may be judged on:

- the **cognitive changes** it is intended to facilitate
- the **behavioural changes** that will be observed
- the **enrichment** it provides through learning experiences
- its **effectiveness** in achieving the learning (obviously).

Because cognitive and behavioural changes are the easiest to observe and assess, courses are usually designed with emphasis on one or the other of these. But enrichment is just as important, since attitudinal change is usually a prerequisite of other learning and results from the nature of the learning experiences and the tasks students are asked to do and the roles they perceive themselves being given (see page 103). In adult education also, enrichment is frequently the major purpose of a course.

You cannot plan your teaching strategy to facilitate the students' learning behaviour before you know what it is. The appropriate way forward is for you to identify:

● what your students are setting out to learn and the changes that need to happen
● what learning strategies and behaviour is likely to succeed best.

Many teachers will say that the strategy is decided for them by awarding bodies or other influential groups such as employers. I am talking here about decisions teachers make which are intrinsic to the learning process, not instrumental questions like methods of assessment of the outcomes of the learning, though it is true that assessment procedures often have an unfortunate effect on how far teachers feel they are free to choose not only the content of their course, but also their approaches to teaching it. There is much more emphasis these days on negotiated curricula, but teachers really do have a great deal more freedom to choose the design of their courses than they might think.

Any strategy, yours or the students', may be more or less successful. People do not usually decide consciously how they are going to learn, they just set off. Frequently they run into trouble because their chosen learning strategy is inappropriate to the intended outcomes. Observe students in your classes who have not grasped what the task is they are asked to do. If they thought about it they could do it more efficiently. The important questions about a learning strategy are:

● Does it work? Will it work?
● Is it the most effective way of learning this?
● Is it efficient in the expenditure of time and effort?
● Are there other strategies? Would they be more effective?

## ACTIVITY 8 | Murder Game (bottom-up/top-down)

Play the Murder Game to see learning strategies in action.

There always seems to be the same pattern of behaviour when a group plays this game. Obviously, it won't work for you since you will have read this description first!

THE MURDER GAME

The purpose of the game is to extract the information about a murder in a country house (a cliché, of course). All the 'clues' and information are printed on individual cards. The cards are shuffled and dealt out to the participants so that each has a fairly even number of clues.

It is a leaderless game: this is important. Everyone in the group has equal responsibility for solving the mystery and the methodology for doing so. No information is given that is not on the cards. No instructions are given. The group has to make up its own rules of play.

Two observers make notes on what occurs – what individuals and the group decide and do, how the mystery is solved. The debrief is concerned with the strategies of learning they chose.

People usually try a 'bottom-up' approach first: 'Let's have everyone read out what's on their cards, I'll start.' 'Let's put the cards on the table so we can see the information.' This soon becomes impossible; there is too much to take in and no shape or order to it. There is a moment of hilarity or panic.

Someone will probably suggest that they should look for patterns. 'I've got something about a knife on the floor. Has anyone got anything to add to that?' This looks and feels more promising. Confidence begins to rise.

Eventually, someone is likely to suggest they write down specific questions and see who has information to answer them: for example, who was killed? when? where? what with? any red herrings? This begins to look and feel like business.

It will be successful if they identify the right questions. This is called a 'top-down' strategy: it aims to ask who has got any information about the weapon, the room, the time and so on. It imposes some logic and structure and pattern on the proceedings which pays off immediately. It is pro-active. Soon, all is revealed.

In the debrief, it is important to ensure that people talk about their feelings as well as their lack of comprehension. How did it feel to be frustrated? to be overwhelmed with information you could not use or make sense of? How did it feel when light began to dawn? How did they eventually reach the result? Was it by little steps, or did it suddenly all fall into place?

The game is experiential, about 'feeling it'. We have to feel these things if we are to know how it frequently is for students.

Case Study 5 in Part 1 used the Table Game, which provides another valuable way to gain insight into learning strategies. How do people attempt to learn the contents of the table? What strategies do they use?

Those who try to memorise a jumble of disconnected ideas fail. Those who can relate things in terms of categories or structures succeed better. How often we choose the first way in so many things we try to learn! How often teachers impose this on students too! Why do they do that?

First find the questions. I strongly advocate the 'top-down' approach.

# Other strategies

These are only a few examples of learning strategies. You will observe both teachers and students using many more. You should try to analyse them: what strategy do you think they are using? Most people do not consciously choose a way of learning something. To help you, here are a few more examples. The paragraphs below are only short summaries of approaches that mostly in practice involve a lot of thinking about.

## Travelling hopefully

This is the strategy most people use most of the time: it is mainly trial and error learning. It is how we deal with life, of course – a Micawberish optimism that 'something will turn up' – and it is often painful and ineffective, an inefficient way of learning. But we are not dealing with 'real life' learning here. What are teachers for? In acquiring skills, maybe it is unavoidable, but learning is much easier if it is given some shape and structure; and it is made much more effective by the use of feedback in relation to identified goals.

## Indoctrination

Some teachers may wish to avoid risks altogether, making all the decisions themselves and avoiding challenge or thinking. Where the importance of demonstrably high standards of performance weighs heavily, with strong emphasis on using the 'right' techniques, it may lead to repetitive practice and rote-learning without understanding.

Many forms of training have used such strategies, but they are less effective than involving the students more actively in decisions about their learning, to give them some ownership.

## 'Cram it all in'

Students faced with examinations frequently adopt the strategy, of 'memorise it, don't try to understand it – that will come later.' Teachers also succumb to it in despair at the size of syllabuses they and the students have to cover.

## Competing groups

This strategy is frequently used in business, on playing fields or even on the factory floor. Many games are used in education and training programmes. Properly managed, they may generate motivation and energy; when badly handled they can destroy good working relationships.

## Interactive and group-based projects

Humans are social animals and they produce better results when they work effectively in groups. This is normal human behaviour. There is also a richness in the experience and expertise of the group members, which is a valuable resource that should be exploited. In problem-solving in particular, generating and sharing ideas and activity is important. But organisation and control of group activities do require special skills. I have advocated the use of the strategy in this book for the development of interpersonal skills and the enrichment that it can achieve.

# Tell and test

I once said to an American friend that I had observed in America a tendency to use this approach. He said, 'Yes, but it's like this. First, you tell 'em you're going to tell 'em – then you tell 'em – then you tell 'em you've told 'em – then you test 'em.' This strategy appears to be efficient in terms of test results, but testing dominates the whole learning process.

# Research and report back

This strategy is used very effectively with students who are well motivated and will work without supervision. Clearly, they have to develop the skills and expertise needed to find information for themselves. If individuals report back to a group to share what they have discovered it is a valuable strategy for enlarging the information base of the group. It also encourages students to take responsibility for their own learning.

# Problem-solving

Challenging students with problems to solve is a well-established procedure in maths and science teaching. In fact, it is integral to almost any 'subject' area with a practical basis or application. Thinking through a problem to a solution is an effective way of learning and can lead to insight. It can be exciting, but also frustrating. It will expose the elements that have not been grasped in understanding principles or theory, and will identify what needs to be discovered or learned. The strategy can be used very effectively with groups.

# Discovery learning

This strategy promotes the excitement and fun of 'exploring' which is a basic instinct of all higher animals. We should try to make learning fun if we can. In the early years of school, learning through play is very effective. Discovery learning, however, is not to be merely play. The less control teachers have of the process, the more carefully the activities need to be designed to ensure that more comes out of it than fun. Many projects labelled 'discovery learning' are intended to be very serious, in science laboratories, for example.

# Closed and open strategies

By 'closed' we mean that the outcomes are predictable. By 'open' that the outcomes are unpredictable and the processes dynamic, that is changing with time. In Part 3, I explore arguments for adopting particular approaches and discuss theorists who have researched and advocated them. Behaviourists believe in closed programmes of instruction: teacher-centred and with predicted outcomes and structured processes to achieve them. Cognitive philosophers advocate 'open', dynamic, student-centred learning.

Deductive approaches to learning/teaching are closed strategies. In these, rules and concepts are stated that lead to predictable outcomes. There is little room for creativity even in student-centred programmes. Learning mathematics for most students, even in maths workshops, is getting right answers by correct methods. Inductive strategies on the other hand are open: 'we're going to mess about in this area for a bit to see what we can discover.' They are about generating questions and problem-solving.

Strategies may be more or less open, allow more or less control of goals and processes. Travelling hopefully is an open strategy. It is unpredictable in both its processes and its outcomes.

Indoctrination is a closed strategy. All the decisions have been made by the teacher; everything is to be predicted, process and outcomes alike. Some strategies employ 'conditioning' as a deliberate means of controlling/shaping learning; these derive from the theory of learning known as behaviourism.

## TASK 16: Strategy and learning programme

You must develop some overview of what you and your students are about – what the relationship is between your activity as teacher and theirs as learners.

1 Try to clarify to yourself what you consider the responsibilities and roles to be, both theirs and yours. How far are you willing to involve them in the decision-making? What are the constraints?
2 How will you communicate with them to share such thinking?
3 What kind of learning/teaching strategy is most likely to help them achieve the learning goals you have in mind for them? How would you justify your choice of that particular strategy?

Design a learning/teaching programme for your student group.

This programme will clearly develop and change, since it covers a series of sessions over time. The strategy you devise will give it overall shape. Within that there has to be a variety of learning experiences that match the learning needs and goals.

The performance criteria below are intended to outline what is good practice in such a design. The statements build on those in Part 1, but are to be understood as implying greater depth. The feedback from reflecting on your experience of using various approaches and methods will ensure there will be development both of the strategy and the methodology through the programme.

Lesson plans and evaluations with consequent rethinking, getting together of materials and resources cumulate into the case study.

PERFORMANCE CRITERIA FOR PREPARATION/DESIGN
1 Students within the group are known in relation to their educational and/or employment background, personal learning goals and motivation.
2 There is shared perception of learning goals in the group and with the teacher, both overall and within each lesson.

3 Teaching sessions are planned and sequenced to meet specified and/or negotiated goals clearly known to all. Links are clear; the students understand how the activities and sessions are intended to progress towards achievement of the overall learning goals.

4 There are clear links with prior learning in the process.

5 Where appropriate, the learning is consistent with requirements of external examining bodies with suitable assessment.

6 Teaching methods/learning activities planned are relevant and appropriate to promote the intended learning and for the students in terms of their background and ability.

7 Sessions will engage students in learning through activities consistent with their readiness to learn and undertake them.

8 Sufficient flexibility will allow for different pace/styles of learning for individual students.

9 The learning materials and aids designed/selected will be effective for the intended learning and of a presentable standard.

10 Assessment of the learning is clearly identified in planning sessions and activities.

11 There is evidence of critical evaluation of the effectiveness of the materials, the activities and the learning programme.

## TASK 17:   Designing tasks

Analyse carefully what it is you are asking your students to do. What is their role? What is your role? How much is required of individuals and how much full participation by the group?

What level of difficulty and challenge do you perceive? How will they see it? Have you thought through what is required to achieve the task? What are the criteria for success? How will they know?

What level of preparation and guidance is there? What resources will you provide and what must they devise?

What are the learning goals? Have the students agreed them? Is it clear what the task is for – how it contributes to the learning? How will the learning be demonstrated and assessed?

It is essential that *before they begin* students know clearly what they have to do individually and together, what it is for, where it is going, how to get there and how it will all be assessed.

## TASK 18:   Designing and implementing individual lessons/sessions

The good practice established in Part 1 should inform what you do. Each learning session will require a lesson plan and teaching/learning activities and materials. The links should be clear, and what is planned should be relevant and stimulating.

Since you will be using these sessions as the main substance of your case study, use a variety of methods and approaches. The criterion must be that they make sense to students in what they feel they are about.

You should also be able to evaluate sessions with your mentor to match your views of what happens and to make your own assessment of progress towards satisfying the performance criteria set out below. There should, therefore, be evidence of this in the way your thinking and teaching develop through this programme. To summarise:

- plan and use a variety of approaches and methods
- evaluate what happens thoroughly and honestly.

PERFORMANCE CRITERIA FOR INDIVIDUAL SESSIONS

1 Each session addresses specified learning goals.

2 Teaching methods and techniques are appropriate/relevant to these goals and the characteristics of the students.

3 Sufficient skill is demonstrated in using the chosen methods.

4 The duration, sequence, structure and content of each session is effective and properly controlled.

5 Where appropriate, the teaching/learning content and methods are consistent with examining board requirements.

6 Learning problems and opportunities for further learning are identified during the session and the programme adapted.

7 Learning and teaching aids are used skilfully and effectively.

8 Individuals and groups are managed effectively. Control of the session and the learning is maintained. The health and safety of the students are assured.

9 Learning is linked, consolidated and assessed.

10 Each session is properly evaluated.

# 16 Teaching Methods – Teaching Skills

## Control and management

The methodology from which teachers may choose ranges through a continuum, from total control by the teacher to total control by the individual student of his or her own learning. Where over the range you, as teacher, choose methodology in relation to retaining control depends on many factors, not least your confidence in yourself and in how far your feel able to trust your students. The table summarises the teacher control/student control continuum.

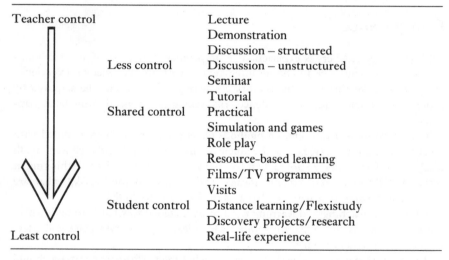

| Teacher control | | Lecture |
| | | Demonstration |
| | | Discussion – structured |
| | Less control | Discussion – unstructured |
| | | Seminar |
| | | Tutorial |
| | Shared control | Practical |
| | | Simulation and games |
| | | Role play |
| | | Resource-based learning |
| | | Films/TV programmes |
| | | Visits |
| | Student control | Distance learning/Flexistudy |
| | | Discovery projects/research |
| Least control | | Real-life experience |

Who makes the decisions? Who chooses the content or sequence, the learning materials, learning goals or interactions? Who controls pace, assessment procedures and criteria for success? Is it the teacher or the students? It depends on so many things:

- the teacher's ability to cope with demands students may make if decisions are left to them
- their ability to cope with the responsibility of choice
- their motivation, and the commitment they have to the learning
- their sense of ownership of decisions that are made
- whether they are used to a totally passive role and, if so, whether they can cope with a greater degree of control – will they know how to learn?

Teachers and students have to learn to use the chosen methods effectively. Choice depends on the following:

- knowing enough about the alternatives available
- having confidence to use the appropriate choice
- having sufficient skill to be effective
- ensuring that it works – feedback/evaluation.

Effectiveness involves:

- suitability of methods for promoting the intended learning
- variety, both within learning sessions and in a programme
- economy of effort relative to learning benefit
- human factors
- proper planning and resourcing within constraints of time
- proper control and management of the learning process
- sufficient skill in using methodology (both teacher and students)
- proper use of feedback, monitoring and flexibility
- assessment of learning, and evaluating process and outcomes.

# Competence

All learning by teachers is experiential. Competence in the use of any methodology involves being able to choose intelligently, with the knowledge, experience and skill to make chosen methods work effectively. This can only be acquired by experience, which requires confidence, risk-taking and reflection on what happens.

The appropriateness of chosen methods of teaching or learning, as noted with regard to overall strategy, is vital. Frequently, the method is hardly 'chosen' at all: teachers and students go for a familiar behaviour pattern without thinking it through. 'Old and tried' usually means 'easiest, least bother'. Ask, 'what are we/they setting out to learn?' and 'what is the best way to do that?'

Methods of teaching and learning need to be matched to what is to be learned, but the conditions and constraints under which learning is to take place will affect both decisions and outcomes.

It is hard, therefore, to specify too closely what the performance criteria should be for success in the use of any method. The measure of success is always how far the students achieve their learning goals rather than the performance of the teacher. Nor is it easy to match one to the other: all sorts of factors that are not within the control of the teacher affect success.

Some of these factors are explored in case studies or elsewhere in the book. They include such things as the weather, unsuitable classroom design and equipment, conflicts between individual students or hostility of groups, the attitudes of employers, demands of awarding bodies, pressures at home and so on. The important thing is to watch students carefully; and to try to discover what is affecting the way they cope with your programme. Consultation may help to alleviate problems.

Any method can be made more effective. Decisions about which you use and what then happens must be carefully evaluated. A mentor to share the experience, to provide a mirror, matters. So too do your students' views. Learning requires controlled risk-taking.

# Lectures

This is a general term covering a range of activities. Some lectures are very formal, given in spacious lecture theatres to large audiences at a safe distance, even requiring use of a microphone.

Lecture-style is used with ordinary classes, too. Micro-lessons may turn into mini-lectures – the skills involved do need practice. All teachers use a didactic style some of the time, even in informal classes and programmes. All lessons have input, even if it is brief (as it should be). This does need to be done well.

Many teachers will point to the advantages of lecturing. It is economic in time and teacher costs. Teachers can deal with large amounts of content relatively quickly and efficiently, possibly with many students. Lecturing allows the efficient transmission of accurate and up-to-date information.

Lectures may be effective not only in ensuring students acquire information, but also in stimulating them to want to find out more about a topic, to become active, enthusiastic learners rather than passive listeners. How can we ensure that happens?

## Preparation

Know your stuff. You cannot teach what you do not know.

Leave nothing to chance. Prepare AVA materials, set them up beforehand and test the equipment. You don't want to have to change a fuse at the start of your lecture. (All the same, I carry a small screwdriver, just in case. Spare bulbs, too.)

Test also for visibility and acoustics. Have things such as handouts and acetate slides to hand, in order and sequence. It is important to control the learning conditions. Practise.

Appear – and be – organised. Impressions count. Take control.

## Structure

Give your students a handout with a key-word structure. It should state your learning goals and your method of assessing the learning, if appropriate. Tell them whether they are to take notes, and in what form: you may decide to provide a summary note-structure for them, leaving space for their own notes. (Note-taking is discussed on pages 156–7).

Bear in mind their attention span – about fifteen minutes, or less if things become physically uncomfortable. Change the focus frequently with visual stimuli. And think two-way. Use opportunities for feedback at intervals, such as taking questions; this is often done at the end of the session, but I find it better to take questions as they arise. Or consolidate by recapping and making a link to the next section. This removes strain and gives students confidence that they do understand the information. Use the key-word structure to check you are not straying.

Another approach is to take questions at the beginning. If a group comes to a lecture properly alert they will have their own questions. This is a good way of knowing where they are starting from, their mind-set, that can help you to direct your input more accurately to their needs. It is very easy for teachers to 'miss' students completely. Your alerting structure must address questions, yours and theirs.

Leave time at the end for a final consolidation. Link your input to what they are to do to ensure they use it effectively.

## Human factors

Watch and check that you can be heard, and that your visual aids can be seen. Ask the people at the back – tell them to keep you up to the mark if they can't hear you. Pitch your voice low, but think of talking only to the person furthest away. Talk slowly. Leave gaps for them to think about what you have said. Watch! If you see attention drifting, consolidate and recap. Consider 'noise' and distractions – don't just ignore them and hope.

## Personal contact and feedback

Language register and use of symbols and/or vocabulary must be at a level of shared experience with the audience; if not, you must explain them. A good strong image is useful to grab attention. Use personal names if at all possible. Humour helps too! Get your audience on your side.

Try to establish eye-contact with members of the group. Don't get trapped by the situation in the lecture-hall. Move around when you can, or even go behind them to teach from the back, especially if you want them to concentrate on the visual material you are showing – you can then see it as they do.

Enter a closer space zone. Become part of the group, discussing what is being shown, so that you can understand how it is for them, and be aware of any difficulties particular students may be having. Ask individuals (by name) to explain things – to give you feedback, a two-way exchange. 'Distance' matters.

Lecturing can create barriers. What is your posture saying to them? What are your signals about personal space and physical distance? behind a desk? on a rostrum? What is the message about roles and relationships?

## What have they learned?/Follow up

What have they learned? How will you know? How will they? You need to consider what is appropriate in terms of assessing learning from input however it happens. They need to do something with it. They need a means of revisiting the learning too. What will they take away in order to do this? Consider that carefully in your planning.

Unless your lecture is a one-off occasion, it should have an effect on the learning process you have devised overall. What part? How does it link to other input or other activity? What is to happen after the input/lecture, however short or long? What do the students need to enable them to use the new material effectively?

## Evaluation

All this forms part of the evaluation of the lecture/input. But if all that is evaluated is the teacher's performance, what has that to do with student learning? What should the evaluation be about?

This is a most important question. The answer includes the factors above, clearly. But was it effective for its major purpose? How did it affect or accelerate learning?

The performance criteria for competence in using the lecture method are not essentially different from those for other approaches and are those set out in Task 18: Designing and Implementing Individual Sessions, above.

## Demonstrations

All teachers are role-models. We inevitably demonstrate to our students what we truly believe to be appropriate behaviour, whatever we are doing, wherever we are working. Bear this in mind, especially if you are working in areas of danger or where good practice in working should be a matter of habit. It is too easy to signal 'do as I say, not as I do!' – if it is unsafe, you *must* not do it. The teacher's overriding, inescapable responsibility is the students' health and safety. In that sense everything we do is a demonstration.

More particularly, we need to consider the formal demonstrations of a skill or a technique, if only how to structure notes.

## Preparation

Much more time is required for the preparation than for the actual demonstration. You have to think it through. Remember that, to be effective, a demonstration has to be short and highly focused. If the students are to attempt to master them afterwards, you can only demonstrate small-scale skills/techniques. Students cannot take in the whole of a long presentation from one exposure. So they have to select what they think they need or what they are alert to. Plan on providing the essentials – never mind the frills.

## Models

Support the learning with an additional model in the form of written instructions (set out clearly and sequentially as 'do this' statements), possibly supplemented with a diagram or a flow-chart.

Think about models. If they know where they are going, what the finished product should look like, say, they will have a model in the head to work towards. Whether the model is a gâteau or a machined part, a step in ballet or a passage on the piano, it had better be a good one. Arthur Cranmer, in his book *The Art of Singing*, tells how Sir Thomas Beecham did not like the way a singer sang a particular phrase. 'Not like this . . .,' he said, and made an awful noise. 'Like this . . .'. He made the same awful noise!

## The whole and the bits

If you plan to give your demonstration only once, it will be hard for students to grasp unless it is very short and/or immediately followed by their doing it.

One way of overcoming the problem is to have what you do recorded on video. This is not to replace the actuality of demonstrating in an appropriate context with the group observing you. That is necessary, but a video-recording of the same demonstration has advantages:

- you do it at normal speed, using your practised skill
- you can watch with them and explain things clearly
- you can replay the video at half-speed (it is very hard for a skilled person to actually do things at half-speed)
- you can put the video-tape on 'hold' to look at details and take questions
- the students can always replay the model.

This last is vital. Learning is most effective at a point of need. You cannot know what you have failed to see or need to grasp until you find you 'can't remember how to do this bit'.

In practice, when the students' turn comes round, they will go through the experience a bit at a time. It is easy for the teacher's demonstration either to ignore the bits or to fail to present the whole properly. It is important to analyse the various steps and skills needed – the tricks of the trade – to show clearly how each is done. But they are to be seen as part of the whole conception, like phrasing in music or brush-strokes on canvas.

## How and why

Although you demonstrate 'how', you are in fact telling the students 'why' this rather than that: your demonstration is about knowledge as well as about skill. So you must explain clearly, as well as show, the skills or techniques they are to learn. This is the part that is easy to ignore or do badly. Make sure you understand what it is they need to know. How will you ensure they know it?

It is much more effective to make the theory part of the 'doing', rather than a separate input session: even if you choose to teach it separately, the link can only be made in a practical context.

Again, the video helps, since you can pause and repeat and so involve the group in question and answer to ensure they understand *why* as well as *how*.

# Where

The environment should be properly designed for the activity. You are modelling good practice, so everything must be right. Set up everything to hand and in order. You can't be hunting for something at a critical moment. Check equipment is working and is what it should be – improvising is wrong. If you are using knives, say, which knife? is it sharp?

Wear the right clothes too. Do things need to be sterile? Are special safety precautions involved? Students must see them used.

# Human factors

Nor can the students learn if they cannot hear or see the demonstration. Later, it is important for them to explore the experience with all the senses, and only then will they fully grasp it – the weight of the knife, the pressure to exert and so on. But in your part, you can get them to handle a piece of equipment or feel the texture of, say, clay, or a fabric, as long as it serves to concentrate attention rather than to distract.

How can you ensure every student can see? This can be a major problem if more than ten are trying to crowd around you. Practical work is often done on flat surfaces, and uses small hand movements rather than large gestures. What angle of view do they need? Even in the round, how can a group of nurses crowd around a bed and all see the same thing? Or apprentices around a lathe, or caterers around a bench?

Some cookery rooms have large mirrors over the bench. Most teachers have to solve the problem in other ways. One way is to show the skill/technique repetitively to four or five students at a time. This is excellent use of personal space, but what will the others do meanwhile? Plan an activity for them – otherwise, boredom.

A video camera may be the only practical solution (you need a technician too). It lets you focus to cut out distracting detail, and can let the students see things exactly as the demonstrator sees them. You can view things from odd angles – from vertically above, say. This can overcome the problem of trying to talk to students through the back of your head too – if you are working at a lathe, say. How can they possibly hear your explanation? Do you talk as you do? talk first? or do, then talk about it? You can't maintain eye-contact so you have no feedback, while the group may neither see nor hear properly.

# Time-management

You need to plan how much time to allow for the various activities. Where do you need to put the emphasis, on what they see or what they do? Indeed, what are they to do while you demonstrate? Time needed relates to the content and complexity of what you and they are setting out to do. Since doing it well has to be properly planned, that needs costing in time too.

## Structure

Structure is concerned with sequencing within a time-plan. The students need to practise themselves, as soon as possible after a demonstration, so that your part and theirs become linked into the learning process. In order to plan properly you must know what the students are going to do to acquire the skill/technique and make it part of their competence.

## Speed and dexterity

You find it easy. Try to remember when it was hard. That is where they are now, and where you need to start from. Their newly acquired ability will be the measure of your success.

A skilled performance is characterised by its speed and dexterity, by not having to think about it, by the memory in the muscles. This doesn't just happen: it comes from doing it many times successfully. It is true of all skills, at whatever level.

It is very hard to teach something slowly that you don't think about at all when you do it normally. Thinking about what you are doing can make you clumsy. If you try to think how you ride a bike you can fall off! If you try to analyse how you balance going down every step of the stairs, or how you hit a ball with a racket, you will see how complex these actions are. It requires practice to do them slowly and to be aware of each step. Practise doing your demonstration slowly – but not in front of students.

Skill in the end is about what it feels like to do something well. It is an internal experience that leads to externally observable behaviour. The teacher provides the mirror to enable a student to do it well, and how it feels to do it well.

## Evaluation

You need feedback from your students. It is not enough for you to feel good about it. Did it help them to gain insight? Do they understand what is involved, and why, as well as how to do it?

## Lecture-demonstrations

Lecture theatres and science laboratories are often equipped with demonstration benches, designed to enable lecturers to demonstrate practical applications of principles they are teaching. In science, the teacher may demonstrate an experiment that students will then also do on their benches. This is an advance on what used to happen in many science classes when the students' activity was confined to taking notes.

The main purpose is to enhance transmission of information to the group by the use of tangible, sometimes sizeable and sophisticated equipment. It is better to see real things actually working than to be told about it. But the ergonomics of seeing from any considerable distance or as a group around a bench are the same as in any other demonstration. Lecturers often need to ask, 'Can you see what happens when I do this? or how this part works?' The answer almost equally often is 'no'.

When teachers wish to use such demonstrations as part of lecture presentation of information, they must consider such factors seriously. No visual material is much good if students cannot see it. Nor is there much advantage in having tangible objects, as against perhaps a video presentation, if students cannot touch them.

Film or video may be much more successful where presentation is to be made to a large group. The ability to focus attention, or to enlarge the image of small parts, or to stop and repeat, adding to the explanation or using two-way discussion, will ensure that what is presented is seen and understood. For small groups there may be greater advantage in the tangible experiment.

Enhancement of the images using a video set-up in the ways described on page 122 may be even better. The group can see both the experiment or equipment on the bench and the person getting it to work, while the camera can focus, enlarge and so on to ensure that everyone gets a first-class view. If the demonstration is also recorded, the re-run can be used along with previous recordings.

# Skills practice

The essence of a practical is 'getting the feel of it'. I feel the weight of a knife in my hand, the danger of cutting my finger off, or the wetness and smell of the clay, the near-impossibility of drawing it up off a wheel. 'Why won't it do it for me when the teacher seemed to do it so easily?' 'Why does my cake sag in the middle?'

Handling a practical is handling frustration for teacher and student. Oh! the temptation to be able to take it out of their hands and just show them again how easy it is! Why is it they can't understand? It's individualised, resource-based learning: all the 'good' words. What can we do to make it easier and more rewarding for them and for us?

We can improve performance once a minimum competence is achieved by a better understanding of what happens and why. No amount of knowledge about balance or moments or forward velocity will help you to ride a bike until you have mastered the ability to stay on it. You must know what it feels like to pedal, steer and balance, to go much faster on the bike than you expect to without panicking.

# Barriers

The teacher cannot be totally in charge of what happens, even if the class 'do it by numbers', army training style. Individuals adopt their own learning pattern and strategy, and bring attitudes and learning barriers to the experience as well as acquired skill.

Clearly, they have to believe they *can* do it. If a demonstration makes it look too magical and amazingly perfect, it may convince some people that they never will.

We have to deal with the confidence of students: success breeds success. At what level of difficulty is this skill/technique? What level of skill do they need before they can even attempt it? A positive attitude is essential.

The learners may have learned behaviour that needs unlearning. It is so hard to unlearn! Established patterns of movement may not help in what they should be doing. A teacher may need to analyse what is getting in the way. Some students have problems anyway with vision or hearing or balance, particularly if they have to wear protection such as goggles. Some may seem clumsy in everything they do, not very skilful at anything: they may need help to develop eye–hand co-ordination.

## Preparation

Students must come properly prepared. To do that they need to be clearly informed of what is required: clothing, what materials they have to provide and so on.

Tasks must be agreed and set out on work-sheets, which also need to show equipment they are to use and their responsibilities.

Performance criteria for successful achievement of each task should be agreed and stated, so that everyone knows what they are. It is hard to find you failed to do something in a way that was expected but which no one told you about until after-wards!

Equipment and materials must be properly organised, in good working order and of the right quality and quantity. Thought must be given to establishing good working practice.

## Rules and safety

It is vital that students establish quickly the right ways of setting about the task. Unlearning is so hard. Rules must be framed accordingly. The students cannot be allowed to work without proper equipment and clothing. They must take respon-sibility for an organised work-station.

The environment must support the learning activity. This may require plan-ning, particularly if person–machine ergonomics are involved. If you are training students to use visual display units (VDUs), for example, you need to make sure that table heights are appropriate, chairs support the base of the spine, screens on the VDU shield the user from glare and possible radiation, and so on. The stu-dents need to sit as directed and observe safe time periods in their use of the machines. You will find pamphlets and guidelines on this and other safe uses of machinery issued by the Health and Safety Commission, and available from your organisation's Safety Officer, or in a public library, or available from the Consumers' Association or Citizens Advice Bureaux.

Students must know what the rules are, for three reasons:

- we are about establishing good practice
- we must ensure that risk-taking does not lead to danger
- disorganisation is costly and inefficient.

# Plateaux and readiness

A practical following a demonstration only makes sense as a part of a longer programme of skills development. Research into skills learning found that learning
curves generally rise quickly, and then flatten into plateaux for a period of embed-
ding and consolidation. Teachers need to look for challenges to shorten this wait-
ing time.

Readiness to take on further challenges and greater tests is for teacher and
learner to judge. The teacher may be able to recognise and use rhythms in an individual's learning. Certainly, much learning is cyclical. There is a need to build up
the whole together and the teacher can take part by creating more interesting tasks
for the learner to undertake. Too big a challenge too soon undermines confidence;
too little will demotivate.

# Action plans: attention, frequency and practice

Attention is also a real problem. Because skills learning is so repetitive, it can easily become tedious. But students need to concentrate and be alert in order to
learn. So more practice, if it is highly monotonous, will not necessarily give a sig-
nificantly improved skill. Tasks have to be designed that give purpose and demonstrable outcomes from the learning activity while demanding improved levels of
skill. Concentration on achieving the task will give meaning and direction to the
skill.

For example, this is clearly what happens in learning to play the piano. A
learner attempts more and more difficult piano pieces. While developing the technical skills to play them, he or she is also attempting to recreate a musical performance. But it is no good someone turning up for a piano lesson once a week and
never touching a piano in between lessons. There has to be a pattern involving
frequency of practice.

Teacher and learner have to agree a learning programme, an action plan that
identifies frequency of practice and study – a kind of contract that identifies
responsibility, goals and schedules. Skills are best learned by practice involving
plenty of variety. In devising learning tasks, the teacher must identify the skills
and how they are to be developed and demonstrated.

And without feedback, one-off practicals make little sense. Skills have to be
seen as meaningful by students in their context and important to them. Tangible
products, cakes or pots or whatever else they may be, assist assessment and evaluation and maintain motivation.

# Perception and insight

For most students problems lie in the complexity of what they are attempting to
do. People learn skills experientially, and do so better when they have role-models
as well as clear 'models in the head'. Knowledge, belief and attitude are the basis
for skill. In the early stages of skill development, learners have to be aware (sometimes painfully) of what they do, and take conscious control of their actions.

127

We cannot begin to be inventive until skills are so embedded that we can think of other things. This implies that skills may be at different levels of conscious control. Once the brain has set up a pattern of behaviour, the skill itself takes less and less attention, less conscious control. Eventually, and as soon as possible, thought can be concentrated on what that skill is intended to allow us to achieve. For example, a driver can concentrate on the road ahead, rather than on how to co-ordinate clutch, gear change and accelerator.

Skill is a means to an end, not an end in itself. Unfortunately, much skills teaching has focused simply on learning the skill rather than using it. More recently, the demands of examinations have shifted away from skill-testing to using the skill effectively, with the criteria for success defined in terms of the context and the product.

Hence, skills learning must be related to individual needs; tasks must be designed as programmes. The students determine their own pace and readiness by feedback from the teacher, using the performance criteria agreed for the tasks. Action plans need frequent renegotiation.

Knowledge becomes increasingly important. The increase in ability in athletics followed extensive research into what makes for a better performance – as much science as art. But theory has to make sense in relation to what it is for.

## Human factors

Students cannot learn without proper well-maintained equipment. Each student needs to 'own' a working territory, although there is advantage in experiencing a variety of similar machines, for example in wordprocessing or engineering. Work simulation, which practicals ought to aim at, requires the right materials to work with too.

What of supervision? How many students can work safely in a workshop or a craftroom or a kitchen supervised, let alone tutored, by only one teacher? How must the room be designed or set out to enable the teacher to see the students, either to spot where help is required or to intervene if necessary? In some situations teachers just cannot see what students are doing: who takes the responsibility then?

## Monitoring

The purpose is to ensure that all students achieve mastery as defined by the performance criteria. The teacher's main role in the practical, therefore, is monitoring progress of individuals, insisting on repetition or finding new ways to tackle something if there is a blockage, intervening where the student is in difficulty or getting it wrong, or to avoid disaster of some kind, and adjusting or renegotiating action plans.

The main teaching skills required are observation, listening and the ability to communicate one-to-one while keeping an eye on what others are doing. Monitoring may be seen as an ongoing tutorial function and depends on established relationships.

## Assessment

The purpose is mastery, so assessment is based on achievement of performance criteria for each task. This is more complex than it sounds. No progress will be made without cognitive and attitudinal change. It is easy to observe 'can do', but 'can't do' requires analysis of what is wrong and appropriate remedial action — which may be dealing with problems of knowledge or lack of confidence, or removing barriers to learning.

## Designing the performance criteria

Performance criteria should state clearly what you believe to be good practice. Achieving the criteria identifies to what extent that good practice has become a matter of habit.

# Group practicals

Practicals are about individuals learning, but in some situations group practicals are essential — for example, in drama, music, languages and sports. Here the skills and insight of individuals need development but relate also to a context where a group of people are working together to achieve agreed and shared learning goals. Group projects (to put on a play or a concert, to perform together, to create a winning team, or simply to share a learning experience — all languages operate in social contexts) are essential to promote these learning goals.

The whole is much greater than the sum of the parts. Individuals as part of successful teams learn quite different skills, insight and behaviour than when learning alone. Here, role and responsibility, commitment to the team and to team goals become even more important. An orchestra consisting only of soloists will make a poor showing in a symphony. This is a major problem in drama training and in the development of sports teams.

As a teacher, your role cannot be largely didactic. You will have to lead, to shape, to manage and inspire. You will need excellent skills of organisation and management, and the ability to win people over. You will provide the 'model in the head' and often the role-model of what the group is to achieve. You must ensure this is communicated clearly, that the sharing to bind the group together happens.

Practical activities are the means by which this happens. One major teaching activity is evaluating carefully with the group what happens and what they need to do as a group and as individuals so as to progress towards agreed goals. In practical situations, when the students are working together, the skill is in observing and analysing what is happening and why, and what needs to happen next and how — to match the model in the head with what actually occurs and to communicate that understanding and insight to the group.

At the beginning of this chapter we discussed the continuum that ranges from teacher control to student control of decision-making/learning activity. How far along that continuum you progress depends on the extent to which the team develops its own momentum and on where the sense of ownership resides. There is no short cut here. You will have to learn how to work with such groups, not only to get the best out of them, to set standards and to ensure they achieve them, but also to avoid teacher-dependence. In the end, the team has to play the game without the coach.

Nor should you attempt to be a one-man orchestra playing all the parts. It is a team effort. Individuals must agree to take on roles, be responsible, make sure things happen when and how they should. Occasionally, you will have to intervene or take over to ensure it happens, but should do so reluctantly. It is your role to provide the overview to maintain proper control.

Performance criteria and assessment are concerned with how far the team achieves its goals as a team. It is hard to identify how individuals are to be assessed in relation to such activity.

# Discussion

In general, discussion is handled least well of all teaching methodology. It seems to come so naturally that there appears no need to intervene. But it is the one area where you, as the teacher, have to be at your most skilful and where you can most easily lose control of the learning.

In teaching, discussion has to be deliberately organised. Since it is one of the most common of human activities this is hard to do. The level of heat in the process depends on context, personalities or passions involved. Discussions can be very unproductive: they can turn into arguments, or even shouting matches or fights. But if well-managed, they can solve problems, promote co-ordinated activity and generate enthusiasm and commitment. They can be used to clarify thinking and ideas, tackle misconceptions and bring to the surface deeply held convictions that may be the cause of misunderstanding.

When we say that communication within a social unit has broken down, we usually mean that the parties (boss and trade union, husband and wife, parent and child) cannot discuss their differences, but are isolated in their own positions. So learning the skills of discussion must be something education should promote: it rarely does. Why? Mainly because teachers tend to lack the skills themselves.

Sharing is two-way communication. Teachers have to listen. They must create the right conditions for such communication.

# Agree the purpose

'Gee, Mr Stravinsky,' said a New York socialite, 'how do you know when to stop?' The maestro replied, 'Before I begin, madam.'

Generally we can tell the beginning, middle and end of some activity. Not so with discussions, which often appear to have none of these. Why is that? They lack shape because they lack a sense of purpose – they appear to be going nowhere.

However much pulsing energy and forward drive there may be in any discussion, students need to know where they are supposed to be going and why they are doing it, before they begin. Only then can teachers hope to control the interactions of people, to monitor what happens, intervene, shape or stop or whatever. Students and teacher alike must know the direction of travel, so that when the discussion starts to stray the teacher can bring it back on course. They must also agree together the rules that govern what happens.

Student satisfaction or frustration depends critically on this, since most adults are impatient of time-wasting, of a feeling of getting nowhere. They want to feel there is progress. People who know where they are going are more likely to arrive there and to have some sense of arriving.

Nor can teachers revisit rambling discussions that have no shape or pattern, or consolidate learning from them. The brain works with patterns and rules; we must assist the process. There has to be some perceived structure and agreed rules.

Committee meetings have agendas, so as to make minute-writing possible. This model is a most useful one. You need to recognise that no one comes to discussion without an agenda. Usually there are as many agendas as there are persons involved, and this is the problem. Misunderstandings are avoided if the agenda is agreed, overt and purposeful, if the rules are understood and if someone takes the chair.

The best discussion has purposeful outcomes, such as action plans involving groups and individuals. People know what it is for: it is to clarify ideas and make decisions. Committees that meet simply to meet are wasting time. We all need to be clear: 'what happens next? as a result of our discussing it here, what is supposed to happen?'

On the other hand, discussion that has no purpose is best avoided. General social discussion as the glue for binding the group can happen in coffee breaks; class time has to be seen to be used purposefully.

## Structure: the teacher's role

Students expect you to take charge. This does not mean that it is always you who takes the chair. You can set up whole class or group discussions, sometimes without leaders, so long as the students have a clear agenda and will know where they are going and when they have arrived.

But 'how do I know what I think till I hear what I say?' or what others say? You will have to encourage openness, a willingness to explore issues, bring out emotions and deeply held beliefs as well as helping the students to restructure their ideas and their thinking by sharing with others. This may be the opportunity to break out of a mind-set, to be ready to listen, to look at things from a new angle, to reconstruct a value-system.

The structure, therefore, is more to do with purpose and process than with content. Discussion of closed questions or where the outcomes have already been determined ('the chairman had the minutes in his pocket when he arrived') are soon exposed. The views of all students must be seen to be valued and taken into account in whatever decisions are made.

All group activities involve group dynamics. These are not predictable even from one class to another. The clearer the structure and goal-setting, the easier it is to maintain control. All groups exhibit patterns of dominance and/or withdrawal. Try to involve all the students, and inhibit those who seek to dominate or use things for their own purposes – to pursue a personal agenda.

You will make the structure loose or tight, you will establish more or less teacher control, in the way you set it up. You can give the group(s) specific questions with guidance as to the kind of answers you will accept, or you can set out a series of structured (but still open) questions, intended to lead discussion down particular paths almost to a predetermined conclusion.

The students should all have a copy of your lesson plan. It should state clearly when and how discussion is to occur, the time constraints and the intended outcomes – what it is supposed to achieve and where it fits with other learning activity. The clearer the guidance the better: preparation matters.

## Chairing

You may appoint a chairperson for the discussion, to keep it going along the right path. You could make it rather like a committee meeting, perhaps, with a secretary to report back. If you want to be more in control, chair it yourself.

Who chairs the group discussion matters greatly. Some will let discussions ramble; others keep speakers to the point, inhibit interruption and defuse conflict, emphasising issues and trying to avoid personal or emotive interactions. Teachers in the chair often seem to have the minutes already in their pockets. It is really another lecture in disguise.

## Reporting back

The discipline of reporting back is important. It concentrates the group's thinking if there is a need to report, to explain to others what conclusions and decisions about actions have been arrived at. The reporting method should be agreed.

One excellent way is to supply each group with OHP acetates and ask them to make a key-word structure for the reporter to talk to. This puts additional discipline on to the discussion; the students have to agree on words and structure and create it – it all takes time, but it concentrates attention on the need for demonstrable outcomes. A composite can easily be made, and comparison with other groups is also simple. If this technique is used in an inductive discussion with the whole class, a student should fill in the OHT rather than the teacher.

Students can take away the structured reports. If they have also specified action, they know what to do and who is to do it. This also serves to consolidate the learning.

The minutes of the effective committees have a strong structure, with minimum reporting of the discussion but very clearly stated outcomes and 'action points' with individual responsibilities clearly defined.

# Human factors

People unconsciously take messages from the arrangement of furniture, and are annoyed by messages that are contradictory or confusing. People sitting in rows, talking to the backs of each other's heads, miss subtleties of communication – facial expressions, eye-contact, humour.

An expectation of committee behaviour is expressed by chairs around a central table. We know immediately what is to happen. But this is only one possibility. We can think about how to manipulate messages, or how to create group space/territory to get people to work more closely together, to identify with each other and break down barriers.

We have to think about sound and vision: groups competing at 'shouting' levels in the same room, for instance. How will they identify their space and their equipment? If there are seminar rooms, use them.

Plan ahead. Define spaces and equip them for what you want the groups to do. For example, some teachers favour the use of flip-charts as against OHP, but to the same purpose: to present key-word structures to the other groups. The sheets can be put up around the walls for others to walk around and compare with their own.

Set up chairs, tables, screens, OHP, flip-charts. Give each group the tools for the job. Make it easy for them. Be businesslike.

# What have they achieved?

Did the students achieve the goals and the intended outcomes? Are they practicable ideas? Does it make good sense? What will they now do with the new structure they have created?

Discussion is not about new information but is a restructuring of the information we have already, making it group-orientated and usable. In the end it affects attitudes and behaviour and leads to action.

# Seminars

No discussion makes progress unless it is informed discussion: a shared and sound basis of information prevents the rehearsing and arguing *ad nauseam* of unfounded but often passionately held opinions. Addition of new information may change suddenly the direction of argument, which may then hasten agreement (or throw things into confusion).

The means of adding information varies. Sometimes a lecture, film or video will be the starting point, sometimes reading matter that the students will be expected to digest beforehand. If the input is complex, it is necessary to revisit it somehow. A seminar's purpose may be to revisit and clarify earlier input and ensure that it is fully understood, to provide fresh input. Seminars should be used to provide or consolidate an information base the group can then work on. Many go much further and generate creative thinking.

Often, someone is invited to lead the seminar, and to make a short introduction to supply a basis and questions for the group to address. A preliminary paper with information and a working paper (with questions and key-words) will help to give shape to the seminar – maybe as 'challenge' and 'defence' as in a debate.

There are advantages in someone producing a draft paper which the group then modifies and improves to present as a group paper. It hastens things along and helps to give shape and direction – it is, incidentally, the best way to arrive at clear action plans in committee.

If the purpose is to encourage all members of the seminar group to research the topic and then share what they discover (and if each is clear as to his or her specific contribution), this can rapidly increase the information available. This technique is valuable when the content of a syllabus seems extremely large and the teacher is faced with problems of covering *some* of it *somehow*!

## Purpose and structure

To be effective seminars must be pretty tightly structured with clear time constraints and schedules. If someone is to produce a paper, it must be available to be read beforehand. Any input must be punchy and short, and discussion must be focused and to the point: it is its narrowness of focus that makes the session a seminar.

A seminar is strongly goal-orientated. Goals must be clear and agreed, and the group must be committed to them. Where action is required it must happen. Everyone carries equal responsibility for process and outcomes, for success.

## Competition

It is not unusual for seminar groups to become competitive. This may be deliberately arranged. 'Games' as tools for learning are based on such groups, which frequently become very tightly knit as a result – with both benefits and costs.

The tasks the groups are given to do determine what happens. Watch carefully how such groups interact and come together. If they are to produce an agreed view to present to others there will be less energy than if they are asked to come up with solutions to a problem, and to discover the best solution, either for kudos or for a prize(!). Many projects run like this. Tremendously energetic seminar groupwork frequently happens.

---

### EXAMPLE 1

---

An elaborate seminar game was used at a weekend Department of Trade and Industry conference. Seminar groups were set the task of designing a science kit that would enable any learner in any country in the world (and without creating language barriers) to learn and understand a principle in science. There were certain constraints: it had to work with minimum technology available anywhere (it must not need electricity); it had to pack flat but be possible to assemble using diagrams as instructions. Similarly, learning had to be experiential, using the kit and diagrams.

To achieve this goal, each group had to decide on a specific principle and then on how the learners would learn it, what they had to do and what equipment they would need and, finally, how to overcome the constraints above.

Each group had a seminar room with OHP, flip–chart, whiteboard, pens, paper and so on: a group territory properly equipped. There was also a workshop with craft materials to make the kit and to ensure it worked. Each group was required to demonstrate a working model to the other groups, and explain how it would be used.

Initially each group had to formulate ideas and a design plan, and explain it to the others: this was to share thinking and ideas and to get feedback. At a later time the final demonstration was required.

One group set out to facilitate learning about kinetic and potential energy. They agreed everyone would have water. Water has potential energy if it is stored at a height. If the water falls its energy is converted into kinetic energy, which can be demonstrated with a turbine. This in turn could be converted into electrical energy and used to light a bulb. The only remaining requirement was energy input to raise the water. If the learners had to put in their own energy they could learn about work. The important thing was that the system had to be a closed one: no extra energy had to be added other than the pupils' own work.

A kit was designed, and then built out of simple craft materials, to raise the water and store it in a tank. A tube with a tap led the water to turn a turbine (slats in a spindle) and so a simple dynamo to light a bulb. The water was collected in a lower tank to be returned to the upper tank by energy supplied by the learner, using a shadoof to raise the water: this energy was the only thing to be added to the system.

The whole thing could pack flat for assembly on site. Instructions for building the kit and running it were given in diagrams. The group wanted to use the old 'flickbook' technique here – flicking the edges of a series of photographs so that the images appeared to move.

This inventiveness resulted from having to compete against others and within tight constraints and parameters.

# Simulation, games, role play

Teachers sometimes confuse these activities. They are different.

## Simulation

Here the teacher attempts to simulate a real situation. The students learn skills and confidence to deal with reality in a controlled environment and context. The constraints can be carefully chosen, and pressures such as the consequences of failure can be removed.

The closer the simulation is to reality, the better. Rules that apply to real encounters apply in simulations. To set up a workshop simulation may involve scaling things down – to what will fit into a booth rather than into a house, say, if we are dealing with plumbing or wiring. But the system has to work in exactly the same way. A simulated committee meeting has a proper agenda and clearly identified roles. We can play roles, but constraints of money, time, production targets, or whatever the committee is about, have to be real. The group is learning to run a committee effectively and purposefully.

Simulations involve time-scales. We need to be able to reflect on the experience, to look at the process and the outcomes. This is easier if the experience is relatively short. But there are many long simulations, such as caterers in a training kitchen and restaurant, or a production team simulation for apprentices to undertake a project in design and construction. In all cases, what is to be assessed is not simply the quality of products or other tangible outcomes but changes in attitudes, insights and skills.

The advantages of simulation are:

- the removal of consequences of failure, leading to a greater willingness to take risks
- opportunity to experience roles and responsibilities which are not one's own, but normally those of more senior people
- elimination of arbitrary problems and control of constraints
- feedback and reflection on the experience; the flexibility to change the constraints, goals, time-schedules and so forth
- simplification of outcomes and criteria for assessment.

Real life experiential learning can be painful, slow and confusing. There are many risks manager and learner deliberately avoid. Much of what is going on is missed because of limitations in sensory perception and the attention we can give it. Teachers in simulations can help learners to see much that they would otherwise miss. And since learners can never acquire all the necessary skills together at once, the learning of skills is easier if they are practised under controlled conditions.

But teachers can also make simulations closed or open. Catering training tends to be closed, almost rehearsing a script with very strongly defined role-models and procedures to follow; invention comes later. Other simulations are deliberately left to develop. A design project requires creativity within constraints. Teachers have to trust the students and monitor what happens closely.

In the end the learning has to be tested in the fire. Most fail to match pressures in the employment base. Other factors beside skills and insights come into play very forcefully. Much carefully trained and desirable behaviour has to be set aside; that may lead to mismatch and disillusionment. This also happens all too often when teachers go away for training courses.

IMPROVING SIMULATION

Ensure that the match with real world experience is close. Unless the learning is transferable it will soon be lost. It is transferability of skills and insight (attitudes too) to real contexts that matters most.

This has implications for the resourcing and organisation of the simulation, and for the methods of assessment. You can only learn good working practice in appropriately equipped environments. In this sense much vocational training may be seen as simulating real world working conditions. Much of this kind of learning is caught rather than taught.

## EXAMPLE 2

Some fire officers on a teacher training course redesigned a course for training firemen to deal with accidents on a motorway. They had available a most sophisticated simulation. An old airfield had been converted into a training ground with mock-ups of ships, tower blocks, railways, motorways and many other structures. Fire could be set, or accidents staged, in any of these. There were also lavishly equipped lecture theatres.

Once they had designed the course making full use of the above, they evaluated it against the agreed criteria. One problem was how to assess the learning. They looked for methods of assessing it *as a course*. It was, however, a simulation with some input lecture style, using video-playback and so on.

They agreed that the only sensible way to assess the learning was to watch the firemen in action. The acid test was whether the trainees, under pressure of the real situation, perform more effectively or not. It was the transferability of the learning that mattered.

# Games

In games the important thing is the pressure of competition. Look at Example 1 above. Games have rules which may be arbitrary and are meant to even out the odds, to eliminate certain aspects of reality to concentrate on the insights the students are intended to learn.

The skills required are not necessarily the same as those that they would need in real situations. The rules can be changed, the situation manipulated. It is the arbitrary nature of games that makes them unlike simulations.

Nor is it intended that what is learned should be practised in any real context. The learning is about insight into human behaviour, how things happen, the factors involved in decision-making, working as a team, competing with others, problem-solving, winning!

Games like Monopoly are played using boards and rules. Others are very physical, involving problem-solving in the round (the Army uses such games to select 'officer potential'). They can be 'intellectual power games', or playing the stock exchange, being Wellington at Waterloo, or solving murders. So many kinds!

To use a game, first think through carefully what is involved and what it is for.

Games are dangerous if handled badly. They can take over, gain their own momentum and become extremely 'noisy' in the ergonomic sense, so that it becomes very hard to know what is being learned. It is easy to lose control of the game once it is set going.

All the same, students love such things and they can be great fun – which learning should undoubtedly be much of the time. But the students know they are playing, it's not real, and the rules are arbitrary. It can still become very serious, raise emotional pressures and anxieties and take over. Students in a losing team can become angry or demoralised.

Students and teacher must agree what the game is for, and what they are setting out to learn. They cannot begin to focus on that while the game is in progress. It has to happen as reflection on the experience. There must be plenty of time to do that or there will be little learning – merely a glow.

Equally, the teacher must intervene if things are really not going in the intended direction or if emotional factors are likely to create negative outcomes.

### EVALUATING AND LEARNING

Simulations and games bring us increasingly up against ourselves. What we learn is not simply how to do something, or even insight into the way the thing works, but most importantly what it feels like to be there, to be under pressure making decisions, taking responsibility, making things happen. 'Can I cope?' 'Is this really me?'

We are faced with the challenge of performance. We adopt roles, take on responsibility: we cannot avoid it. We learn what it means to try to work in a team, relying on others and they on us. With any luck, we find a good team and lots of support, but this doesn't always happen. Some people may be badly hurt, their self-esteem and self-image damaged not improved. That is what real life does to people!

To draw benefit from simulations and games, students have to focus on the positive learning that comes from the experience, both for them personally and for the team. Tutor support is essential if they are to gain fully from these learning activities.

It is difficult to define learning goals as specific, demonstrable outcomes in activities where much of what will occur is unpredictable – deliberately so. It is possible, though, and in some cases, such as the catering simulation mentioned above, is desirable to make the outcomes 'closed' and quite specific as learning goals to be assessed.

To consolidate the learning, students need to agree what learning occurred as a result of the activity, as a process of reflection on it. To assist that process, it is helpful to agree a statement of intended learning, what the activity is for, before they undertake it. As an example only, the list might include:

- to understand the value of teamwork and planning
- to gain insight into roles and responsibilities
- to discover what my strengths and weaknesses are
- to discover how to work effectively in a team
- to discover how to tackle problems systematically
- to discover how to deal with frustration and stress
- to discover skills such as [ . . .]
- to gain confidence and coping skills.

Knowing what you are trying to learn before you set out will help you identify questions to address to the experience when it is over.

It is obviously difficult to specify clear learning goals in such activities since much of what occurs is unpredictable, unless it is 'closed' like the catering simulation mentioned above. It is necessary, however, to have agreed learning goals that can be assessed and evaluated by both teacher and students at the end. Otherwise, consolidation becomes impossible.

## Role play

Many simulations involve taking on roles. Sometimes, as we have seen, there is a script (actual or implied) that controls what is allowed of the characters. Often, specific characters are needed to make the simulation more real: in a committee, for example, those who are eager to get things done, those who want to block things, those who are pursuing a personal agenda, those whose personalities clash. Teachers can deliberately identify such personalities.

When exploring roles takes precedence over other factors the exercise becomes role play. When someone goes into role, they must adopt a level of belief about themselves and the person they have become. There is a liberation in role play you must watch: 'There are a hundred different me's trying to get out,' said one student.

Since it is not 'me', the usual constraints on my behaviour may be relaxed. This is great, if that is what we want to happen. Many students can only get past their own inhibitions this way, and this can be most important in learning languages, or in learning to deal with people in social situations. Here, such methods can be used with excellent results.

In most contexts, role play should be used with great care. It is a very powerful tool, and teachers can use it effectively or dangerously. It may be largely discovering feelings, emotions, images, stereotypes, values and so on that lie hidden in our subconscious and are released by the role play. Both adults and youngsters can be quite startled by what they do, since they are not consciously in control. The most hilariously funny things I have seen anywhere have occurred during role play; so have some of the most traumatic. We are asking people to discover things about themselves, about relationships with others, perhaps about deeply held values too.

Taking on a role may uncover one of the 'hundreds of me's trying to get out'. It may release inhibitions and barriers that make it difficult for people to talk about things rationally. Relationships, like sex and space, are hard to talk about. Acted out, we may discover what we really feel and truly believe, even if we may wish to deny these feelings and beliefs. It may be best to avoid role play which explores suppressed strong emotions such as anger or fear or jealousy.

To use role play as a learning tool the teacher must maintain control, be fully in charge, in an activity where it is impossible to predict what is going to happen, and be ready to intervene if things take off in ways that are not helpful to the intended learning.

Be prepared for participants to use stereotyping they hardly know they have, even when roles are incidental to simulations: union negotiator, manager/boss, wife or husband, mother-in-law, customer and so forth. They are exploring their image of such persons. You will need to evaluate such images with students and help them to talk through where they have come from, and what effect such stereotyping has on their own behaviour.

Use role as a way of getting at aspects of learning that students find difficult because of attitudinal problems or inhibitions. There are so many examples: speaking a foreign language is a good one. Another is to get students to negotiate a price for a catering buffet, or for a product they want to sell.

### GUIDANCE

There is no value in going into a role play without clear guidance to everyone concerned as to what role they are to play and what is to be discovered from the exercise. It is not always easy to set out guidance since people will only see what they expect to see. They usually just look at the name on the label and not the contents of the bottle. It is the same with any information. So ensure that there is a preliminary session in which things are carefully explored and explained.

Get them each to tell you what their role is so that you can share perceptions of it all before they begin. This will help the evaluation at the end, of course.

> As part of your course design, consider the place of any of these methods within your lessons. A lesson is itself a mini-strategy. It is important to build in as much sensible variety as you can.
>
> To learn you must tackle them systematically and look carefully at what happens and why afterwards. You will discover where you are lacking in skill and understanding so that the next time you will be better prepared and tackle that method more effectively.

# 17 Managing Flexible Learning

As the continuum of teaching methodology becomes more student-centred and controlled, the discussion takes on new dimensions. New factors are involved.

## Using resources

The teacher is an important resource for students, but not the only one they may use. Some teachers put intolerable burdens on themselves to deliver because they feel all learning must be funnelled through them. But the emphasis has changed. Increasingly, teachers must become managers of learning that uses all manner of resources, not least those the students bring with them.

Teachers need different skills to become such managers. They are handing over much of the responsibility for learning and control to the students. Teachers need confidence and trust in students and their own ability to cope. 'I want them where I can see them,' cries the insecure teacher who finds it hard to let go in case the class gets out of control.

Much managed learning happens under strict control. A workshop is a major resource: individualised programmes with the students using lathes and work-sheets is an example of managed learning. So is reading an English literature text quietly and discussing it in groups, or writing an essay to show insight into the writer's style under supervision. There is hardly anything revolutionary here.

What is intended is a total change in methodology, with different roles and responsibilities for teacher and students. There are to be teaching teams to concentrate on designing learning as whole programmes. They will plan how students will learn, what they will need in order to learn, where they will learn, what materials they will use, and what guidance and equipment they will need. How progress will be managed, possibly framing action plans, individual programmes of study and tutorial support. Development of materials, organisation, supervision, monitoring, assessment and handling feedback will be major functions. So will setting targets and schedules and performance criteria, and assessing achievement, all things that are very familiar to the reader of this book.

The responsibility for the learning is firmly with the students. The teacher is to manage the resources and the programme, ensuring that students have access to what is needed, and controlling the process.

All this requires redefinition of teaching time and scheduling. Decisions have to be made about input sessions and group activities. Do they happen regularly week by week or as needed to maintain progress? Since programmes are individualised, there has to be time for tutorials. How is it to be paid for?

Costing of programmes becomes important. The cost of making the materials is offset against the freedom teachers then have to do other things that are perhaps more effective than regular classroom teaching. Preparation pays off, but setting it up is expensive. The time and effort to design and create useful, valid resources will have to be paid for out of whole budget planning.

Managed learning programmes work well if:

- learning structure and design are carefully thought through
- tasks and assignments are well-designed and well-presented
- the learning is interesting, stimulating and relevant
- there is clear understanding of 'activity' and criteria for successful achievement/completion of the tasks
- there is sufficient finance and good support facilities
- students are taught how to organise their own learning
- feedback is immediate at a point of need, and is supportive and positive – preferably in a tutorial context
- there is flexibility and adaptability to individual need
- record-keeping and tracking of achievement is maintained
- there is a team and resource-base for developing materials.

## Task design

This is the essential skill. Patterns help. Establish a format that is understood. Ask yourself what the students need in the way of information and guidance in order to do the task. Provide an overview of how this task fits into the whole. In setting out to do it, they need to know clearly what they are setting out to learn, what they have to do and why, what they will use in order to do it and where it is to be found, how they will get hold of the resources they will use.

If the task is to achieve a product they must know the form it should take, and/or the criteria for success. They must understand what the assessment process will be, and how it will be handled, how the achievement will be recorded and profiled. It must therefore be clear to them what successful achievement of each task contributes to achievement of major learning goals.

The tasks need to be appraised for the demands they make on the students. Pace, readiness, ability to meet a challenge have to be thought about. Is there sufficient flexibility in the guidance and criteria to allow for variations in individual ability to cope with the demands, and/or to interpret the tasks to meet their personal learning needs?

Above all, clarity and simplicity in the guidance matter.

## Process

The students will do tasks in some sequence: how will that be known and who will make the decisions? How will targets be set? What time constraints are there, what 'complete by' dates? How much of all this is negotiable – or renegotiable – with the tutor?

They may need to be guided through early tasks, finding out where they can get help and additional resources, how to use the library/multi-media centre or other resource areas, how to deal with equipment. If a programme involves seeking help, information or exploring major resources elsewhere, they must be shown how.

Some tasks deal with people more than with books or things. Especially if the learning is concerned with developing social skills and ability to work with others, students may need help in dealing with people, perhaps interviewing them or conducting negotiations or a survey. None of this can be taken for granted: it is courting disaster just to ask students to do such things and hope it will be all right.

Teachers will not know what is involved, how hard it is or what difficulties will occur unless they experience it themselves. All tasks therefore need validating by experience.

## Assessment

The process of assessment and the process of learning are closely linked. One feeds back to the other. It is possible to treat each task as separate for the purposes of assessment, with its own criteria. But this is to lose the process completely and to concentrate entirely on outcomes. The tasks become a series of coconuts in a shy.

This will have an unfortunate effect on motivation. Tutoring must be concerned with overall learning goals and progress towards their achievement. The tasks identify the process by which progress is made. To develop an action plan with a student the tutor has to monitor what is learned or achieved by completion of any of the tasks and what has been identified as learning need. That is what assessment is for.

This requires careful monitoring and regular review, preferably in tutorials, if students are to appreciate the nature and extent of their learning. In this context you can draw up fresh action plans to meet their learning needs as they emerge. You need to keep careful records of what has been achieved and what is still to be done. These records are, of course, shared with the student so that they can feel they are in charge of the development of their learning.

You can use a 'tutorial log' pro forma to keep track of students' achievements. This is a simple form showing goals achieved and new goals set in the tutorial. These log sheets make up the basis of the student's Record of Achievement at the end of the course.

## Evaluation

Programmes of this kind need constant review. All aspects of the process need revision in the light of experience. Each task must be evaluated for its level of difficulty, the way in which students coped with it, its effectiveness in promoting the intended learning. The same is true of resources, guidance, support and so on.

The aim must be to make the programme as effective as possible. It could be argued that if students fail to learn the fault is with the programme, either its design or its operation, or perhaps the nature of the tasks or the assessment process: it is not necessarily the inability of the students to achieve the learning goals that we are measuring or addressing.

Evaluation therefore is team-based and should lead to teams revising their programmes, techniques and action plans.

# Real life learning/discovery

Teachers cannot control what students learn from watching films or TV at home, or what they pick up in places where they work or visit. This learning is almost all unconscious, but it is far too important to ignore. It constitutes in fact the bulk of what people learn. It is all the more likely to become part of someone's perception of reality and to control his or her value system than learning in a formal environment, simply because it is acquired when they are relaxed and enjoying life in what they see as 'their normal world'. It is also shared with groups they want to be part of. When people know they are learning, as in an educational context, they often put up barriers to learning that are not present when they are at ease.

But students need to focus this 'unconscious learning' somehow: to have a view of what they have learned. They can then evaluate it and integrate it with learning controlled by teachers.

When learning which has been gained in work or family or leisure settings is analysed formally and put forward for certification, as nowadays it can be, it is known as 'prior learning'. Systems have been set up to help individuals present such learning for assessment, alongside conventional learning from courses. If the learning is accepted, it is 'accredited' as part of the student's overall achievement, and is then certificated.

The richness of this resource is immense, but usually it is left untapped. A major problem with using it is its lack of structure. How does one select what is good, relevant and valuable? After all, no one said there would be a test. Clearly, many occasions will arise when the learning can be tapped. If there is shared experience it can be used in groupwork. Students should constantly be asked to match what they learn against their own experience in life.

There is increasing pressure for teachers to work closely with employers to integrate 'real life imperatives' – those felt by employers and the community – with what teachers feel important.

One aspect of the real world which has been more fully integrated into learning recently is the workplace. Whereas traditionally students went from the workplace to colleges in order to learn, they now frequently study workplace tasks, processes and procedures on the job itself. They can then be assessed in the workplace to see if they meet the standards of real life interaction, pace and quality required by employers.

Teachers have to develop skills, not only in working with students, but with those who also have important relationships with them at work and elsewhere.

They will have joint responsibility for the programmes students undertake and they need to ensure their coherence.

# Distance learning/Flexistudy

Flexibility of response by educational institutions is required to tackle the difficulties so many adult students have in getting at training and education opportunities. Programmes of study and training have to be devised that allow learners (or employers, or whoever requires the service) to negotiate how the learning is to be achieved.

This may take any pattern. It may (or may not) involve attendance at the educational institution, either on a regular basis or as a negotiated provision, perhaps related to the needs of the employer. It may involve sessions on other premises. It may be based only on tasks and assignments, supported by input through reading and other materials designed as a distance learning programme. The teacher is tutor to individuals, and may be contacted for consultation in a variety of ways. There may be blocks of time when groups of students can come together (Saturdays, weekends, maybe even a residential week along Open University lines).

# Effective use of visits

Students are often taken on visits to extend their experience. The students may be faced with an overwhelming amount of information to try to take in. Again, they will select. They are visiting 'foreign' territory.

How can we help them to make sense of it? What are they in fact trying to learn? Do they know? How does it fit in to learning on their programme? What are they going to do to reflect on the experience? How will they use the learning? All this needs clarifying and agreeing beforehand. As with other methods alerting, structuring, revisiting.

A video presentation beforehand showing them what they are going to see, with clear explanation, makes it familiar, less foreign, when they arrive.

They could take a set of structured questions to address. It may be no bad thing to set it up competitively in terms of what they can report back. This provides incentive: the level of motivation is important.

Younger students need to know exactly what rules they are to keep to, the constraints on their actions.

There are always rules. What dress do they need? It's not a good idea to go down a coal-mine in a short skirt. What do they need to take to make notes, to record information and so on? Have it all clearly stated on a handout well in advance.

There must be time for reflection after the experience. The learning has to be properly focused and consolidated. They must do something with it to make sure it has 'value'.

# Roles

In the future, teachers will need to adopt many new roles, which will require training and development of novel skills and techniques. A teacher may be a 'manager of resources', 'liaison officer with outside agencies' (such as employers), 'adviser', 'external assessor', or 'counsellor'. In all these areas, teachers need to approach their changing roles with a view of themselves primarily as teachers. This means that the skills and insights developed by the programme in this book will remain as relevant as ever.

# Monitoring progress

For a new teacher it may be enough to know that all the above possibilities exist. But one role that teachers will find themselves undertaking more and more is 'tutor' to individuals within a group of students. As students take more responsibility for their own learning, it becomes increasingly important to monitor and control the learning programme with each student. One obvious effect is that time must be found to spend with each individual.

# Tutorials

Tutorials serve many purposes. They are necessary to check on progress and to give support. They may also act as small-scale seminars to clarify ideas or create action plans. But they are expensive of time and teaching cost, usually one-to-one or at most one-to-three.

An easy-going tutor is of no benefit to students. Tutorials must be cost-effective: contract-based and strongly goal-orientated. Student and tutor are both responsible for achieving the goals. The major skill required is in handling this relationship.

There must be two-way exchange – a tutorial is certainly not a lecture! Tutors have to listen, indeed to act as a mirror. The agenda must be agreed, not imposed. Students must feel able to control the agenda to meet needs they perceive if they are to trust the tutor and be open in discussion. It is their learning programme, their action plan.

Tutorials provide feedback in both directions. The students need to know how they are progressing relative to agreed performance criteria. The teacher needs to know whether the tasks the group or an individual has been set to do make sense to each student, and whether each can cope: how to make progress or whether to renegotiate the programme in some way, or to put in additional learning activity or support.

Checking on progress is vital. Schedules matter: they are targets agreed and to be met. But there has to be flexibility, since individuals learn at their own pace and bring their own barriers and problems. The major purpose of assessing is to advance the learning, not to put a mark on it as a grade. Tutorials are an important part of this assessment/learning process, to shape individual learning paths.

The frequency of tutorials relates to the way the programme has been designed. They support individual learning through agreed action plans based on assignments. For time to be available for tutorials, less time has to be used in full class teaching. The programme should be sustained by student learning activity, group and individual tasks.

## Handling tutorials

Choose a suitable environment. Set it up to give the right messages. Appear organised and serious. It is terrible if the student feels the tutorial is simply a formality. You have to listen. Eliminate 'noise': make sure you won't be interrupted by the telephone or by other people. The tutorial needs your full attention as well as that of the student. Come prepared, too. Know about this student: what he or she is doing and what has happened already.

Think about personal space. Chairs should preferably be soft or at least comfortable. Avoid obstructions like desks that create distance. Chairs should be close but not confrontational: they are better set at an angle so that eye-contact can be made and broken easily – looking away must not be a problem.

Timing matters. Start on time. Students need to learn how to handle time effectively, to say things clearly but succinctly. More time does not mean better. You need to do this too.

Listen carefully, and wait for the student to say it. Teachers tend to be impatient. One of the skills you need to develop (and with class interactions) is how to be patient and wait. Jumping in to fill a silence too soon stops important things from happening. When teachers do this as a matter of habit, students just let them get on with it. Things need space and time in order to happen, as in the theatre. Encourage, but don't take over.

To listen is to show concern. How hard it is to find someone who actually wants to listen to you, who will find the time to do it! You are a mirror. Try to see it from where they sit so that you reflect back accurately what they say and do, then to match it against the agreed criteria – where we are going.

Students mainly need support and reassurance. If they are slipping in terms of targets, they have to perceive the need to achieve them. Tutorials are about feedback, enabling them to see things more clearly themselves. They do not usually need bullying. Target-setting, keeping to schedule, yes. Most students want to succeed. Matching the programme to individual needs is the tutor's responsibility.

Keep records of tutorials, with a copy for the student. The negotiation of the learning programme and action plans for individuals (and the revisions) need documenting. Targets or progress need monitoring and recording. Be businesslike.

## Records of Achievement

Full-time students build up a record of achievement (RoA) as they go through their studies. This is a national system administered within colleges. The RoA folder is intended to provide a picture of all the student's achievements both inside and outside the college – it is about the whole person, not just about examinations. Both tutor and student write statements about the student's progress; these accompany the vocational or academic record. If you are involved in this process, a college tutor will explain to you what you are expected to do to support the students and to fill in the record.

# 18 Student Guidance and Support

You will have noticed a great deal of emphasis in further and adult education centres on supporting students while they are learning. This applies particularly to full-time students, whether they are 16–19 year olds or mature students, but part-time students are also offered a wide range of what are called 'support services'. These services can include information, advice, guidance, tutoring and counselling. The process begins before students enrol, with Advice and Guidance evenings or Open Days. Here teachers and current students describe the learning opportunities on offer, and specialist staff give guidance on matters such as grants, help for people with disabilities or language support for people whose first language is not English. There are then many other sources of help available throughout the learning period.

## The current scene

Changes in the curriculum and Government intervention have had a major impact on the kind of provision made for these services in institutions. Potential students need far more guidance than formerly to discover their best learning route.

- There is now a wide range of qualifications available, some in modular or unit form, some with core and optional studies, some with placements or work experience; in addition students can claim credit for prior certificated and uncertificated learning (APL).
- Full-time students are now taught for fewer hours and encouraged to work independently of the teacher in workshops and resource centres; they need help with the study skills which make this a viable learning route – time management, self-motivation, use of catalogues, use of information technology.
- New client groups are coming into further education, e.g. mature students on Access courses, refugees and asylum seekers, women returning to study. There is an increased need for guidance on financial, legal and welfare matters as well as language support for those for whom English is not their mother tongue.
- The Government has set ambitious National Training and Education Targets (the percentage of the working population with qualifications by a certain date). The funding received by colleges is now dependent on them taking in

more students each year. Many of them are unused to systematic study and require considerable help with study skills, as well as induction to the expectations and requirements of college life.

- Many students are unemployed or receive benefits; they need advice on how to combine job seeking with studying, on sources of financial assistance and on welfare services.
- Too many students drop out because they have chosen the wrong course, have inadequate study skills, or have too many personal difficulties to enable them to cope. This is tragic for them, disappointing for teachers and unfortunate for Government figures; consequently funding has been tied to retaining students until they achieve their qualifications. The effect of this has been to raise the amount and quality of guidance and support available at all stages of the student's programme.
- Colleges are in competition with each other and with schools for the 16–19 cohort of students; a major marketing advantage is good student support services, particularly in view of the school tradition of pastoral care.

As a result of these trends and direct intervention, advice and guidance services have become centralised rather than peripheral, systematic rather than *ad hoc*, better funded and operated by a team of qualified professional staff. They are now seen as vital to the business success of the centre.

## The support team

There is no one model because centres respond to their own context and students, but in most centres you will find a team of people who work together to offer students advice, guidance and support on academic, study and personal matters. There may well be a core team who organise and manage the service, a wider team of specialists looking after medical, legal, financial, career, disability and child care matters, and teachers with particular responsibilities, for instance for ESOL students or for Basic Skills (literacy, numeracy, IT). There will also be support staff in library and learning resource centre areas who advise on finding and using information.

In addition to this team there may also be teachers who act as academic advisors about particular subject areas and courses, who may also help students with applications to higher education and further study.

## Being a personal tutor

Teachers also have an important role to play. You may find yourself asked to be part of a personal tutor system. This is a system of support and guidance, mainly for full-time students, managed by a senior member of staff who briefs, trains and supports the teachers who act as personal tutors.

How does this work? Groups of students are attached to a member of staff, who may or may not also teach them, for the period of their studies. You, as their tutor, are responsible for first line support. You help them settle in, keep an eye on their progress, discipline them if necessary, respond to their requests for help of various kinds and refer them to your team of specialists for further help if you think it appropriate. You may also be asked to help them complete their Record of Achievement. This is a document in which students and staff collect material which shows how the student has progressed and lists achievements; it will contain certificates and statements about progress from teachers and the students themselves.

In order to work with the students in this way you set up tutorial sessions, either on a one-to-one basis or with them as a group. Younger students tend to prefer the group setting. In some centres there is a Tutorial Programme of activities for the year which you can run in these sessions. The most important of these is probably the Induction period, some of which will be organised centrally; you follow this up in sessions with your own tutees.

## Your knowledge and skills

You will need **to know** about the following aspects:

- the support services available in your centre, the names of the key advisors, the locations and times of access.
- the courses/programmes on which the students are studying and the staff involved (with whom you will need to liaise).
- the duties and responsibilities expected of you, particularly the **boundaries** around your area of work and the reports you are expected to provide.
- where to go for information and help on your own account.

## The skills you need to develop

The most important element you bring to the tutor role is your normal friendly relationship with students. You are not expected to be a social worker, priest and lawyer all in one. You are there to help with a range of fairly everyday difficulties; the team of experts is there to pick up the more specialist work. Your chief skill is that of knowing your limitations and when to refer. Other skills are:

- noticing if a student is acting out of character and approaching them sensitively to see if they want help
- listening attentively to what they tell you
- clarifying your understanding of what they have said
- exploring possible courses of action
- helping them to decide what to do
- maintaining contact while they work on their decisions
- acknowledging their progress and success.

## Attitudes are all important

How you are is as important as what you do. Students quickly identify the people they can trust, whether or not you are designated as a tutor. They look particularly for people who have time to listen to them, who accept that they have a problem but who do not designate **them** as a problem, and who have a generally positive attitude to the whole business of sorting things out. They **do** require confidentiality. You don't need to be a personal tutor to behave like this; it is an extension of your normal teaching role.

## Sorting out the terminology

You may be unsure of the difference between the various terms. Most of us would see advice giving as something fairly directive, based on information which we make available on request. Guidance is seen as showing people the options available and suggesting some courses of action. You don't need to be involved with the enquirer to carry out these functions. Tutoring and counselling, however, are dependent for their effectiveness on a **relationship** which you build up with the other person. This lasts over a period of time during which you get to know the person so that you can understand how best to help them. There are some crucial differences, however.

**Tutoring** is closely related to study matters; the tutor takes the lead, organises activities, can be directive about the tutee's behaviour and discusses their behaviour and progress with other staff. The **content** of the exchanges is fairly routine. In **counselling** the content is deeply personal and around serious issues. Strict confidentiality is essential. A formal contract between the counsellor and student is set up with agreed boundaries, times and location. The counsellor works to help the student explore routes which might be taken to resolve difficulties. These solutions are likely to be long term and involve more than academic matters.

Counselling is a highly skilled professional service, which should only be offered by those qualified to do so. You may find yourself using some of the basic counselling techniques in your tutoring or helping relationships, like listening for example. But the centre will have designated staff to carry out counselling and it is to them that you refer your students when you think that they have this need. Your professionalism lies in being able to make that judgement. Don't be tempted to think that you should do it yourself. This is not in the student's best interests.

Task 19 will help you to sum up this chapter.

---

**TASK 19:   Support and guidance services**

Imagine yourself to be *a student in the institution or context in which you are teaching*. **Construct** a 'coral diagram' (see page 153) to show what is available to support students. Most of the information you need is in this Appendix, but you will need to look carefully at your own context, too.

Students could share this Task, with the teacher in a tutorial role. They may co-operate in completing the chart, perhaps in groups.

---

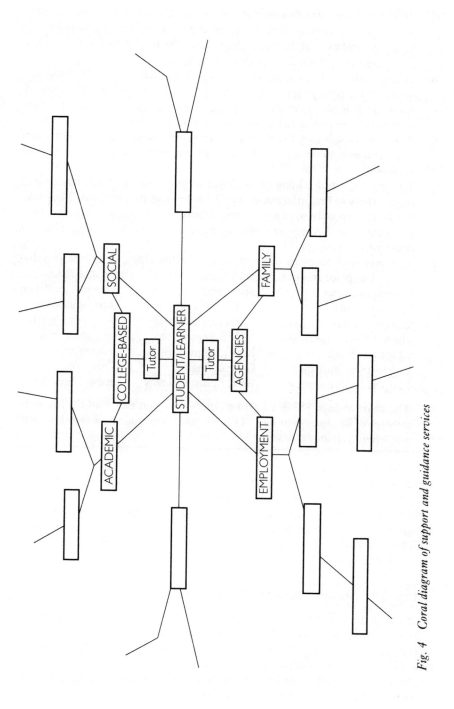

*Fig. 4  Coral diagram of support and guidance services*

A   You, *the student*, are naturally at the centre. What support and guidance services might there be that you could approach or have access to to help you? You will need all kinds of advice and help since your life is complex; you are not simply a learner in this institution.

B   Where is *the teacher, advisor or tutor*, within the framework? Will the students see the tutor as the first line of approach, as an anchor while they are learning? It is the tutor that will bring it all together for them: they may wish to refer to him or her as well as to the specialist services.

C   The services will vary from place to place and will change. It may require some research to discover: what is available, where it is located, who to approach.

D   You may continue adding to this chart as you (tutor or student) discover more; where to find information or which services are provided. They may not be located only within your own institution. Many government, local government and employer based agencies are available to help. This is a constantly changing field.

E   You may wish to place some of these into the chart, or others you discover. The place and order of such things in the chart need discussion.

| | | |
|---|---|---|
| Careers guidance | Study skills support | Academic guidance |
| ESOL support | APL/APEL guidance | Tutorial guidance |
| Grants, sources of funding | Child care facilities | Mentorship system |
| Home Office Regulations | DHSS Regulations | Accommodation |
| Learning difficulties | Equal Opportunities | Chaplaincy |
| Employment guidance | Counselling | IT support |
| Basic Skills: Numeracy | Basic Skills: Literacy | Medical Services |

F   The chart of page 153 is a starting point only. You may find the headings unhelpful, so *choose your own*. This is your chart, your framework to help you where you are.

# 19 Developing Study Skills

It cannot be assumed that students can cope with learning on their own. Most people have poorly developed study skills; your own may well need further development. In this chapter you will find some ideas and activities that should help you and your students to improve the ability to learn.

## Targets and short-term goals

All skill learning depends on practice and repetition. You will achieve the skill as long as you clearly understand what it is you are trying to do and set yourself targets. Skills arise from habit-forming practice.

There is a problem with motivation. Long-term goals take so long to achieve and may seem to get no nearer; they may become disincentives. So, we need short-term goals and targets obtainable within days or weeks, which can then build towards our long-term goals. The same is true for our students.

Think of useful things. Set yourself attainable tasks:
I will master the Dewey Decimal system in the library.
I will learn how to use the microfiche catalogue.
I will make a list of books and materials in my field and where to find them.
I will learn to use a wordprocessor.
I will increase my reading speed by searching documents/books and other material for answers to my questions.
I will look carefully at any documents I produce to make sure they are clear and easy to understand.
I will cut out unnecessary words in memos and so on I send.
I will find out about electronic mail and how to use it.
I will learn how to use computer databases and networks.

All this sort of activity will encourage you to work closely with staff in resource centres and libraries, who will support you. It is essential to develop these skills so as to create or gather a bank of resource material that your students may learn from, as well as to be a creative member of a team with your colleagues.

ACTIVITY 9

ACTIVITY 10

# Learning from lectures

To be followable the lecture must have a structure. Properly handled lectures make the structure plain, with a structure plan employing key-words. The listeners can add notes of their own.

The worst kind of notes are verbatim scribble. Listening, watching and addressing questions to the lecturer are more important than getting down everything that is said. You cannot do both.

If you listen carefully a pattern will emerge, with 'alerting' words about the links, or 'now I want . . .' statements, or rhetorical questions. Key-words are usually not too hard to pick up if you listen out for them.

This skeleton, or pattern, is what you need to take away. You will need to look at it again, revisit as soon as possible afterwards, and reorganise the structure so that it makes sense to you. This allows you to clarify it as you review it. Look again at my advice in Part 1. Approach a lecture like this:

1  What are you hoping to learn? Are you ready and alert?
2  Be ready. Create your working space.
3  Listen to the preamble. If the lecture is part of a series, there should be a recap and links to previous learning. Note the links. There should be a 'map' of what is to come, even a plan which will help you to know where you are – in case you or the lecturer wanders, as lecturers are prone to do.
4  Listen for key-words, structural statements and recap statements – to consolidate as it goes along – opportunities for feedback, voice inflections, gestures and so forth that show important points.
5  Watch: if there are OHP presentations, they should offer key-words or patterns you can note down.
6  Use key-words only. You have to listen, not write.
7  If you lose track, if the lecturer wanders, or if you do not understand, *ask*. The lecturer knows it already, but cannot know your difficulty unless you say so – you are trying to learn. The lecture is not intended to be a sermon in church.
8  Listen to any summary/consolidation and check your notes.
9  **Review soon.** Within twenty-four hours you will have lost 70 per cent of it.

# Learning from written materials

You can employ similar techniques to written materials such as this book. It is important to identify clearly the structure the author uses, and how parts relate to the whole. Your needs are not the same as those of other readers, nor are you starting from where the author is. Approach the material with your own questions as well as those the author seems to address.

You should certainly make structure notes. In Part 1 I discussed the problem of 'forgetting' and the need for revisiting. This is made much easier to tackle if you make notes and review them whenever you come back to them.

In any case, you will change and your perception will change with a fuller understanding of the author's intentions and growing experience to make comparisons of your own. Be proactive.

All books have maps – use them. Take charge of your learning.

# Making notes

Why make notes at all?

- to be attentive, proactive learners. Humans are exploratory animals and need to be 'searching' in order to learn
- to get at the structure in order to see the whole and how it all fits together
- to produce a pattern we can absorb, match with our knowledge and experience
- to avoid the necessity of constantly rereading everything
- to enable us to revisit and review and so consolidate: it is important that we learn it 'right', for unlearning is harder than learning
- to challenge and restructure our own understanding.

## ACTIVITY 11

## Using television advertisements

How to practise? You need short, repetitive activity. Television advertisements provide the shortest, most accessible and punchiest means. These are highly efficient in the use of time in getting the message across. Within about thirty seconds, they grab attention and hold it. They convey a message (of some kind). They have to make it memorable, not necessarily simple in meaning but effective for the purpose of the advertisement. They may appeal to us in quite subtle ways, which it is interesting to analyse and explore. They are very efficient in the use of words and compelling images.

One advertisement will usually be repeated several times, so that you can check what you do. Be proactive: address questions to the experience. Once you have the skill, you can apply it to any experience, including this book. Write down the questions; revise them as new ideas occur to you.

Try to see the script behind words and images. Visualise the script into camera shots, which hardly ever last more than a few seconds. Then add the words. It is unusual for sound and vision to be recorded together.

You are trying to get behind the presentation to the structure to see how the thing has been put together and how it works. Nothing happens without a great deal of design-work first. Find the questions the designers posed to themselves:

How many camera shots? how long for each shot? why choose those?
What is the message? how is it built up, conveyed?
What are the words? how do they work with the images?
What is the advertisement appealing to? and to whom?
Is it effective? What makes it so? If not, why not?

## Structures

# Patterning and sequencing

Notes are not verbatim reports. They are for you. To be useful they
must provide:

- triggers to facilitate recall
- a means of showing links, patterns of ideas that make a whole.

You will develop your own pattern for notes. Some people prefer to
make linear structures, to see a spine of argument developing. Others
prefer to start with a central idea, and then to use links by key-words to
related but not necessarily sequential ideas, forming what has been
named a 'coral' structure (after the branching coral). Figure 5 illustrates
these two different types.

Both rely on key-words as triggers. Other clues to structure and
relationships can be added: you can draw circles and boxes to enclose
related ideas/words, and arrows to show direction and connections.
You must develop your own methodology of making sense of the
information.

Once you have something that works well for you, you can use it to get
the message across effectively to others on hand-outs or OHP
transparencies or on the whiteboard.

Experiment with different structures of notes. See which one is the
most useful, the most meaningful for you. Remember, students will have
their own way of visualising and dealing with information you present.
Some will respond to linear structures, others to patterning. Do not
assume that what works for you works for everyone.

### A. Linear style

#### COMMUNICATION

| Individuals | Channels | Groups |
|---|---|---|
| barriers | signals | sharing |
| self-image | messages | boundaries |
| attitude | interference | identifying |
| mind-set | noise | signals |
| emotions | redundancy | measures |
| prior learning | (radio/TV) | rules |
| experience | | bonding |
| knowledge | | common goals |

skills
convictions
messages
reading
interpreting
sending
concepts
formal thinking
vocabulary

teams
support
individuals
personal needs
common language
concepts/group
experience
leadership
roles
decisions
action plans

**B. Linking pattern**

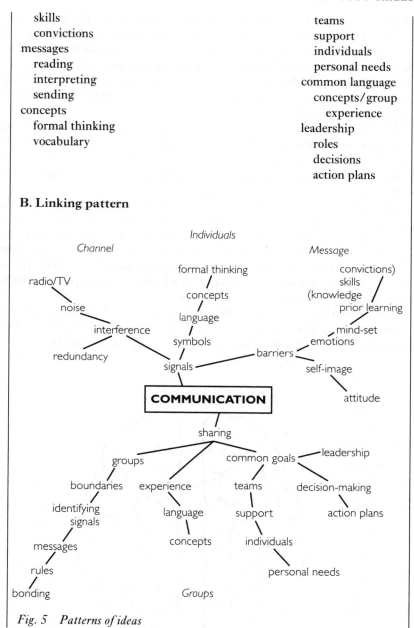

*Fig. 5   Patterns of ideas*

# Brain behaviour

Brain behaviour appears to use pattern-making and rule-making. It seems this may be to do with the ways in which the two halves of the brain prefer to work:

159

the left and right hemispheres appear to be different. In the 1970s Dr Roger Sperry did pioneering research that led to conceptions of dominance in brain behaviour. Studying brain electrical pulses of people doing different activities, he and his colleagues found that each hemisphere appeared to be involved in one kind rather than another. They 'specialise'. Studies of people who have suffered brain damage, or whose brain hemispheres have been physically divided, show this differentiated behaviour.

The left hemisphere is responsible for logical thought, language and mathematical processes, reasoning and analysis. Left brain dominance leads to goal-seeking, logical and linear thinking, a preference for analytical behaviour. It seems to be concerned with rule-making and linear structuring. Centres for language, reading and writing are located there (see Figure 6).

The right hemisphere deals with rhythm, colour, spatial concepts, imagination and synthesis. Right brain dominance is characterised by patterns and 'wholes', rather than by analysis. It facilitates the rather mysterious insights and 'leaps in the dark' that all of us experience. It seems to allow us to respond intuitively, emotionally, sensitively. It works with images and pictures, internal representations, models and patterns. It tends to work also on numerous parallel paths, matching and hypothesising to produce new structures.

It is a simplification to say all this is to do simply with the different hemispheres of the brain. But it is a fact that we do exhibit these quite different ways of behaving in the way we think about and deal with the world and social life.

*Fig. 6 Hemispheres of the brain* (derived from a paper presented at the Industrial Society, 1989)

They are clearly different kinds of activity. One promotes more creativity, essential in order to go about problem-solving and exploring alternatives. The other is essential for planning, getting things done, organising and communicating in a logical fashion.

It is an unfortunate feature of modern education that emphasis is put so heavily on left brain behaviour. At school and at work it is left brain behaviour that is valued, considered 'clever'. The creativity and imagination of students are not rewarded with high marks in examinations which more easily test memory, logic and so on. Consequently, we tend to try to do everything logically. There is a preference for linear structures. We cannot analyse our own thinking: we cannot watch ourselves think. But we can have a view of our preferred patterns and seek to exploit those fully, while ensuring that we improve where we need to those activities that we personally find less attractive.

## Studying

Studying requires us to be able to handle both pattern-making and rule-making. We have to be able to grasp the whole in order to see how the parts make sense. But we also need to see the structure. We do need to follow the logic of argument and to analyse the validity of the evidence, but we also need to match it with experience and insight gained elsewhere so as to construct our own picture of it all.

In setting about studying, you need to be aware of how you perform best in order to maximise the benefit. Establish for yourself what you find the most effective procedures for you. This is experiential learning, trying various approaches to see what works best. Once you have settled on a formula which seems to work well, you should make what you do *habitual*. Habits are patterns of behaviour we do not have to think about. Some are beneficial, others not. In learning, it is important to establish good habits and eliminate those that inhibit you, get in the way and slow you down.

## Networks, electronic mail and interactive video

New technology has revolutionised the way we think about 'information'. 'Searching for information' on networks and databases using computer modems, electronic mail-boxes and so on appears to be far superior, access is much simpler, than reading or searching for what we want to know in books. One is limited to what has been put into the databases, but the range of material is increasing geometrically by the day. Publishers have agreed to books of all kinds being published on CD-rom with study notes and interactive study programmes, so that we may buy packages to use on a desktop machine; or we may get them via networks. Many dictionaries, thesauri, and other standard reference books are now available on CD-rom. How much more convenient it is to 'look up a word' using the powerful 'search and compare' facilities of a computer: and then to print out information as we need it!

Such techniques are to be encouraged, to promote the *proactive learning* we need to develop ourselves and to have our students enjoy. From a very early age, many have already become quite at home with computers; these are becoming cheaper, more accessible and far more sophisticated. Computer games fascinate young and old and encourage them to 'interact' with machine-generated images. Educational institutions and teachers should make positive use of the new enthusiasm for learning this creates.

Interaction with a computer is not the same as passively, mindlessly watching TV. The brain is alert and active, even on video games that may seem to be highly repetitive. The sophisticated techniques of interactive video, which combine video material on laser discs, more recently CD-rom, with computer programmes, enable students to interrogate both the video material and a great deal of other information in other forms. The volume of such information is staggeringly large now.

A problem with material recorded on film or video-tape is that its sheer volume, its very richness, makes it verbose and hard to comprehend or use. But this richness should be exploited.

Teachers can try to overcome this problem by explaining the structure, creating a list of questions to address to the material, or by selection. Computer programmes linked to video material, however, allow anyone to search for answers to questions and to select the parts of the visual material that are relevant to each question. This selection is usually programmed in. Of course, it would be better if one could ask one's own questions rather than only those stored in programmes. Nevertheless, the technique allows students to plan their own learning paths through the material. 'Fully structured training programmes' use feedback loops to try to ensure a thorough grasp of the material by repetitive questioning.

The computer can be used to test learning; or may be linked to a wordprocessor, printer and other machines. Information may be made available in different formats: on screen, in print, recorded on discs, as instructions or in visual form. One great advantage is that the information can be kept up-to-date, which is much more expensive to do when it appears in book form. This makes it particularly valuable in areas like careers advice or economic forecasting when a student needs accurate, up-to-the-minute data.

Training in the use of new technology is straightforward for teachers and students. Using wordprocessing programmes will allow anyone to record their own materials, so making them accessible along with other database materials. They can be stored on a computer disc or as video material where appropriate. Anyone can print out what they need on paper (maybe using electronic mail even from home or office).

Teachers will be able to accumulate visual and textual computer-based material specifically for their own use via networks and databases – or develop their own which can be shared with others through a network. Electronic mail and networks may be used for sharing, not only information but the excitement of creative activity, problem-solving and so on. Groups or individuals who are far apart, even on separate continents, can work together on projects with ease.

This does not mean that books and other printed material are no longer of value. It is essential that people continue to read: for enjoyment, for information, for stimulation of their own creative faculties and to share and generate ideas – not least to develop a feeling for language and vocabulary. But libraries have become 'multi-media centres'. Teachers must be at least as comfortable with 'multi-media' as students; and exploit its possibilities to the full.

Like any map, this brief description of the nature of new technology and its effect on the way teachers and learning interact will not come fully alive until you actually see it and use it yourself. Try to work closely with the manager in your 'multi-media centre'.

# 20 Teaching and Learning Aids

## TASK 20: Teaching/learning aids

Design, produce and use a variety of teaching/learning aids.

For each session, the activities planned for students and teacher should be clearly identified within the lesson plan. Aids and materials to support that activity should be designed or selected to be appropriate and effective. Where they are produced it is expected that they will be of a presentable standard.

All these aids and materials need careful evaluation after use. They will accumulate to create a resource file which you should frequently edit, organise and keep up to date.

PERFORMANCE CRITERIA FOR TEACHING/LEARNING MATERIALS AND AIDS

1 Learning materials are designed to stimulate and challenge while building links and structures to earlier learning.

2 Learning materials use symbols and language and require the students to undertake activities appropriate to their needs.

3 Learning materials are easy to understand and clear in what they say. They are well produced and sequence learning in a sensible and supportive way.

4 Teaching aids are well designed for their purpose, and of a presentable quality.

5 Teaching aids are simple, taking account of known difficulty students have in comprehension. They show an understanding of the principles of designing such aids.

6 Teaching aids and learning materials are used skilfully and effectively in the session and are adapted sensitively to student needs as they arise.

7 All are evaluated for effectiveness or redesigned as needed.

8 Teaching aids and learning materials reflect the culture and assumptions of all members of the group.

## Audio-visual aids

The major purpose of audio-visual aids in the classroom is to focus attention. If you switch on an OHP, attention moves from your face to the screen. This helps by providing variety and regenerating interest – attention span is normally no more than fifteen minutes – but is obviously self-defeating if the OHP is then just left on. Use it only as needed; otherwise, it becomes 'noise'. Students need to concentrate on you when you wish to engage them in two-way exchange.

Visual stimuli are in the control of the teacher and should be used effectively. Clear the board and the walls of distracting material, including work from previous classes. And don't inflict your material on others.

# Visual images

Since we learn 70 per cent of our information by seeing, visual stimuli are particularly powerful. They should be chosen or designed with care. A picture can be worth a thousand words, but not if it is a bad picture or misleading or irrelevant or difficult to interpret.

Pictures are extremely rich in information, and simplified diagrams are often much clearer and simpler to grasp. They let you eliminate everything except what you want to show. You can also build up the structure using overlay techniques on an OHP, for example. Focus on essentials, and select out noisy detail.

In choosing a visual stimulus, you must appraise it for what you want to achieve by using it. How effective is it for the specific purpose you intend? It may be to show how the parts relate to the whole, or to concentrate attention on fine detail. Both are necessary to understanding and good diagrams or pictures can make understanding very much easier. But they are a means to an end. Support them if possible by physical exploration of the reality.

In constructing images, certain factors improve effectiveness:

- **simplicity**: the brain simplifies – searches for patterns; to help we too should simplify our images where we can
- **closure**: we like to perceive things as 'wholes' rather than in bits; we should ensure that the whole is clear even when we want to concentrate on details
- **clarity**: the brain tests hypotheses about figures and will try different ones; avoid ambiguity or lack of clarity
- **boundary**: to see we must differentiate things; clear boundaries will help, and the use of colour can also be effective.

A good example to visualise is a child's wooden train. Think of the simplification of the complex engine into horizontal and vertical cylinders, cubes and circles, especially if these are differentiated by being painted in bright contrasting colours.

# Audibility and visibility

Consider the acoustics of the room and the lighting conditions. Do not assume that people can hear or see. The screen may be masked for some students by others, or by the OHP. Even the greatest visual aid is useless if it can't be seen. Always ask the people furthest away or at the widest angle if they are having difficulty. When possible test it out yourself – walk around to see. In particular, check any material you have put up on the board for its legibility and structure, preferably from the furthest point. This has the added advantage that you can make personal contact with students and experience it from their point of view. It is easy to remain rather fixed at the front when using AVA.

Think about the personalities involved. Are there any in the group with poor eyesight? (They may be too embarrassed to put on their spectacles – this quite frequently happens!) Is anyone there colour-blind (6 per cent of males are)? Maybe colour differentiation is important. Some people cannot distinguish lines that are too fine or present narrow angles. Ask people to move if it might help. Think about brightness of illumination or contrast with general brightness in the room. Draw the curtains or switch off lights. There may be angles at which reflections make it hard to see. Experiment; move the screen (or the class). Take control.

Deafness tends to be more embarrassing and more difficult, and people are often less aware of the onset of deafness than they are of failing vision. Both affect people gradually, usually as they get older. A physical decline seems inevitable, though often people compensate with greater effort too. We need to be alert to problems, to clarity of diction and pace of delivery.

## Listening skills

Listening skills require a great effort. We are surrounded by a cacophony of sounds. Students have been conditioned to be unhappy with silence. Some people wake up listening anxiously to silence in the middle of the night. So we routinely block out most of what we hear. Listen to a tape-recording of an hour of your life in normal circumstances. What sounds are there you do not 'hear'?

Yet teachers expect students to listen more than to do anything else, without recognising the problems involved. Students may be talked at for an hour or more. They are also often expected to take down notes at the same time. Apart from the difficulty of trying to do two things at once, there are many problems of inaccuracy, mis-hearing, misunderstanding and so on. Many teachers take a cynical view: 'As long as they've been given the information, what the hell! If they can't make use of it, it's nothing to do with me.'

All social behaviour depends on listening to others; most people are very bad at it. Teachers are also notoriously bad at listening to students. Parliament is a public display of egotists talking and no one listening. Eventually people have to scream and shout, even become social vandals, to get others to listen.

## Alerting signals

If you want students to listen it is essential that you give them cues, alerting signals, questions to think about. They need to be able to follow your structure easily. Give them the pattern. It can be built up using key-words. There should also be opportunities for feedback, two-way communication, loops or links to consolidate learning at least every fifteen minutes or so.

166

Take stock of your delivery. How fast do you talk, and how monotonous is your voice? Inexperienced teachers tend to let their voices rise, become rather strangled or shrill. Relax, slow down. Slower pace gives you and them thinking time. Try to pitch your voice lower, and to vary its pitch; it will be nicer to listen to and will probably carry better. Try to improve your diction, too. Do you miss consonants off the ends of words? Are there difficult acoustics in the room? What do you do about that? For instance, the hum of the OHP is a distraction, so turn it off whenever you do not need it.

Listen to yourself on a tape-recorder after a class. Better than video, it can be quite revealing.

## Structure

Students need to take away a pattern, a structure, in order to learn it. If they try to listen and copy out they are likely to select and distort information, and embed misunderstanding. If you are using a lecture approach, it is best to give them the structure of your lecture beforehand so that they can use it to follow what you wish to present. It may be in the form of headings with gaps for their own notes, but they need to be helped to structure them with key-words and patterns to make sense of them.

If the method you choose is inductive, you must genuinely build up on the board or OHP what they discover or suggest. But it will need to be written up into a comprehensible structure afterwards, to ensure it makes sense as a whole. Produce your own version as a handout when you make the links to the next class.

## OHP: projector and screen

The OHP is a most versatile tool. It has the advantage that you can prepare material beforehand, but also add to it or adapt it in the class. You can maintain eye-contact with the students while you use it, and encourage their participation. (You have to turn your back to write on a chalkboard, and risk losing the contact.)

You can also sit to appear part of the group when appropriate, or invite them to work with you. You should, in any case, develop techniques that will not divide you from your class. Some teachers treat the screen as if it were a chalkboard and do all the explanation at the screen, so losing the advantage of the OHP.

You can point out relevant detail on the transparency, perhaps using a pen to lie as a semi-permanent pointer, moving it as needed to focus attention. You can reveal and mask parts of the structure or diagram as you want to concentrate on particular things. You can use a host of visual clues, exploiting the four basic factors set out on page 165.

All that I emphasised earlier about structure and sequence applies to the use of the OHP. Once you have a clear structure, take the students through it. Too much all at once is difficult to grasp, but they will need to see the structure as a whole by the end. Build it up gradually, revealing it a bit at a time as you elaborate the key-words or diagram. It helps to black out all the image except the bit you want to concentrate on (easily done with ordinary paper), and then gradually reveal the building blocks. Remember that the OHP is an aid for your explanation, not a substitute for it.

Think, too, about the density of information and verbosity. It is easy to make A4 printed pages into transparencies, and teachers frequently do. But the result can be illegibility and incomprehension. An OHP transparency must be read at a distance, while a paper is held in the hand. Keep the difference in mind.

## Setting up the projector and screen

Where are you going to place yourself in relation to the OHP? The OHP allows you to face your audience, maintain eye-contact and so on. You do not have to stand, presentation-style. You can use it with a group in a much more relaxed way. You can sit beside the OHP, which signals that you are part of the group. It also allows you to interact more easily with the group rather than with the screen. This kind of teaching is about sharing, not telling.

Make sure that the machine itself is not preventing students from seeing the screen. Try putting it on a low table (or even a chair) rather than obstructing the sight-line for people sitting down (see Figure 7). It helps if the screen can be tilted forward at the top.

## Building up resources

OHP transparencies form part of a developing resource bank. This requires organising too to allow for order and retrieval. The transparencies need to be

*Fig. 7* (Left) *Impossible to avoid obscuring the screen for some people, and when you write or point on OHP: you could raise the screen. Also puts a table between you and the group: creates distance, formality.*
(Right) *OHP not on sight-line or dominating. Screen needs angling forward. Easier to see in most illuminations, feels comfortably closer. Barriers removed.*

168

framed and covered. Using such frames, you can make transparencies that use several acetate sections as overlays, although this is probably only worth the effort if you intend to use them more than once. Have the acetates firmly located in their frames so that the overlays fall easily into the right place. Start with a 'stripped' diagram or structure, and add complexity using slices of acetate with the additional information or detail. Provide students with the basic figure as a 'gapped handout' on paper for them to fill out as you add information, such as labels.

Resource rooms will have appropriate cutting and pasting equipment. They should have acetate sheets in different colours, frames, a cutting board and a sharp knife. The simplest way to add colour is with felt pens, which come in different thicknesses – some colours become almost illegible when projected, however. White lettering on a coloured ground can be more effective.

Experiment. Prepare your transparencies beforehand, since only then can you design them properly. Make sure print is of a suitable size and density, with good colour contrast if possible. Think too of the four rules above. OHTs are about the bones of the teaching, not the flesh.

The photocopier can be used in conjunction with OHP to produce good-quality transparencies quickly. A structured lesson plan, for instance, should be in handout form, but also on OHP acetate to provide an overview of learning goals and activities.

# Boardwork

Structure matters in boardwork too. It is easy to use a board as a jotting pad; this is quite helpful to concentrate attention and move the focus, but it doesn't produce a pattern that is easy to remember. Plan your boardwork whenever you can, or at least determine some structure within which you can make notes on the board. Look at it at the end and see if the pattern makes sense for them to take away. You need a 'model in the head'. You can put up an outline before they come. White boards have the advantage you can use colours for boundary.

Write legibly. This requires practice – it's quite different from any other writing you do. Can the people at the back read it? If it is too small or the letters are poorly formed, no! Try to look at it from the back, to see it as they do.

You could use columns, circles, or section off the board, or use lists with headings or careful use of arrows to show relationships between ideas. The coral diagrams on pages 153 and 159 work well on a board. If you do add information, words and so on on the board as you go along, you must differentiate information by boundaries (lines) around each part and indicate the links somehow. Go through it with students to consolidate at the end if you can.

# Handouts

The most valuable, least understood resource is the photocopier. It tends to be used merely to reproduce masses of 'stuff to give the students' without thinking through what they are going to do with it, or whether it will contribute effectively to learning. As with every other aid, a handout needs careful planning. What is it for? How should it look? When do they need it? What is to be the sequence? Here are some useful examples.

1 It is most important that students read widely. It is also much better if they do this *before* a session, so that what they have read forms a basis for their work. It is easy to use material as if it were a textbook, to let it run the class. Better to see it like a committee paper circulated as a basis for discussion, to take as read – somewhere to start from.

A teacher has to assume knowledge, breadth of experience, to be able to concentrate on what can be done in class. There has to be a lot of learning elsewhere. A handout ensures that all have the same accurate and up-to-date information. (Of course, they have to read it!)

Students should be encouraged to find their own reading too. They will need access to photocopying in the library to make up a reading portfolio. They should be encouraged to adopt the approach I have set out in my advice on the development of study skills, in Chapter 2.

2 Reduce a handout to be used in class to a skeleton of key-words, which students can flesh out with their own notes. Use it to help students to grasp the structure and pattern of the whole, the flow and sequence. Wordy handouts are confusing 'noise'.

Structure and linking, alerting and outline notes, are much better than the (usually) selective and inaccurate notes that students scribble while their attention should be on listening and watching. The brain cannot be alerted with questions while the ears are trying to catch the answers.

A 'gapped handout' can assist note-taking and consolidation, by enabling students to recall accurately what was covered in class. It can also be used to test recall, words, whole sentences, labels – or whatever needs to be tested. It can be filed for revision.

3 A handout can be designed as an instruction sheet, an action plan or a working document. Guidance, drawings to complete, questions to find answers to, maps, treasure hunts – there are so many ways of using handouts creatively. But they all need design so that they are effective to their purpose. This is much better than inventing the material on the hoof and then getting the group to copy it down from the board. Distortion and misunderstanding become inevitable.

Once you have designed a handout, always get it validated by someone else for clarity, ambiguity, what it is like for someone who is coming to it fresh and possibly not already knowledgeable.

## REMEMBER!

*. . . Check your handout, especially if it contains visual material, to see that it does not use stereotypes or other material which could offend some students or distract them from their learning. Be particularly careful with humour. Material, visual or in words, that*

*seems innocent or amusing to you may be offensive to someone else of another gender, age or culture.*

4 Use handouts to 'share'. As with OHTs for groupwork, handouts can ensure that all accumulate the same ideas – and can focus them through revisiting – and have the same richness of resources to work with.

## Resource bank

A most important feature of handouts is that they accumulate as a personal resource file. They need organising: given headings and dates, and perhaps colour-coded. Using different colours for the different kinds of handouts can be extremely helpful.

Sensible use of handouts ensures a well-structured, clear, non-verbose and accurate information-base with a linking pattern. It is unhelpful for students to try to revise from material that is as wrong, incomplete, ambiguous, illusory or fictional as student notes so frequently turn out to be.

Simple learning materials are often as effective as complex ones. All AVA is expensive in time and effort. Time spent making AVA or handouts will only make sense if the products solve a real problem in learning; it is also far better if they can be used for more than one session or class. An advantage of working in a team, or with colleagues, is that you share ideas and the effort of creating resources. There should be a team resource bank to use.

## Problem-solving

One good exercise is to identify the real learning problems in your field of teaching. Then with colleagues think of creative ways in which you could tackle the problems. You could use models as well as OHP presentations or slides. You could think of games or activities that require setting out as instructions.

I have seen extraordinarily inventive ideas in a wide range of disciplines from such an exercise. I gave an example in Case Study 7, in which a doll's house was used to help students who had difficulty in visualising things, and to 'see it happening' somehow.

A group (or an individual) might pose themselves a learning or a visualising problem: for example, to show how far away the nearest star is by taking the sun to be the size of a pea, and where the planets are on the same scale. Or how you might explain planetary motion. Or to convey the idea of a standing wave in physics, maybe, or the menstrual cycle or the circulation of the blood. Or dealing in stocks and shares, or decision-making in a business enterprise. Or to analyse the action of the four-stroke engine.

These have all been designed as models, charts (some with parts that move), board and card games – some were highly competitive. If a visual stimulus can be helped with action, all the better. Think of the 'sculpting' in Case Study 6.

# Team-based resources

Teams share their expertise and creativity in building up a team resource bank of teaching/learning materials. Awarding bodies and examining boards increasingly promote team approaches which help to integrate areas of the curriculum. Students are to learn through projects that cross subject disciplines, while teachers work as teams to produce the learning materials.

A resource base is needed where materials can be located and are accessible to the team. It needs to be equipped not only for the storage and retrieval of materials but for creative work too. This is a base where the team can generate ideas and activity-work for a whole curriculum programme. Clearly, since it consists mostly of handouts and consumables, there must be a system that tracks usage and ensures replacement. All team members carry responsibility. The production of AVA, models and so on requires work-benches, wordprocessing, video machines, materials such as acetates, and so forth. The control of expenditure and decision-making is important, and record-keeping must be well organised too.

In a previous chapter, I suggested ways in which teachers can develop their skills to contribute more effectively to such work. Many institutions have set up multi-media and/or resource rooms with technicians and other support staff. If you are lucky enough to have such support for teachers, you should make sure that you work closely with them. They are often linked to the library, now frequently called by more general titles such as the multi-media centre to take account of the technological changes in the use of computers, networks and so on. It makes economic sense to put major resources of this kind together with trained staff to ensure they are used as effectively as possible.

# Wordprocessing and desktop publishing

Do learn to use a wordprocessor. It makes the production of good-quality handouts much easier. Handwritten ones are untidy. You can manipulate text in a wordprocessor to ensure that it is presented in the most effective way without the tedium of having to rewrite (or retype) things. Learn to compose, to 'invent', at the keyboard.

Most computers have a range of fonts and allow the use of graphics which will enable you to produce excellent OHP materials also. You can make transparencies from text produced with a wordprocessor.

All computers can now support desktop publishing programs that allow teachers to produce materials that look as attractive and well produced as a printed page, but at a fraction of the cost. Once the basic text and diagrams have been set up, they can be manipulated into all the ways magazines use to make them visually exciting. But you can also make them work with the way in which learners learn using all the visual techniques mentioned above – simplifying, structuring, sequencing, headlining, marking strong boundaries using lines and boxes, and integrating diagrams and other images with the text.

Poor visual presentation of teaching materials fails to stimulate, and can simply switch students off. Look at almost any commercially produced material and see how it depends on visual impact for its effect. Even quite awful content can be made compelling reading. Teachers need to exploit every possible technique to the full.

# Films and television

There are good and bad ways of using films and television programmes. All these are by their nature 'verbose': they contain far too much information and visual imagery for students to make sense of, certainly if they see it only once. Their main purpose is to entertain, or to stimulate interest. Where they set out to inform, they have to assume some general audience they are addressing. Students will find it hard to select what they need. Even instructional films may not be particularly easy to digest. Most information is selected out by the lack of attention we can give to it – and usually, too, the dimly lit and comfortable environment is not conducive to giving attention. Only the strongest of images will be remembered.

## Using films and television well

You must see the material first (simple advice, but often ignored). Analyse the film into structure to see how it is put together – after all, someone planned it. Provide students with this structure (as key-words) to help them grasp the parts in relation to the whole.

Alert students for what they can learn, what to look out for – pinpoint the questions the film addresses; otherwise they will not know what to look or listen for, and will certainly miss most of it. And it's no good asking them afterwards, 'did you notice . . . ?'

Even better, select those, possibly short, parts of the film or programme that contain what you want students to learn, and show only those. This has the added advantage that you can show these parts more than once.

Using this technique:

1 Prepare the students with questions and structure.
2 Show them relevant and important extracts from the whole.
3 Revisit these with the questions to elicit answers – or maybe more searching questions.
4 Reshow the extracts to consolidate the learning and link it to other learning experiences.
5 Evaluate the learning with them.

If this technique is used with video-recordings, the students can have material available as part of a data-bank (for example, in a library) to consult when they need to revise.

173

# Visits

Films and television are ways of bringing the world into the classroom. Often, but not always, it is useful to take the class to the real world. Apart from the logistics of doing it and the time it consumes, the benefits can be great. Look again at **Effective use of visits** on page 145.

# 21 Barriers to Communication

In order to make progress in engaging students in the learning process, we must ensure that we and they recognise the barriers to learning they bring with them. We, as teachers, should be able to recognise specific problems students create for themselves or behavioural characteristics. It is not easy for us to see our own.

## Mind-set and emotion

Emotional or attitudinal barriers result from cultural conditioning or response to past experience. We all have a mind-set about things that relate to us, a self-image that inhibits our willingness to believe we can do certain things, attitudes and beliefs we defend against overwhelming evidence.

Perhaps you know someone who is a banker. What image does that word conjure up for him or her, and for you? 'There are certain things bankers do, wear, enjoy, don't do, don't wear, don't enjoy, aren't there? I couldn't possibly . . .' and this will inhibit certain kinds of behaviour. Some girls (or their parents) still reject the idea of engineering as a career: 'Do women actually enjoy engineering or science or maths? Isn't that what men do, not women?' Some men believe that nursing or primary school teaching is an inappropriate choice of career. Where do such attitudes come from?

They clearly relate to our perception of ourselves, a powerful self-image we have developed as a result of our experience. Many, such as that of the banker, we derive from models around us. It is not unusual to meet students who genuinely see themselves as 'thick', not 'clever like these other people'. It may be a result of painful experiences in education in the past, or a defensive posture to protect them from possible failure.

We have our needs for personal space and territory. Our value-system, our likes and dislikes, are often firmly embedded: they are inextricable from 'me – who I am' and exhibited both in words and in body language. We can all read such body signals easily.

Someone who has a mind-set that says 'I can't do maths' is not going to succeed in maths, however hard the teacher tries, unless that mould can somehow be broken. This learner has had past experience of maths learning, perhaps reinforced with some role-model that has established a conviction that it is not worth trying. The same happens in most areas of learning. Ball games defeat some people utterly; some are all thumbs in craftwork; some are word-blind; some cannot draw a straight line. You will have heard people say these things. They are self-fulfilling prophecies.

It is far from easy to tackle such attitudinal barriers. Equally, when someone discovers a way through such a barrier, the effect on their self-image and on their lives can be quite dramatic. The discussion above on motivation (page 107) may suggest ways forward.

# Information theory

In 1949, the Shannon–Weaver mathematical theory of communication was published. These workers made a distinction between 'information' and 'informational channels': between what the information is about and the way it is transmitted, person to person. Shannon and Weaver were concerned to improve radar and radio transmission: 'we want to maintain a high-fidelity transmission so that messages don't get garbled on the way. We also want a lot of redundancy and clarity: we don't want noise interfering with the transmission.'

'Noise' and 'redundancy' are technical terms. Noise in radio is the jumble of background sound that may prevent us hearing what we are trying to listen to. We have all had the frustration of noise when we try to hear a concert or a talk on the radio; it can be even worse when television pictures break up, develop strange images or disappear. It is often referred to as interference. Redundancy refers to an excess deliberately put into the signal to ensure that something of the message gets through. The theory is about effectiveness in sending and receiving signals.

We are dealing here in metaphors, so this account is not be taken too literally. Problems in classrooms that affect information transmission, whatever the kind of signal, increase with distance. The further people are away, the harder it is for them to read our signals, for us to read theirs. So much of what we wish to share is to be read in the way we say or demonstrate it. Subtleties and nuances are lost.

Distraction in the classroom is one kind of 'noise'. For example, I was running a discussion with a group of teachers. A colleague who was with me said at the end that he had had great difficulty in concentrating on what I was saying because a woman sitting opposite him had such 'noisy legs'. After another session a group of students told me they found the design of the sweatshirt I was wearing so fascinating they simply couldn't follow my arguments.

Conflicting messages, emotional stress, aggressive behaviour may also act as 'noise'. The problem relates to the learner's 'attention'. Learners need to concentrate on what is to be learned, but so much can get in the way. Anything that interferes with attention is noise.

But so is lack of clarity in the signals and messages we wish to convey. The means of transmission – the tone of voice, perhaps, the words we speak or the visual materials used – all need to be clear and easy to understand. Monotony of delivery will become 'noisy'. Rooms with difficult acoustics, rooms that are too hot, lighting conditions that prevent proper vision, seats that are too hard (or soft) can all get in the way of the message. Try to experience it as students do.

Redundancy implies that a message is so strong that it overcomes any noise likely to be around. A tale may be so absorbing that listeners ignore everything else; people can 'lose themselves' in a computer program, a book or a film. Most people are actually quite good at doing this.

Chaotic presentation of information with little or no structure will produce a great deal of noise. Ask yourself: How hard is this for students to understand? What exactly do I want them to take away? What can I get rid of so that they can grasp essentials presented?

It is notoriously difficult to write instruction manuals. Here again, structure is all-important. There has to be a clear learning path and action plan. Often a simplified diagram helps. And a correctly sequenced structure is vital. In one jet aircraft, the instructions to the pilot to eject were set out on the pilot's canopy: the first instruction was 'Eject the canopy'. Think about it.

## Ambiguity

'Crematorium Pedestrians Only' reads the sign.

I remember writing a memo to a colleague telling her to arrange a week's leave with her team leader: 'Do you think Corfu would be nice?' she said.

Sometimes ambiguity can be dangerous. Which switch? when? in what sequence? 'I didn't mean you to plug it in there!' Whose fault is it if there is an explosion? It is essential to get a third party to validate any set of instructions, to ensure there is no ambiguity.

## Selection

The brain selects from experience. However hard we seem to be concentrating, we will select some things and ignore others. Teachers who recognise this can try to ensure that the important things do not get selected out. Repetition and redundancy, as already mentioned, are important here: hence the need for revisiting and consolidation.

A reasonably effective way of doing this is to get students to explain what they understand or what they have to do – what the thing is about or how it works. In trying to explain it to someone else there is not only an alerting of the brain, but also processing of what has been learned into the student's personal knowledge structure.

Repetition of material, revisiting, presentation of information in several different forms (OHTs, discussions, handouts) may be useful redundancy. It is very hard for students to grasp something they are only exposed to once.

## Verbosity

Sheer volume of information is noisy. An overloaded channel or receiver obviously cannot cope. Have a look at the OHP transparencies you use. How much of the information can possibly get through, and how much is noise? What about the learning materials you use? Are they clear? Could you simplify it, make it easier to grasp? Could you structure it more clearly? How much is essential?

You need to be constantly alert to problems of distraction and the need for clarity. *Less* may actually mean *better*. It is so easy to believe that the more that is said, the clearer it will be. Frequently, the opposite is true. Teachers tend to be verbose, to put too many words and symbols into OHP acetates or into instructions. Structure and key-words matter more than the information they contain. The message is: simplify it.

## Incomplete information

The opposite problem can arise, however, Sometimes students are not given all the information they need by the teacher or the instruction card or the work-sheet or other task guidance. It is easy to make unjustified assumptions about what the learner knows already or will bring to the activity, or to fail to think through what it is that they need to know.

Using jargon can also lead to incompleteness. The purpose of jargon is to share understanding, to be unambiguous. It fails if the student does not know the words or the symbols.

---

**TASK 21:   Noise**

Before you start a teaching session, remove distractions. Check for 'noise'.

Use a minimum of information in materials you present but ensure that it is structured as a learning path, or where appropriate an action plan. Use key-words and indicate direction clearly.

Sequence your instructions, and ensure they are complete.

Validate your materials for ambiguity and omission.

Be positive, not negative (the Ten Commandments fail this test).

Familiar words (watch out for jargon), short sentences and active verbs ('do this . . .', not 'It is best to . . .') are the easiest to grasp.

Use a variety of presentation to ensure useful redundancy.

---

## Language barriers

The cartoons in Figure 8 are taken from a refreshingly different way of helping adults to come to terms with what are called *kanji* in Japanese which means 'Chinese characters'. When a native Chinese speaker reads these characters he or she recognises them as words conveying meaning, and each has a particular monosyllabic sound; e.g. 'kan', 'ji'. In Japanese *kanji* is one word, since the characters are usually in combinations of two or more to make complete words, as Japanese is a polysyllabic language.

It is easy to misunderstand someone if the words they use, even when they seem to be the same as words we use, carry all sorts of implications, references to values and expectations that are different from our own. We are not 'coming from the same place'. How much more likely is it when they use words or symbols

*Fig. 8  Fun with Chinese characters* (T. H. Peng, Straits Times Collection, Federal Publications, Singapore, 1980)

which are less familiar to us! Do you in fact share the same cultural value system as your students? Even when you speak apparently the same language, are they interpreting your words as you intend?

Words can be said more accurately to have uses rather than meanings. There is a strong cultural element in all language use, so that it is almost impossible to understand a speaker of any language, including one's own (!), if you have no insight into the values and assumptions conveyed by the words he or she uses. All language works by accumulated meanings or nuances according to the context; we need to know who is using the word and for what purpose.

I remember one tutor telling me of an occasion when she was talking with a group about children and how important security was to them. She discovered after half an hour or so of discussion that some of the class thought she was talking about Social Security.

In many subject areas, there is a large specialist vocabulary to be learned. The use of symbols is vitally important in others. Interestingly, symbols of all kinds work very similarly to *kanji*: the meaning of the visual symbol is quite independent of the word that may be used to 'read' it. Consider the arabic numbers which may be expressed in many different words even in English let alone in other languages, but convey the same visual meaning. Jargon (which includes symbols) is

179

intended to facilitate sharing between those who work in a particular field. But initially at least, jargon, specialist vocabulary, use of symbols and so on are more likely to confuse than enlighten and may become a substitute for clear thinking. Maybe, we could help students learn our symbols in an amusing way as these cartoons do with the *kanji*. But we should make sure they do understand them: we have a shared context of meaning. Students quite often feel isolated in class; they may feel they are visiting 'foreign parts'.

Look again at Case Study 3 on page 26. Sandra wanted her 'students' to experience, to feel what it is like to face something 'you just can't make head or tail of'.

Language register is also most important. We choose a style of speaking which is appropriate for the context we are in. We use a range of styles, words, phrases, sentence structures, formal and informal expressions and tones of voice. These are our 'language registers'. Consider the difference between making a speech at a wedding and chatting in the lounge with friends. Would you address your boss in the same way you would your husband or wife, or one of your children? Or your dog? What about your 'tone of voice'? In some cultures, choosing the right level of politeness in speech is more important than what is said. In others, anything goes apparently (though probably not!).

The words we use, our whole language register, show how we value the other person relative to others and ourselves. 'Talking down' to adults is to show that you do not value them as equal to yourself. On the other hand, if your choice of vocabulary is wrong, your sentence structures are too complex or idiosyncratic, or the speed at which you talk is too fast, you will fail to communicate with them.

## Your words

ACTIVITY 13

Look carefully at the words and symbols you use in your teaching, and at the language registers you choose.

There are many questions you could ask yourself. For example:

How much of what you say is 'jargon', part of your specialism? How will you ensure that your students understand and are comfortable in using these jargon words and will use them accurately? How much is still a foreign language to them?

How far are you conscious of your use of language at all? When you talk, do you consciously choose words and your 'language register' to ensure that your students share a common level of understanding with you, as well as among themselves? Are they, in any case, a homogenous group?

In your handout material and teaching aids, do you look at words and symbols as carefully as you should to ensure that they are within the comprehension of the students? Are they clear, unambiguous, easy to follow and so on? Are they culturally 'neutral' or at least inoffensive?

How complex do you make your sentences? Can students follow you easily?

Any evaluation you make must be a preliminary to action you take to make things better if you can, of course.

# Questions

Many classes seem to operate like the showing of holiday slides. There is no communication, because there is little sharing. Students are excluded. It is essential that they approach the experience alert and with a questioning brain. Humans are exploratory animals, so curiosity must be an important trait. If the brain operates by pattern-making and rule-making it must be searching to find the patterns and the rules. Exploring is a trait we share with the animal kingdom. Progress requires challenge, tackling and solving problems. Much of it is inherited behaviour; how else would you explain what beavers do?

What distinguishes humans is the ability to distance ourselves from reality and to construct concepts – mental models that we describe in words. Exploratory, discovering activity is organised into concepts constructed to explain or control our experience.

It is this level of curiosity that questioning relates to. Most children are full of the word 'why?' A baby is asking a question when she puts a rattle in her mouth to explore hardness. Questions really require language, words, concepts; but would a child develop concepts without this physical exploration?

Questions have to do with alerting the brain to some new experience, idea or word-pattern that is coming and which might challenge our present understanding. Knowledge, according to Jerome Bruner in *The Process of Education* (1977), is a process of constant restructuring of concepts. It is not lumps of stuff to transmit somehow from here to there. Nor can you just hammer knowledge into your students' brains: they must be made ready to restructure, to deal with what is new. Information can only become personal knowledge when it is processed in some way. The radio must be switched on, as it were.

Without preparation the brain cannot deal with new information. It will ignore it, as it ignores most of the sensory data around us most of the time. We just do not notice it. We perceive consciously only the things we alert our brain to – the rest passes unnoticed and apparently unrecorded. That we have in fact recorded it can be shown by hypnosis, but concept formation depends on conscious alerting. What do you remember of the last twenty-four hours? Why those things and not all the rest?

Hence the importance of questions. Rote-learning, although powerful, actually has no effect on what people think or do. The learning is not part of our own structure of concepts, they way words work for us. It belongs to someone else.

# Levels of questions

We can alert the brain to explore present experience or revisit past experience. Questions work at various levels:

Level 1: direct experience – focusing on what is happening now
Level 2: describing experience, to ourselves and to others; this is a second level of abstraction

Level 3:   comparing and interpreting experiences (a third level of abstraction) –
this involves mental models/patterns; we restructure our conceptual
understanding when patterns do not match

Level 4:   thinking creatively, generalising, transferring learning to new contexts,
using it to solve problems.

Much brain activity is to do with processing information. We may use questioning
to make the brain receptive to take the information we want it to have and to provide us with perceptions of the world, and of our internal mental ideas. We need
to do this all the time to be able to deal competently with our world.

But we can set the brain actively thinking to form new concepts and abstractions from experience, patterning information into new insights. There is a social
function of language that allows us to share and bond: we experience this when we
try to tell others how we are perceiving this information and experience – what we
now know. We can compare it with the new structures they have created, and
which they in turn express in their words.

This working with other people helps us to refine our ideas, to create hypotheses about the world and people that allow us to attempt to predict what will
happen or what people will do. We need to explain and to predict in order to try
to control what happens. This is how technology works – and most human and
social activity too. It is also how words acquire their meanings.

## Teacher's questions

How can teachers handle questions? What should teachers do?

These two sentences are alerting statements, pseudo-questions, rhetorical questions: all teachers use them. They are not looking for creative response, but
merely aiming to alert the students' brains.

They prepare them for 'my' answers, without stimulating them to find their
own. Having a student actually discover answers different from 'mine' can seem
to be bad news for many teachers. They want students to remember the 'right'
answer, in other words 'mine'. Great weight is given to this procedure through
the examination and testing system. The level of restructuring by the student
depends not so much on curiosity as on extrinsic motivating factors such as the
teacher's pleasure or anger, or passing the exam, or just 'getting it right'.

It depends critically too on how easy it is for the student to link the information
or concepts into what is known already. If the pace of arrival of new information
(or new words or new definitions) is too fast, or if the volume of information is
overwhelming, learners cannot deal with it. In any case, just being exposed to it
once will not work. It has to be revisited and rethought. It has to 'arrive' – to be
put into familiar language or symbols. Teachers need to pitch it at the right level
and recognise the barriers to learning that all of us have.

Effectiveness depends on the students' readiness to learn and on the control
exercised by the teacher, who must manage pace and volume and the form in
which the information is acquired. It must match the students' readiness and
receptivity.

It is easier for learners if the structure is clear, and if it leads them through identifying questions which build one from another, even if they are presented in the form of statements of key-words only. This will ensure alerting of the brain to deal with the information and assist processing.

## Closed and open questions

Closed questions assume the 'right' answer exists. They can often be answered yes or no. Many tests are of this kind: true/false, objective tests, computations and so on. Much of education seems to be about closed questions. Teachers often have a preference for them in many of their classroom interactions.

As an alerting exercise a closed question can be successful. But to be effective as a technique the teacher must name students who are to answer. General questions addressed to the whole group are ineffective in alerting all students, since most will leave it to clever-clogs to answer. It is realised that this is teacher's game: I don't want to play at guessing teacher's right answer. Why don't you just tell us, sir?

The teacher is not looking for competing answers, nor even for students to reframe the information into their own words. This last is vitally important and questioning can be used effectively to promote level 2 activity. The questions may still be closed. But if students are to achieve level 3 or 4, they need open questions that stimulate them to think.

Inductive methodology is the use of open questions.

---

### EXAMPLE 3

A television programme on teaching methods showed a teacher using an inductive approach. A military sergeant was teaching cadets in a very crowded classroom. He asked questions in order to elicit a structure of ideas that could be used to formulate a problem.

He asked a series of questions. After each one, he walked halfway down the class and took the answer from one particular cadet. He then returned to the whiteboard and put up the answer. At the end, he produced an OHP transparency with the same answers ready in the same structure but neatly presented. It was rather like a committee meeting in which the chairman arrives with the minutes already typed out in his pocket.

Clearly, this was not inductive methodology. The sergeant knew which cadet would give him 'teacher's right answer'. No other answers were sought or taken, although many cadets offered. In particular, he ignored the only three girls in the class, who had sat at the front eager to learn. He walked past them every time, perhaps deliberately. It seemed the last thing he wanted was competing answers. It was a good example of closed questions.

---

Open questions receive unpredictable answers: 'messing about here for a bit to see what we can discover'. Indeed, their purpose is not to elicit answers at all, but to generate increasingly searching questions. Open questions are about an attitude of mind, stimulating natural curiosity to explore and find out.

They also involve openly valuing each student's answer, however improbable it might be. It is very easy to demotivate students from even trying to find answers or generate ideas. Most can experience damage to their self-esteem if they find themselves competing with others in discovery learning. The most successful approach is usually to set students up in groups to explore problems and ideas. They feel less exposed and can give mutual support.

A great deal of wasted effort is also caused by asking questions which are of the wrong kind, looking for unhelpful answers. First find the right questions and validate them to make sure they alert the students to useful activity, and they will look in the right sort of places.

Structured questions that define a linking path are better than a series of unconnected general questions, at least until students have sufficient experience to structure their own paths. But the students may still arrive at the 'wrong' answers or go off in the wrong direction. A teacher using inductive methods has to decide when to intervene, certainly if discovery learning is intended. Unlearning is much harder than learning, so students need to get it right first time. There is frustration in letting them get into a mess with it, nor should they be trying to reinvent the wheel.

The appropriateness or otherwise of discovery needs appraising. Again, it is a matter of clearly formulating what has to be done and controlling the learning activity through structure. The main purpose may be to promote group bonding rather than what they in fact discover for themselves.

## ACTIVITY 14 Your use of questions

*Examine carefully the way you use questions.* The following is intended to help you.

A  What level in the above hierarchy are they operating at? What level of mental activity do they demand of students?

1  Level 1: 'focusing on what is happening now'.

Think, for example, of an experiment in science: the students need to observe and record accurately what happens. Learning activities in all subject areas from practical skills like dressmaking to the study of a text in a literature class require the same level of concentration and accuracy. Clearly, students need to be alert and questioning what is happening for them or around them. To observe accurately they have to develop the right skills.

This is only the first level of questioning, however, and many fail even to achieve that satisfactorily. In a hierarchy, higher levels will depend on successful achievement at lower levels of skill as a prerequisite of further advance.

2  Level 2: 'describing experience'.

It is essential that students achieve at least level 2. In order to do this, they need questions to address to the observations they have made. It is questions like: 'What have I observed? What has actually happened?', that will give shape, and meaning, to the new information. This requires construction of a frame of reference and language or symbols to describe the observations. One valuable effect of this learning will be an enlarged vocabulary.

3   Level 3: 'comparing and interpreting experiences'.

This requires concept formation and the ability to think in abstractions. Reflection on the learning will be necessary for achievement at level 3. Students need to match a new experience with previous experiences and with knowledge already acquired. They must be given activities that ensure processing of new information so as to link it with previous knowledge into a structured whole. It is this process we call 'understanding'; it may also lead to leaps to new mental models or structures we call 'insight'.

Questions that promote activity of this kind are much more searching. 'Compare the results of this experiment with those you got in Experiment C.' 'What do you think is happening here?' 'If we change xxxxx, what do you think will happen? Why? Think of the principles we discussed yesterday.' Questions may not be in obvious question format as you can see here.

4   Level 4: 'generalising, thinking creatively'.

Problem–solving involves first having a clear mental picture of the problem to be solved. We should not assume that most people can 'visualise' problems or even the context within which the problems exist. Modelling in the head is a sophisticated skill that many find almost impossible. Tackling problems, however, can accelerate learning dramatically, so long as the problems are set at a level appropriate to the 'readiness' of the students. Problems that are too complex or assume knowledge or experience they do not have will simply defeat them.

Questions at this level will be related to problems to solve. They do not have to be particularly clever questions. I have seen problems set to children in a primary school which are effective in getting them to think creatively, 'to turn the problem over in their minds' and suggest possible ways of tackling it; and then argue for one solution against another one. For example, a class was asked to come up with ideas about keeping pets in school. Teachers can help their students to frame the problem in a tractable way through structuring their questions. If they fail to tackle the problem successfully, it may simply be that the questions they are addressing are unhelpful and are not setting enquiry off in the right direction.

B   Are the questions in A above closed or open questions? At Level 1 generally, they will be rather closed since we are concerned with accuracy of observation. It may depend, however, on the kind of answers the teacher will accept or is looking for. Even at this level, it is perfectly possible to encourage students to explore their observations, as in a programme of 'discovery learning', so long as what they observe is described properly at Level 2. On the other hand, even problems tackled at Level 4 may be rather closed if the students are informed that there are 'right' solutions to them. The emphasis may be put on the methodology used by the students or their understanding of the nature of the problem to be solved.

*Now look carefully at your use of closed and open questions.*
How do you handle class interactions using questions? Have you thought carefully about why you do what you do?

When you use closed questions (all teachers do, frequently, to keep students alert to what the teacher is trying to teach), what techniques do you use to ensure that all your students are in fact alert?

How far would the use of open questions work with your students in your context? If you chose to use more open questions, what would you need to do to ensure that the students found them helpful rather than disruptive?

# 22 Ergonomics/Human Factors

Ergonomics (called 'human factors' in the United States) can be defined as 'managing work'. It is a study of the interaction of human beings with things they use and environments where they work. It is concerned with the amount of effort it costs to do something, and what can be done to make it more human, less inefficient in the way it affects the people concerned. All objects, or whole environments, intended for human use should be designed to take account of the human users, of what is supposed to happen and what is to be done there.

How often do teachers have to battle with badly designed rooms or workshops? How many are expected to teach in environments 'designed' on assumptions about what is going to happen as learning activity which are no longer valid? How hard is it for them to get things they need, or to do adequate preparation? How hard is it for the students too? How can you maintain motivation if it is too hard?

Certainly, industrialisation has forced workers into desperately uncomfortable, exhausting environments: noisy, machine-dominated, production orientated and inhuman. Think of the early cotton-mills; imagine what it was like to drive and stoke great steam engines on the railway, where a man had to shovel six tons of coal between Leeds and London while the engine bounced around at high speed. Until quite recently, factories survived where riveters had to work inside huge boilers with the result that they became deaf.

It is all grossly inefficient. The cost of the human has to be measured in with the cost of machines and buildings. As teachers we can try to ensure that factors under our control support what we ask the students to do rather than get in the way.

Read again Chapter 11, 'Control of Environment'.

## Risk-taking

Studies of road accidents show that compulsory wearing of seat-belts has not brought about any dramatic reduction in deaths in the UK. Why? We need 'arousal' to keep our 'perception of risk' and our 'sense of danger' in balance, so psychologists argue. They are very good at inventing 'new speak' words: they say we have 'risk-compensation' to keep our 'arousal' at an acceptable level. What this means in practice is that straightening roads merely makes people go faster. With our sense of security, or lessening of our sense of risk, when we fasten our seat-belt, we drive faster and brake later. We tend to maintain a balance between our pleasure and excitement in doing something and what we perceive as the risks involved in doing it. Of course, the point of balance varies with the individual.

All human activity, even lying in bed, involves some kind of risk. To be alive is to be in danger of dying. But those who 'play safe' learn very little. We all need to take risks in order to learn. I wonder if children know this somehow. The development of adventure playgrounds on bomb-sites after the war was a response to what children actually did in play. The builders thought: let us create an environment that is as adventurous, as exciting as these ruined houses, but where we can supervise and control the risks they are taking.

Teachers must take risks, too. It is risk-taking in every human activity that leads to progress. It is obviously risky to share decision-making with students, to experiment with new (to you at least!) methods of teaching/learning, or to let go control in some measure over what occurs: maybe to send out a group to do a survey of traffic, to ask questions of people, or to do a piece of field research, or to use resource bases, rather than to keep them 'where I can see them'. Growth as a teacher must involve a willingness to experiment, the growing confidence to let go control, to involve students and so give them 'ownership' of their learning.

But it has to be controlled risk-taking. The purpose of building the adventure playground was not to minimise risks, but to supervise and control them. Your responsibility for the safety of students is a legal requirement. If the environment poses hazards that are avoidable, you must take action. You are also a role model: 'do as I do.' Risk-taking is necessary, but it must be controlled and purposeful. Students need to accept their share of responsibility. To do that they need adequate guidance and organisation: you must define clearly what they can and cannot do. We want the right kind of risks taken to bring about the most profitable kind of arousal.

### REMEMBER!
*... Your principal responsibility is always to ensure the health and safety of your students.*

# Personal space

Personal space is felt as an area surrounding a person's body in which there are boundaries for interactions with other people. It is defined by zones of social contact. The types of possible interaction vary with distance, which is shaped by the context and environment.

A study by Hall simplified this into concentric circles. He identified four zones: intimate, personal, social and public distances from the centre (see Figure 9, opposite). The behaviour of a person whose space is violated may change considerably if the 'wrong' person enters a zone or if 'wrong' interactions are attempted there.

Closeness increases the effect of one person on another. There is increased sensory stimulation; smell and sound are added to sight. And the amounts of physical contact allowed between individuals varies in different cultures: for example, it seems greater among the French and Italians than the English, who like to keep each other at arm's length (a distance confirmed by research). Middle-class people seem to be more likely to hug and kiss each other than are the working class, and women more so than men – except on the football field, perhaps.

People who work together tend to use close social distance, while business is conducted more distantly. It has to do with seeing the whole person: with the enlargement and importance of the head as people approach, and with maintaining eye-contact. This distance is important also in screening out other people. Public distance is well outside a circle of social involvement, and at this distance other communication problems occur.

Establishing right relationships relates to identifying appropriate zones for social contacts. To be intimate in behaviour, one has to be close and to be comfortable there. Men and women behave differently in this zone. Invasion may seem threatening: there may be tension, discomfort or even flight. Drama training uses techniques to overcome such barriers to physical contact, and they are also broken down in sports like rugby. Working together in a physical way requires contact; indeed, team behaviour requires a redefining of everyone's personal space zones, perhaps creating group space instead.

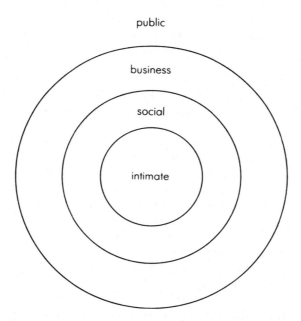

*Fig. 9   Personal space* (derived from *Silent Language* by E. T. Hall, Fawcett, 1959)

A typical reaction to invasion of personal space is to face away, avoid eye-contact, become stiff, pull in the shoulders – leave! Defensive behaviour is typified by lack of verbal response, or by abusiveness. Hall says, 'We treat space as we do sex. It is there, but we don't talk about it.'

Studies of crowding and empty space on trains identified a stress chemical in the urine of passengers who had travelled in crowded carriages. Invasion created responses that were complex, but intended to distance the intruder from the victim: leaning away, turning, or more simply withdrawing into oneself. In crowded trains people shrink their private space and control their discomfort by staring at the floor or into space: their body language projects non-relating to non-persons.

# Territoriality

Concepts such as personal space and territoriality are borrowed from behavioural analyses of animals to explain how such factors may affect performance. You will have watched a dog mark out his territory. Most male animals seem to have some means of doing it, so why not humans? And is it only males?

Like personal space, territoriality is a concept that has social, unwritten rules of space behaviour. Infringing these rules will cause discomfort and often hostility. Territoriality differs from personal space in that territories are fixed locations, and do not move around with the people who define them. The boundaries are sensory, marked by stimuli such as scent in animals, and visible cues such as coats and bags with humans. You will see students mark out their territories in this way. Why do people feel more comfortable if they always use the same seat or table?

We all know the rules that govern territory. We can all distinguish that which is 'mine', such as a house or flat which can be controlled even when 'I' am not there, from that which is for everyone like a park, and from that which becomes semi-private – claimed by someone on a temporary basis, such as a seat on a train.

Behaviour related to semi-private territory is of importance to teachers. It appears when students reserve seats and mark seat boundaries in a class with 'ownership' of equipment. Studies in trains showed there was little verbal exchange; passengers had territory markers like bags and coats on the adjacent seat. Students use bags and books. An invader is forced to ask for a marker to be removed – 'is this seat taken?' Removing it oneself breaks the social code.

Well-designed teaching spaces need to take into account not only the more obvious things (often ignored, though), such as acoustics, noise levels, temperature control and ventilation, but also the spaces that are occupied for particular purposes. Teaching spaces may be rendered ineffective if seating arrangements are such that students are unable to mark territories (they can't spread out), or if they feel impelled to withdraw into themselves to preserve their need for personal space. Density and crowding are threatening both to personal space and territoriality. Having too many students in a class also makes social grouping difficult.

Teachers need to control the spaces students occupy. They should try to define group territories where they want group activities. Having students sitting in rows merely defines the teacher's space.

Consider again Case Study 12 on page 79. Gillian had set up her classroom in an open square with students on three sides of it so as to promote communication not only with her but with other students. Unfortunately, the students had decided to occupy the three sides as separate group territories: girls, boys and mature women. Gillian had lost control of the interactions between herself and two thirds of the class. She maintained eye-contact and exchange with only the mature women who sat in front of her. The younger students took no part in her lessons, partly perhaps as a reaction to her unconscious messages. We need to be constantly watching: what are the messages we are giving and what are our students' reactions to them? If students define group territories, we should make sure they are used to good and effective purpose.'

Activity has to be planned in relation to physical distance, eye-contact, territorial identification of working groups and their resources. It needs to be restructured frequently to prevent the fixing of small cliques, and to ensure that space is right for each particular learning activity. Variety is important.

---

**TASK 22:  Environment, space and territories**

Make a detailed study of the environment where you teach.

What factors influenced the design? What was assumed to happen as learning and teaching activities? Is that still appropriate?

What would you consider to be the right conditions, taking into account all factors involved in achieving your learning goals?

What action and by whom is necessary to create these conditions?

Look carefully at use of space and territory in your class.

1 Do you mark out your territory? How? Some teachers have a desk with their papers in between themselves and their students, perhaps as a protection. What signals do you use?
2 How close do you get to students, or let them get to you? Where would you place the socially acceptable zones around yourself? How do you indicate those to the students? (Remember that they will take you as a role-model.)
3 How do individuals define their personal space or territory? What if this creates difficulties? What should you do?
4 Has the class broken up into more than one group? Are they defining group territory or group space and behaviour?
5 How can you ensure that there is positive use of space?

It is up to you, as teacher, to take control, to establish the rules for group behaviour, to define territories if need be by moving people around, to set up different groupings for varied activity. And whatever you do, do not let groups settle into one fixed pattern.

---

# Managing your group

Watch your class carefully as it becomes a social group, and in particular if people join the group late. What happens? Why?

What action should you take if they form not one cohesive group, but several cliques? How will you ensure they come together and agree purpose, goals, rules, patterns of sharing and working as a team together? How will you help them define their boundaries?

---

### TASK 23:  Managing groups

Demonstrate skill in managing your students and group behaviour. Consider carefully the performance criteria below.

PERFORMANCE CRITERIA IN COMMUNICATION

1 Students establish with the teacher a supportive, positive group identity: they have agreed and shared purposes.
2 Social and personal interactions are carefully observed. Groups as they form are noted, together with the behaviour of students in them.
3 Dominance patterns, effects of personalities and personal factors are noted. So too are the students' reactions to teacher language and behaviour. The teacher takes appropriate action.
4 The teacher responds to feedback. Teaching method, language and behaviour are modified to match student reaction.
5 Teacher language and stimulus material are appropriate.
6 The teacher is sensitive to learning problems and to the students' difficulty in comprehending information and instructions.
7 There is variety of pace, presentation, activity and skilful use of open and closed questions.
8 Individuals and groups are managed well.
9 The teacher is respected by students, and has established an acceptable role relationship with them and with colleagues.

---

# Community

Human beings are social animals. Communication is 'sharing' within a community: a group with defined boundaries, shared purposes and duties, and a common language.

## ACTIVITY 15 — Social groups

1 Think about the groups to which you belong. How are they defined and what are their boundaries, shared purposes and understanding?
   What did you have to learn and do to become accepted as a member?
2 Consider the social group that is your class. Try to clarify:

● what you consider to be the purposes that you all share
● how those purposes are to be identified and agreed to
● what the rules are that should regulate group behaviour

- what roles you expect your students to adopt
- what role(s) you see for yourself
- how you ensure students 'join the club'
- how you should deal with outsiders coming in.

## Exploring and social behaviour

Learning is an activity on the part of learners in which teachers may play a minor role. We talk about a picture, or a building or a statue, communicating with a person. What can we mean? Clearly, pictures just hang there. The energy for anything to happen has to come from the viewer, whatever skill the artist had.

Albert Einstein invented the 'thought experiment', to explore the behaviour of objects approaching the speed of light. Here is a thought experiment for you to do, preferably with colleagues.

## ACTIVITY 16 | Contexts

What can we learn about communication from the contexts below?

- visiting an art gallery alone
- listening to a classical music concert or a rock concert
- going to a foreign country for the first time
- becoming a member of a club
- practising with a sports team
- watching a television programme
- telling friends about a holiday, using slides.

The important thing is to think: what actually happens there?

With colleagues you could divide into groups of three and report what you have discovered to the whole group, to see if any principles about communicating emerge that apply to all the contexts.

## Joining groups

In looking for the bases of communication, we should bear in mind the idea of the group with boundaries. Competition between groups will define boundaries more sharply. Members of each group will invent all sorts of glue and banners to proclaim 'us' against 'them'. In extremes, it can turn into secret societies with handshakes and coded signalling, but frequently it is a matter of dress or uniform and other open signals. In most societies we recognise groups that adopt pseudo-military uniform and indications of rank: the police, fire service, ambulance service, nurses and so on. When people put on a particular uniform they also adopt a behaviour pattern with it.

One hidden purpose is to ensure that 'the whole is greater than the sum of the parts'. Groups that gel – that is, that work well together – achieve much more than the same individuals would on their own. Where does this added value come from?

We can see analogies in the animal world. Some are mysterious. The ant-hill, created by termites, is a remarkable structure with a complex ventilation system including chimneys that heat up and extract stale air, so generating air currents through the tunnels. But where is the 'model in the head' that enables termites to build it? There is no possibility of the parts existing alone, so how do individual termites know in their tiny blind world what each has to do to construct the whole? Communication, we know, is by chemical pheromones excreted by the queen. In human groups too there is a mystery as to how purposes and direction arise, and how they are communicated to all involved.

Joining a sports team carries with it the competitive element. A team spirit is exhibited in dress and observation of specific rules and codes. It is derived partly from agreed purposes (goals!) and partly from perceived antagonists (other teams). Team members rely on the others, and display a commitment to the team that supersedes other social commitments. The same is true of a drama group or an orchestra. We exploit this competitive glue in setting up learning games.

Group behaviour imposes a need for individuals to discover a role in the group. This is no less true for you, as teacher, than for any other members, unless you choose to remain as an 'outsider'. To be the disruptive outsider cannot be right.

To be effective, you will have to establish that you are working with the students as part of a group while you are together – to be one of 'us'. The unhappiest experience you can have as a teacher is to find a group ganging up against you and to be fighting to establish common ground. Your own behaviour may even help to create that distance. Your first job as the teacher is to establish the class as a group with agreed goals, roles, rules of behaving and responsibilities.

We may think of an evening class as a club. Complicated things may be going on. There are rules which govern the operation of the club: what are they for? how are they arrived at? Anyone joining has to learn and observe them and has to take trouble to see what this means. People who have dealt with adult groups know that breaking into established groups is difficult and disruptive.

It is easier if the rules are stated explicitly, but important ones are usually exhibited only in the behaviour of the club members: what is considered acceptable and what is not. Peer group pressure and a desire to become, or remain, one of the group ensure that members learn rules quickly. New members arrive feeling 'foreign', but wanting to be accepted as one of 'us'. They look constantly for clues as to how to behave and are extremely sensitive to modelling and feedback: they will conform in dress and language use, even if it feels odd or wrong. They will absorb values and ways of thinking too.

# Sharing

Sharing is clearly an important aspect of communication. Searching, wanting to share and to belong is another. Being part of a group, or a valued and effective member of a team, working with others to achieve a goal is all part of our sense of community. Being an outsider is a painful experience. Being isolated by language or cultural differences is also highly disturbing, particularly if it involves loss of self-respect because you can no longer do things for yourself, such as use the telephone or order a meal. This can happen in joining new groups or classes at home as well as when we travel abroad.

In many aspects of communication, the energy has to come principally from you. We are more acutely aware of this in activities we do alone than in those we share with others. In looking at pictures or walking through a city, we respond in individual ways to the stimuli about us. We may quickly get bored or we may experience a high level of excitement, depending on our receptivity to the stimuli. In other situations, even if we are totally passive, as when listening to a concert in a concert hall, or watching a play, or an opera maybe, on stage in a theatre, we are infected by shared emotional responses. Rock concerts make these shared responses much more uninhibited and dominant.

Television has become the major source of entertainment world-wide and has had a profound effect on the traditional cultures of many peoples. Though for us it tends to be a 'private' experience, except when sharing the excitement of a crowd watching a football match, say, it absorbs us like reading an interesting book. We share experience not just with those who make the programmes; we know many other people are sharing it, too. It is such a powerful educational tool mainly because we learn more readily if our attention is strongly focused, and we are not putting up barriers to the learning. We do not know that we are learning, we are 'having fun'.

# 23 Assessment and Testing

In Part 1, you were introduced to basic principles and practice in feedback and assessment within the learning process. You are now going to take those ideas further.

Assessment is an important process, one which is taken seriously by learners and teachers alike. You will be aware that it is also of interest to the Government, which regularly intervenes in the way in which the achievements of both school-children and adults are assessed. It devises policies and sets up bodies to regulate assessment according to currently held beliefs about learning and achievement.

For the past 10 years Government-backed bodies have been developing a national system of assessment for vocational qualifications based on learners demonstrating their competence. If you do not already know about National Vocational Qualifications, Scottish Vocational Qualifications, and General National Vocational Qualifications (NVQs, SVQs and GNVQs), now is the time to find a colleague who will show you how they work in practice. You will be introduced to some of the theory in this chapter.

First, however, you are going to look at assessment in general, picking up on the ideas you explored in Part 1 of the book.

# What is assessment?

Assessment is the process of finding out about the nature and quality of the student's learning. When you assess, you measure achievement against a previously laid down standard. You compare what the learner knows and can do with what the standard says the learner should know and be able to do, at a given level and in the kind of test which you are using.

There are three kinds of standard with which you can compare the individual learner's performance. In **criterion referenced assessment** you measure achievement against a standard (a set of criteria) which represent mastery or competence at the level concerned. The learner must meet all the criteria to qualify for a pass, and pass represents 100 per cent of possible achievement. National Vocational Qualifications use this approach.

In **norm referenced assessment** you measure the learner's achievement against the standard normally achieved by a candidate at that level in that kind of test. These standards or 'norms' are arrived at by piloting the tests on very large numbers of people – this is called 'standardising the test'. In this kind of test you can set the pass mark at different levels; 40 per cent is common, but it could be as high as 80 per cent. You can grade the learner's achievement by deciding beforehand on bands of scores which will represent, for example, pass, credit or distinction. You can use numbers to indicate grades, e.g. 85 per cent = distinction or letters, e.g. A–G. Large national examinations such as GCE A Levels use letters.

In this case 'pass' equals good enough or acceptable rather than mastery or competence. Unlike criterion reference assessment which tells you that the person is competent in all the areas assessed, norm referenced testing does not necessarily show the learner's areas of strength and weakness.

In **self referenced assessment** the learner's performance is compared with their own previous performance in the same kind of test at a given level. This kind of testing is appropriate for measuring attitudes where there is no absolute standard, e.g. confidence or responsibility. It is also used for learners with learning difficulties and disabilities who may only be able to achieve a small amount of progress at a time.

# The purposes of assessment

Your reasons for assessing will determine the kind of approach to testing which you adopt. We said in Part 1 that tests produced information about learners' achievements. Such information is very useful to people such as employers or admissions tutors on further courses. It tells them how capable the applicant or worker is. Such people want unambiguous information on which they can rely. Part of the rationale for developing NVQs was to reduce the bewildering array of qualifications from a host of awarding bodies. It was difficult to see how the various qualifications related to each other, and people with the same qualification might perform very differently in practice.

But, as you saw earlier, the primary function of assessment is to tell the **learner** how well they have done; it is part of the learning process. None of us can learn without feedback on our performance. Students come into formal learning situations partly so that they can receive this feedback and so come closer to their goals. This is as true of those who attend leisure classes as it is of those who embark on national qualifications. This process of receiving **formative feedback** is very valuable to the learner and calls for great skill from the teacher.

Formative assessment also helps the teacher, in that it can show up areas of strength and weakness in the teaching in time for corrective action. If all students do poorly in one area while achieving a spread of marks in the other areas, it is reasonable to assume that the fault lies with some aspect of the teaching.

Assessment at the end of a period of learning, **summative assessment**, yields information for different purposes. It can enable you to compare one student with another in that group of learners or another group or with a whole national cohort if you wish. It can help you to predict how that learner might go on to perform at a higher level of learning or in a particular field of employment. It can be used by you or other people to allow or prevent the student's entry into other spheres of activity.

Unfortunately there is a tendency within the education and employment systems to allow achievement at one particular time and in one set of circumstances to remain an indicator of ability and value (or lack of it) for years to come. When it is used as a label in this way, assessment may come to be seen as a barrier rather than an aid to learning.

## Your role in assessment

You may be involved in operating tests which have been devised by others or in creating your own. Some of the tests used in further and adult education are externally devised and marked (GCE A Levels for example). Your role might be to prepare your students for such exams by carrying out mock assessments. In these the students practise on questions which you have devised to be as similar as possible to the ones you expect them to encounter, and which you mark at the same level.

If you are working on an NVQ programme all the criteria and other assessment requirements will be laid down for you by the awarding body. Your role will be to check your interpretation of these criteria with your team (or with your internal verifier if you do not have a team); to prepare your candidates for assessment; to observe their performance, question them, scrutinise any written material or items they may have produced; and then to make your judgement and give them feedback. There is more to be said about these various stages of the process later in this chapter, including the role of the internal verifier.

You may have a part in devising GNVQ assignments with a team according to national criteria laid down by an awarding body such as BTEC. You may be given sample assignments as models, and there will be guidelines to the grades of achievement available so that you can judge how to mark the work. These GNVQ assessments are also checked by an internal verifier and, periodically, by an external verifier.

You may, however, be able to design your own tests and assessment activities for your own students, which you mark and on which you give them feedback.

At whatever level you are working you will need to follow certain principles if you are to conduct assessment in a professional manner.

# Aiming for good quality evidence of learning

The assessment process is designed to enable you to find out in detail about a learner's abilities. A properly constructed test can give you a great deal of information. What the learner does in the test, whether it is a practical, written or spoken activity, is proof or **evidence** of their learning. It can also indicate what he or she still needs to learn/master.

You began to explore in Part 1 the need for evidence to meet certain criteria if it is to show a true picture of the learner's abilities. Some of these criteria are obvious, for instance that the evidence must be the learner's own work (**authentic**) and that there should be enough of it to convince you that they are truly competent (**sufficient**). You also need a picture of their **current** ability, not something they did some years ago (this is common sense if you think how rapidly some skill areas have changed, like computing for instance). Usually you will be testing students in the present; but if you are involved in accrediting someone's prior learning (APL) you will need to check that their knowledge and skills are still up to date.

The two most important criteria by which we judge evidence arise if we ask: are the tests we are using **valid** and **reliable**? Look back at Part 1 where these ideas were introduced. You will see that we say that a test is **valid** if it does the job it was supposed to do. Does it really test the knowledge and skills you targeted? Does it do so at the right level? Does it discriminate between those who understand and those who don't? You need to be very clear what it is that you want back from the test before you construct the questions; drawing up a model answer is quite a good guide. So is discussing the questions with colleagues to see how they interpret them. If possible, try the test out on a group of learners to see if you get back what you expected. And check that successful answers are indeed based on knowledge and understanding, and not just the ability to speak and write fluently.

You will also need to ask whether the test is **reliable**. Does it produce results other people can rely on? Would it produce a similar spread of results if given again to a similar group of students? Can you continue to use it with confidence?

The most reliable tests are those whose questions have only one right answer. The objective or multiple choice test is an example. In its simplest form you choose one answer from a choice of four possibilities. The wrong answers will have been designed to be as plausible as possible, so that it takes real knowledge and discrimination to pick out the correct option. Objective tests can be marked by computer, which cuts out any risk of subjective judgement by the assessor. Essay style questions are far less reliable. The greater the range of possible answers or interpretations, the more carefully the criteria for acceptable answers have to be specified. Awarding bodies commonly organise checking systems whereby assessors standardise their marking on sample questions, so that they will avoid significant divergence of judgement.

Reliability may also be increased if internal tests (set and marked by college assessors) are combined with externally set and marked tests, as with GNVQs.

You will probably need a very thorough test or series of tests to feel that you have **sufficient** assessment information to determine the learner's abilities. One demonstration of practical competence is unlikely to be enough. Your judgement will be more reliable if you have sampled the learner's knowledge and skill by means of several different kinds of test, such as written assignments and an oral assessment and a practical performance test. Within the test itself there needs to be a sufficiently wide range of questions to cover the area of knowledge.

If a learner has chosen to be a student on a course you will be able to assess them either as they go along or at the end of the learning programme. This will give you **current** evidence of their abilities. However, some candidates for an award may judge that they already have the knowledge and skill to enable them to proceed directly to assessment, without undertaking a course of study first (as some people do with the driving test). The tests will then either show that they were right in their judgement, i.e. competent, or show up areas of work for further practice, after which they can be tested again.

Where a candidate for an award is asking for their competence based on previous learning and experience to be judged in an APL (Accreditation of Prior Learning) system, it is very important to be sure that they have the knowledge and skill claimed **now**, however extensive their previous experience may appear to be. This is probably most obvious in relation to vocational qualifications, where the commercial or industrial context may have changed radically in just two or three years. This is why the role of advisor to an APL candidate is so crucial; they can help the applicant to review their learning in relation to the criteria for assessment, so that they have a very clear picture of what is required before they opt for assessment.

The **authenticity** of a student's work is carefully monitored on a continually assessed course, and there are elaborate safeguards built in to public examinations to prevent cheating. However, you would need to check carefully on the ownership of material presented for APL. Oral tests or practical performance tests can usefully be combined with written submissions to check authenticity.

# Being fair

The criteria for good quality evidence described above all contribute to a system which aims to be fair to all candidates. Tests which have high validity and reliability will be based on relevant material at the right level, and will be sufficiently rigorous in gathering a suitable amount of proof that candidates cannot succeed by coincidence or luck. A great deal of work has been done by individual teachers and examining bodies to eliminate bias in test questions, just as they have established test procedures to give everyone the same opportunities to succeed. This involves looking very carefully at the way questions are phrased so that there are no ambiguities which could mislead candidates. You also need to be sure that the questions do not rely on an understanding of a cultural context or access to an experience which some candidates might not have, e.g. going to the opera or using ultra modern equipment.

# What are you going to assess?

You need to think about what exactly it is that you want to assess – what knowledge, which skills, which attitudes. You cannot make decisions about the kind of tests you will use until you have decided their purpose and content. Once you have a clear idea of what you are aiming to achieve through testing, and the areas of ability which you want to pinpoint, you will find it relatively straightforward to choose or devise an appropriate set of tests.

Basically you test mastery of the objectives or outcomes of the subject/skill area which have formed the basis of the teaching on the course of training in the workplace. Students are entitled to expect to be assessed on what they have been taught or led to believe will be in the assessment schedule. One of the advantages of NVQs is that the whole area to be tested is set out for the candidate from the start. By contrast in some public examinations, although the syllabus has been outlined, the questions can sample the candidate's understanding of any part of it. Some candidates may be lucky in getting questions in which they are particularly proficient.

If you are designing your own questions, remember that you should have the same pattern of emphasis in the test as you had in the teaching. If you stressed that one area was particularly important, this should be reflected in the test.

# Setting the level

## Assessing knowledge

You will need to decide what to include and what to leave out (if there is a choice), where to put the emphasis and what **level** of knowledge processing you wish to target. Selecting the level of questions or tasks and then phrasing them correctly to imply this level, is the most challenging of these tasks.

You will very seldom be assessing facts alone unless perhaps as a simple **recall** exercise before going on to develop the ideas behind the facts, e.g. recalling mathematical formulae before going on to use them to solve problems. You will be more interested in getting students to demonstrate their **understanding** of the facts by manipulating them in some way, e.g. explaining their significance, selecting those which support or destroy an argument, describing relationships between them and so on. You want the student to explore the 'why' and 'why not' and 'so what' of the facts. You also want them to **apply** their knowledge and understanding by solving new problems which depend on their grasp of principles which they have learned. These three levels, knowing (recall), understanding and applying, make up about 50 per cent of the testing we do in college and adult centre courses.

You may wish your candidates to demonstrate their knowledge at higher levels. You could ask them to **analyse** a situation, to pick out the important factors within it, and the way they interact, for instance the factors contributing to an economic recession. You could require them to take existing factors and link or **synthesise** them into a solution, for instance proposing ways in which juvenile crime might be reduced in urban areas, or a business returned to profit. Finally you might ask them to **evaluate** a situation, weighing up its strengths and weaknesses and recommending ways forward, e.g. carrying out a feasibility study on setting up an irrigation system in a desert area or introducing road safety awareness into the senior school curriculum.

You may have noticed that the higher you go in setting your level, the more your learner will have to demonstrate the knowledge processing skills they have learned in order to deal with lower levels. If you think of a case study in almost any subject area, you will see that to deal with it successfully students have to recall facts, understand their significance, apply them to a problem situation, analyse the causes of the problem, propose solutions and weigh up the feasibility of their proposals. This is what makes the case study such an effective assessment instrument.

The key point is that you need to choose assessment tasks at the right level/s for the course and award concerned. If they are too low or too high your test will lack validity and may well be unfair to the candidates, especially if it is higher than the level which they have been led to expect.

## Assessing physical skills

The same general points about level apply here too; in judging performance you will be looking for levels of accuracy, coordination, speed and economy as well as technical proficiency and, in some cases, imagination and style. You can add to the demands the task makes by combining certain skills, changing the context or increasing the pace. You must ask yourself if the tasks you have set are appropriate for the type of candidate and award concerned. Are they, for instance, foundation, intermediate or advanced level? As you saw earlier, you will find it very helpful to compare your perceptions with those of your colleagues. You will also remember that you should check that the tasks reveal **sufficient** of the candidates' skills for you to make a valid judgement of their abilities.

## Assessing attitudes

It is more difficult to set a level for attitudes, but it can be done by describing the behaviours which you want to see demonstrated. You may have to add a time dimension, so that the candidate must demonstrate the required attitude over a period of time and on all occasions, i.e. habitually – does the lathe operator habitually use the safety guard, does the chiropodist habitually treat the whole person? You may also need proof from more than one assessor. This has the advantage that you can compare your perceptions and interpretations; and it is likely to be fairer to the candidate, since judgement of attitudes is more subjective than judgement of skills.

When assessing attitudes you will either be working to a given set of criteria or you will have devised your own. Naturally you will have explained these to the learner so that they know what is expected of them. When we say that someone exhibits a particular attitude we are usually referring to lots of small pieces of behaviour which add up to the approach required. It is these which you need to list so that you can check that they are really there and that you are not being misled by a general impression, or bias based on other factors. Here is an example from customer care for a leisure centre receptionist:

- is punctual on arrival for her duties
- is correctly dressed
- has a good standard of personal hygiene
- gives priority of attention to the customer over routine duties, e.g. answering the phone
- looks alert and interested (sitting and standing)
- greets the customer with a smile
- gives the customer full attention while dealing with them
- listens carefully to any requests
- gives full explanations to queries
- makes generally friendly but not personal comments if appropriate
- acknowledges the end of the encounter; e.g. with thanks.

If you still find the idea of a checklist difficult, try compiling one describing appropriate teacher behaviour towards students in class.

## Compiling tests

You are now armed with much of the information you need to put your tests together, if this is your role. You know the syllabus and its objectives, the level of the award, the areas of knowledge skill and attitude which you want to assess. You know the characteristics which your tests must meet to produce good quality evidence. You may or may not know the actual students who will sit the tests, but you do know what they have been expected to learn. You can now decide **how** you will assess them; i.e. what kind of assessment instruments (tests) you will use.

You can choose from a wide range. We have already mentioned that objective (multi-choice) tests can sample specific knowledge, that essays are useful for explaining processes and that case studies can sample several levels of knowledge. You know that skills are best sampled through practical performance tests. We have also mentioned oral questioning as a way of supplementing practical performance (getting at the underpinning knowledge) and assignments as part of continuous assessment. You may know from experience about written short answer tests and you may have experienced oral and aural tests if you learned a language.

You may find it helpful to think of these tests in three groups:

- things you ask candidates to do
- things you ask candidates to write
- things you ask candidates to say or explain.

These groups are not necessarily separate; in fact you may well be increasing the validity and reliability of your assessment if you combine tests from each group. You might want a candidate for a catering award to cook vegetables in several different ways; you might ask them questions about the processes they have used, and you might ask them to write about the nutritional value of the food. Together this will give you a reliable body of evidence of their skills and understanding.

## Suited to its purpose?

When you choose or devise a test, you need to be sure that it is suitable for its purpose. You would not use a written test to assess someone's competence in life saving, for instance. If you want to test competence in physical skills you need a practical performance test. You might couple this with an oral test to ensure that the candidates knew why they were carrying out certain actions in certain ways, and that they understood the consequences of their actions. However, if you wanted a candidate to produce a reasoned argument setting out the advantages and disadvantages of a process, say the use of a new drug regime in an intensive care unit, an essay question format would give you the best opportunity to assess the candidate's analytical thinking skills. If you only wanted to know if the candidate was familiar with the names and uses of certain drugs, you could use a multi-choice objective test, since there are no shades of meaning or interpretation involved.

The point is to make sure that the chosen test is appropriate for the kind and level of abilities which you want to assess. This is part of your check on the validity of the test.

To see if you have chosen the right kind of test for your purposes you could subject it to the sort of checklist which follows.

## Checklist of characteristics of an effective test

- it tests what it set out to test (valid)
- it does this whenever used and whoever marks it (reliable)
- it discriminates between those who know the (correct or appropriate) answers and those who do not
- it is relevant to the learning objectives
- it is not biased against any candidate by reason of language, background or culture
- it is at the right level of difficulty
- it is interesting in itself and will promote learning
- it is clearly expressed in appropriate language
- its instructions (rubric) are clear and straightforward
- it covers a reasonable amount of material
- it does not take too long to administer or mark.

The best way to find out if you have made the right choice of test is to pilot it on a group of people and analyse the results. If you can't do this, meet with a colleague to go over your test questions and procedures rigorously, looking for potential hazards and misunderstandings.

## A word about timing

An effective test could still be a disaster if introduced at the wrong stage, say in an assignment-based continuously assessed programme. The following test was proposed as the first assignment for a group of Access to Social Science students, mainly mature students returning to learning after a career and study break, several without formal qualifications:

> 'Investigate the recent changes in employment law as promulgated by the European Parliament. Prepare a short paper which covers the implications for employers and employees and estimate the likely consequences for small employers in the UK. You will have 10 minutes to present your key ideas to the rest of your group and to answer questions on them.'

Where possible the tests chosen should suit the learning group. The above is an assignment which **midway** through the course could be a source of great interest and learning. But what is it testing? At the outset it begs all sorts of questions about familiarity with library accession systems, with academic papers, with techniques of oral presentation, and it demands a challenging 'public' performance before the group has had time to establish a dynamic. Clearly, these students would need lots of preparation in much more than the subject matter before it would be fair to test them in this way. They would need induction and practice in study skills and techniques of information retrieval as well as practice in pair work and individual tasks within the group to build up their confidence.

You might like to consider whether this test would have met the criteria for validity and reliability which you looked at earlier. The key to validity is the learning objectives. For this test to be valid the objectives for the learning programme would have had to include these areas:

- be able to retrieve information from paper and electronic storage systems
- be able to display knowledge about employment practices and their legal base, in the UK and Europe
- be able to apply that knowledge in the analysis and evaluation of specific cases
- be able to précis the knowledge for report purposes
- be able to plan a presentation taking into account target audience, language register and time allocation
- be able to communicate orally with a group in a formal setting.

If the teacher had set out to help the students to develop this range of cognitive and interpersonal skills, it would be fair to assess them. The test concerned would then be relevant to the objectives, at the right level, would discriminate those who had the knowledge and skills from those who did not. The test would be invalid if either the cognitive skills or interpersonal skills were not in the objectives of the learning/course in the first place.

Would the test be reliable? Would it yield the same results if it were used with a similar group of students on another occasion? Could you trust the results it produced? The test **would** be reliable, provided a set of assessment criteria had been worked out for it which matched the objectives. These would have to be unambiguous so that all assessors interpreted them in the same way. Each assessor must then keep strictly to the criteria when marking the test.

You might consider whether as an 'activity' designed to promote learning it has an appropriate place in your learning programme. If so, at what point could it be undertaken successfully? If you identify carefully the criteria for success in presenting such an analysis, you should begin to understand the complexity of in-course assessment in a field such as this.

# Frequency of testing

You will need to decide how often you are going to use tests with your students. An important consideration is to make sure that the testing process does not dominate the learning process. You can use tests very effectively as progress markers, giving students feedback on their strengths and weaknesses in a way which remotivates them and prepares them for later summative assessment. But be careful of overloading the learning time with tests which check on but do not enhance the learning, or which seem to be an end in themselves.

You will need to draw up a scheme of assessment if you are working with a group of learners over a period of time. Remember that you will need to leave time to teach the material, to give students practice in the thinking or skill acquisition required, to prepare them properly for the testing process, to carry out the assessment, to mark the tests and then to give the students feedback. If you are operating a scheme of continuous assessment you will have to do all this formally, and compile the appropriate records. If you are using this kind of test framework to prepare students for an external examination you can be more flexible, but none of the stages above should be skimped. Getting the balance between learning and testing takes thought and practice; if the assessment tasks can promote higher order skills and imaginative thinking, this is obviously an advantage.

# Making and recording assessment judgements (marking)

The secret of making judgements on work submitted for assessment, whether that work is practical or written or in some other form, is to have a very clear picture of what you want to see as evidence of understanding and competence. This should **always** be written down, never left to your memory.

When you design the assessment and draw up the assessment checklist you should allocate marks to each group of criteria, unless this is already done for you. These marks represent the value which you are giving to aspects of the performance from a total number available. At its simplest you might have 10 marks available and 10 key points which you value equally, so that each point gets 1 mark. You may decide that all 10 marks must be gained for a pass, or you may decide that 4 out of 10 is acceptable. If you express this as a percentage, then 40 per cent is your pass mark. If you want to grade the marks you can decide that 5–7 inclusive represents a credit grade (50–70 per cent) and that 8–10 inclusive equates to a distinction (80–100 per cent). This is your marking scheme.

In the example above all the points counted equally. This is a very simple scheme; you can make it progressively more complex. You can give more weight to some points than to others. You could make some points half a mark and others 2 marks to achieve this. You could say that a pass could only be achieved if certain points were achieved as part of the necessary 40 per cent, rather than any 4. In a written paper this might mean that certain questions were compulsory while others were optional.

You need to be sure that whatever you decide matches the emphasis placed on topics or skills when they were taught or outlined in the scheme documents.

It is also vital to **record** your decisions correctly; assessment information is among the most sensitive information with which you will deal. It should only be passed on to those with a proper right to know about it. One of these people, if you are working on an NVQ or GNVQ, will be the internal verifier for your team. An internal verifier's function is quality control. They check that what should have happened did happen. Did you follow all the procedures correctly? Were all candidates treated fairly? They do this by sampling some of your assessments, so they will accompany you while you assess a practical performance and look at the way you handled submitted work. This process is designed to ensure that all candidates get a fair deal and that the level of the award is kept up. Their work in turn is checked by an external verifier who works directly for the awarding body.

# Weighting

You can weight the marks so that you acknowledge the greater importance of higher levels of skill than lower levels. For instance, it is obvious that students need knowledge of facts and formulae before they go on to use them in argument or calculation. If the point of the assessment is to test application of the facts and formulae rather than their recall, you need to give more marks for the more difficult operation. You can make this distinction within one test question or over a whole test. Certain maths tests commonly give 20 per cent of the marks for recalling formulae but 80 per cent for using the formulae to solve problems.

Let's take the question 'Show how the effects of global warming might influence agricultural practices differently in different parts of Europe in the next 30 years'. Here the student could obtain 20 per cent of the marks for knowing about current agricultural practices in relation to geographical area, 20 per cent of the marks for knowing what the effects of global warming are, but 60 per cent of the marks for discussing the **changes** implied by global warming in a sufficient number of geographical areas to show an understanding of the principles involved.

## Dealing with failure

Tests are inevitably linked with the idea or fear of failure for many people. The consequences of failure have been used too often as a threat. One of your roles is to prepare the students for assessment; this should include being as positive as possible about what happens if they do not do as well as expected. With NVQs this is a positive process where first of all the candidate is advised to delay assessment until they feel that they are competent, thus reducing the likelihood of failure (this can also save everyone's time). Then if they do not meet all of the criteria they are given feedback about their areas of strength and weakness, and a new action plan is drawn up for a date by which they can prepare themselves to retake the test.

Within your teaching you can manage testing processes so that they are routes to learning rather than events to fear. You can be very influential in setting the appropriate tone here, and in demonstrating its reality through your constructive feedback to individuals after in-class tests. You can help them to feel that if they fail a national examination there are always further opportunities, and that failure at this particular time does not mean that **they** are a failure. If you act as a personal tutor to a group of students, you may be able to give them some positive guidance during the run up to examination periods.

## Your scheme of assessment

You have looked at approaches to assessment, its organisation, and what you need to consider for a single test. Now extend your ideas to analyse what you want out of an overall scheme of assessment, i.e. one which spans a period of time and includes several types of test. Here are some questions you could ask. They form a summary of much of the material in this chapter.

Will my scheme of assessment:

● cover all the knowledge, skills and attitudes which I need to assess
● match the objectives and outcomes of the course
● suit the types of group and learners
● use only valid and reliable tests
● provide sufficient evidence overall of the candidates' competence
● fit into the pattern of learning without unbalancing it
● communicate its requirements clearly
● give candidates interesting things to do
● have fair deadlines, reasonably spaced out
● use straightforward administrative procedures?

You are now aware of the basic requirements for assessing, but it is an area which can be taken much further. The following books (available from City & Guilds, Sales Department, 1 Giltspur Street, London EC1A 9DD) will be helpful:

Assessment Handbooks (priced):

1 *Setting Multiple-choice Tests* (compiled and edited by Norman Gealy)

3 *Setting and Moderating Constructed-answer Question Papers* (by Chahid Fourali)

*Glossary of Terms* – used in standards development, curriculum design, assessment and accreditation (by Chahid Fourali).

# Part 3

# *The Theory Behind it All*

# Introduction: Discoveries in Psychology

When I complained to my Head of Division in a Florida college that the sheer size and volume of the humanities syllabus made it unteachable, he replied, 'It's only a survey.' I think he meant it amounted to a 'naming of parts'. They were to be 'covered' briefly, so as to ensure the students had heard about them. What for? I wondered. Why learn these things unless they are to become significant to you in some way?

What I hope to show in this part of the book is that psychological discovery as it can be applied to learning and teaching is exciting and fascinating. It is not 'out there somewhere', but fundamentally important to what teachers do. Even if I had the space of a large book devoted exclusively to it, I could not cover it. I can only provide a glimpse through chinks in the curtains at some major theories of learning. It is my hope you will want to read more, and use what you find out to try to understand what is happening for your students.

A great deal of what happens, even in good teaching, is intuitive. Teachers learn by trial and error and role-modelling, sometimes by *diktat*. They do not always know why something works, but are glad that it does. They are just too busy to be curious, and do not have the time to stand back and think or to read the educational literature. Nor, in any case, will the reading have value unless they think about it in relation to what they decide to do with their students in their context.

This book started the other way about: to try to develop good practice and test theory in teaching before exploring theories in any depth. The test of a theory is whether it works: does it predict usefully what will happen *here*? It is not enough that it should offer an explanation of what *might* be going on. There could be many other equally valid explanations. The history of education is littered with failed theories, even those that were the result of years and years of research.

The model of teaching/learning set out in Parts 1 and 2 is not invention arising simply from my own experience. There is well-documented research in psychology and practical teaching. I have worked closely with many teachers of adults also in many contexts, and I have benefited from their knowledge and experience. It is usual in academic texts to direct the reader through use of footnotes and references to sources for statements and assertions made. I have resisted doing that, as I do not find such texts helpful.

The literature on learning and teaching is vast, however. I have attempted below to direct your attention to those beliefs and thinkers I believe have had an important influence on what has happened: to try to show the sources of the ideas and practice exhibited in the model in this book. Moreover, academic books present a dispassionate, non-advocative description of learning theorists. This survey is intended to go beyond that: there is a thread of argument. Selection and therefore distortion are inevitable. I urge you, where you can, to read original texts for comparison. The 'Suggestions for Further Reading' at the end are intended as a guide, not a comprehensive list.

# 24 Behaviourism

In the 1900s, psychology was dominated by the school of behaviourism, under the leadership of John B. Watson. The school was inspired by brilliant results in animal psychology achieved by Morgan and Thorndike. Human beings, Watson declared, should be studied like any other animals. 'Behaviour' should be observed like the phenomena in all other natural sciences.

No behaviourist, Watson declared, has observed anything that can be called consciousness, sensation, perception, imagery or will. All such terms are unusable in descriptions of human activity. This assertion was held to be true and self-evident. Experiments were to be confined to objective observations of the results of stimulus and response.

Decision-making was effectively ignored, as was 'thinking it through'. These are mentalistic terms which some examiners still think you cannot test and therefore for the sake of objectivity must ignore. For the same reasons 'goal-seeking', 'the will' and other attitudinal terms cannot be part of the examination/criterion-referencing system, although they were to be accepted by some behaviourists, such as Tolman, as important. Why such puritanism? particularly since they seem to exclude intelligence in the behaviour we are trying to assess (and improve?).

Mental 'representation' or 'conjectural modelling' of the world is an idea the early twentieth-century psychologists tried to eliminate in the effort to give their discipline the appearance of an objective science. 'Any reference to consciousness was carefully excluded for fear it would introduce the scientifically unmanageable idea of a causal principle that was not immediately accessible to public observation' (George Miller in *States of Mind: Conversations with Psychological Investigators*).

The behaviourists developed a programme of research based on the assumption that behaviour of all kinds could be explained in terms of the measurable stimuli impinging on the sense organs and the nerves which controlled the muscles. Stimulus-response bonds most often quoted are reflexes such as the knee-jerk, and the reaction of the iris of the eye to light. There is a stimulus, light, and an immediate unlearned response of the iris muscles. The important thing is that it does not have to be learned.

It is obvious that most behaviour, in all plants and animals, essential for dealing with the world is of this kind. A baby is born with peristalsis in its digestive tract, for example. Without conscious control, it pumps blood around its body and constantly produces the thousands of proteins necessary to its functioning as an organism.

What then is learning? What is it necessary to learn? How is it learned? How does it become embedded so that we do not have to employ consciousness? The behaviourists thought they had discovered the mechanism by which this happened: the **conditioned reflex** – a reflex that was transferred somehow from a direct stimulus to a surrogate stimulus. They believed that, by analysis, it should be possible to show the 'chaining' by which each of these conditioned stimulus–response bonds came to be the behaviour that they were studying, however complex that behaviour might appear to be.

The idea of the conditioned reflex that was built into the doctrine of the behaviourists began with observations of dogs by I. P. Pavlov early this century. In studying the digestive system, he noticed that his dogs would salivate without the presence of food – just the sight of the man who would give them the food would do the trick. Pavlov showed that any stimulus a dog can perceive could be made to evoke salivation after it has been paired with food often enough. Pavlov offered, it seemed, an objective way to explain how ideas become associated: as Pavlov's dogs associated food with seeing the caretaker.

The salivary reflex is not under conscious control. You cannot say: I will now secrete saliva, and thereby cause your mouth to start watering. You could think about dinner, and that might make you salivate: this is a conditioned reflex. Psychologists came to believe that they could build any arbitrary system or hierarchy of behaviour by simply conditioning people in the same way.

Bechterev, a rival of Pavlov's, experimented with voluntary movements, like lifting the paw, rather than involuntary reflexes. Pavlov's ideas, with Bechterev's methodology, were then picked up by John B. Watson and others. In the 1920s, the behaviourists redefined psychology as the science of behaviour, not the science of mental activity. They wanted to exclude the mind from psychology.

As different people introspect differently, they thought a researcher could not rely on what people said about mental activity: 'there's no way I can verify you really had the experience you told me you had.' Behaviourists knew they were conscious, but they thought they could not study conscious experience scientifically. They had to be hard-headed scientists: so nothing was allowed that a physiologist would or could not do.

They thought any complex pattern of behaviour, such as human speech, could with sufficient analysis be reduced to reflexes, and to chains of reflexes. When a stimulus elicits a response, and that response in turn becomes the stimulus to elicit the next response, and so on, the result is a reflex chain. How simple! they thought. People are not complicated after all. Psychologists had discovered the unit of analysis. Given a response they should be able to figure out what the stimulus was that led to it, and so on back up a chain of reflexes. This would allow control of the process.

What was being studied was transfer of response to stimuli of one kind to stimuli of another kind. Learning was defined as **relatively permanent change in behaviour** that could be observed and measured. The programme was to analyse and simplify the complexity of behaviour so as to describe it as chains of stimulus–response bonds. A trained person could then teach by controlling and reinforcing each of the links in such defined chains.

# Teaching programmes

The facts are hardly in dispute. Dogs do salivate if they hear the sound of the bis-cuit barrel. I can be made to feel fear in the cinema by visual or auditory stimulus – made possible by conditioning. It makes it easy for the advertising and propa-ganda industry to work on people's emotions. **Conditioning happens** – it is very powerful. What is arguable is how it works, what the mechanism is, and how it can be used in teaching/learning. Later psychologists of the behaviourist school sought to extend and modify the early doctrine – to make it viable as a means of instruction.

B. F. Skinner (born in 1904 and formerly Professor of Psychology at Harvard University) set out to identify the 'how'. Skinner argues that a learning process is accelerated by **reinforcement**: a stimulus that increases the probability of a response. He claims that one can describe behaviour in terms of external stimuli and their positive or negative reinforcement.

In **operant conditioning**, the important stimulus is that which immediately follows the response, not that which triggers it. In order to predict how a person will behave, we must look not at his expectation of the consequences that will fol-low his behaviour, but at what happened as a consequence of similar behaviour in the past. This may seem rather mentalistic after all. What Skinner is trying to avoid is the idea that future expectation – goal-seeking – affects present behav-iour. It must relate to what has happened in the past in terms of reinforcement. This shapes our behaviour by using our desires and our fears. The strength of a response can be determined by the intensity of the stimulus. Prolongation or repe-tition will also increase the intensity of a stimulus.

For instance, if an animal such as a rat is starved, the stimulus of food and the reward of food will be greatly increased. Skinner used this to show how rats can be conditioned to find a path through a maze with food as the stimulus. A rat, which is an exploratory animal, searches a box until by trial and error it discovers how to get food. It can then be conditioned to follow more and more complex paths through a maze to get the food. The experimenter can control the behaviour of the animal and establish patterns in that behaviour. From this, Skinner believed that you could predict behaviour – you could control the process of learning and shape the behaviour as you wished.

The systematic application of reinforcement has been his principal study. Skinner believed that a technology of learning/teaching can be devised. It could be all predictable (in the scientific sense) and so programmed. So teachers should not be learning by experience in the classroom. 'Teachers need the kind of help offered by a scientific analysis of behaviour.' This kind of programme has been attempted, and with some success.

# Comment

Does conditioning work? Yes, certainly. Animals and children, and no doubt adults, can be conditioned. It happens in normal nurturing. We observe strong conditioning into sex roles and status expectations. I find it very difficult to prevent making responses that have been conditioned into me, even though I am conscious of it happening. The advertising industry uses emotional engineering to control our responses to their images.

Skinner did it most effectively, at least with rats, by systematic use of his techniques. Parents and teachers use conditioning much more simply, through rewards and punishments, to shape the behaviour they want. People can condition themselves to need salt, nicotine, alcohol – almost anything. With an effort they can also decondition themselves. Much human behaviour in social situations (membership of particular societies, groups, tribes) can be seen to be the result of conditioning.

But powerful as it is, conditioning is not the only type of learning. It cannot be ignored and teachers should take careful note of what has been discovered about reinforcing learned behaviour. As a systematic approach to education or even training, it fails to take into account many other aspects of human behaviour, most notably motivation and attitudinal change. For this reason it tends to fail to achieve the intended programme. Humans develop resistance to conditioning. And it is not clear how conditioning is to promote cognitive and intellectual skills. Surely, teachers need to promote intelligent thinking.

# 25 Neo-behaviourism: Structural Analysis

Probably the most influential of the neo-behaviourist psychologists since the mid-1960s has been R. Gagné (born in 1916, and Professor of Psychology at the Universities of Princeton and Florida). His concern is the structural analysis of learning processes and the design of teaching models to match the kinds of learning they are intended to facilitate.

He devised a systematised approach to instruction which strongly influences design of many teaching programmes. Learning is seen as 'a change in human disposition or capability, which can be retained, and which is not simply ascribable to the process of growth'. He makes a comparison with organic processes in the body such as digestion to describe a process taking place in the learner's brain. It is a 'total process' – not fragmented but systematically described. It starts for him with **apprehending** what is in the environment – the stimuli – followed by **acquisition**, then **storage** and, finally, **retrieval**. The analogy is a computer program.

Learning is analysed into descriptions of 'changed behaviour in terms of an observable type of human performance', with five major categories of 'human capability that are outcomes of learning':

- verbal information
- intellectual skills
- cognitive strategies
- attitudes
- motor skills.

Clearly, this goes a long way beyond Skinner in identifying a range of types of learning. Each one requires a different learning strategy, and teaching that recognises the type of learning and the strategy in order to match the appropriate process of instruction to it – certainly not simple stimulus–response bonding. It is behaviourist in placing emphasis on a structure imposed from outside. While acknowledging the importance of process in the learning, outcomes are seen as the main criterion of successful instruction. Instruction must be designed with different characteristics 'that depend on which particular class of performance change is the focus of interest'. But the range in the types of learning that are to be 'systematised' is limited.

Gagné sets out eight conditions or types of learning:

1 **signal learning:** stimulus–response at the level of signals
2 **stimulus–response learning:** involves discrimination between stimuli

3 **chaining**: stimulus–response bonds are chained in sequence at a motor level – what others might call 'memory in the muscles'

4 **verbal discrimination association**: verbal chains are formed – involves making of individual links, discrimination and chaining to 'associate' (in Pavlov's sense)

5 **multiple discrimination**: more sophisticated discrimination between apparently similar stimuli – with correct responses

6 **concept learning**: responses to 'classes' of stimuli – recognition of relationships or 'classes'

7 **rule-learning**: chaining concepts: a rule is 'an inferred capability that enables the individual to respond to a class of stimulus situations with a class of performances'

8 **problem-solving**: a natural extension of rule-learning where the most important part of the process takes place within the learner 'who discovers relationships'.

This is a 'hierarchy' of learning. The word is taken from the organisation of priests, and implies a pyramidal structure from many at the base to one at the top. By extension, however, as in this case, it implies that each capability has within it and necessary to it all the previous lower capabilities. For example, I cannot chain stimulus–response bonds unless I am capable of making the individual bonds first.

Gagné proposes use of 'instructional sequences' related to the hierarchy:

- informing the learner as to what form of performance is expected after completion of the learning
- questioning the learner to elicit recall of previously learned concepts
- using cues to elicit the formation of chains of concepts or 'rules'
- questioning the learner so as to obtain demonstration of rules
- requiring the learner to make a verbal statement of the rule.

As a teaching programme this is clearly desperately limited, and entirely teacher-centred. Gagné identifies eight phases in an act of learning which implies voluntary learning activity only:

1 motivation: goal-seeking – induced by creating expectations
2 apprehending: differentiation of stimuli by focusing attention
3 acquisition: storing the learning by encoding it
4 retention: extended memory storage
5 recall: the process of retrieval
6 generalisation: transfer of learning to new contexts
7 performance: demonstration of what has been learned
8 feedback: the process of reinforcement.

# Comment on behaviourism

Gagné's programming of learning derives from how he believes the teaching–learning interface operates. Certainly, statement of learning goals is of major importance – but who identifies the goals? The teacher? Gagné sees the teacher as the designer and manager of the process of instruction, the provider of immediate feedback to the learner to reinforce learning (Skinner-style), and also the assessor of learning outcomes. Assessment is the teacher's prerogative.

This is an attempt to 'systematise' instruction. A great deal of effort in training in particular has gone into such systems. It has dominated much of the provision. There is little room for dynamic or organic change within such a programme. It has within it an implied conditioning of the learning through the process of shaping and reinforcement.

Nor does it acknowledge that humans are exploratory animals. Decision-making is for the instructor. How can this produce independent learners, let alone independent thinkers? The emphasis in the end is on demonstrable, observable performance. Those aspects of learning which Gagné identifies as important, such as the developing of cognitive strategies and attitudes, since they are not demonstrable in performance are ignored in instructional/assessment/feedback programming.

The eight phases of instruction appear to relate systematically to outside rather than inside need – to the American style of instruction: 'tell and test' orthodox right answers. Where then are 'discoveries of relationships' or 'leaps ahead beyond the evidence'? It would be impossible to imagine 'leaps' that miss out whole parts of the chaining.

Yet we know that the human mind does make such leaps. Often enough we leap to conclusions, usually with very inadequate evidence, and then fill in the gaps in the chain afterwards. Desperately untidy for such a system as Gagné proposes. Where is 'trust in the students'?

Science, it was thought, worked by the accumulation of experimental 'facts', analysis, theorising, the demonstration of proofs, and replication: a misconception of how science works that was prevalent until the last war. The whole behaviourist programme was based on this misconception. Behaviourists thought they could build up a supremely thorough-going system which would inevitably be effective, since it was designed on the basis of 'scientific' research. It could be systematised: each building block was to be made up of conditioned behavioural patterns, using reinforcement techniques (totally teacher-centred stuff). Gagné appears, like Darwin and Freud, to wish to impose a rigid finality that cannot allow of challenge from the learner.

Dynamic, unpredictable change must imply unpredictable outcomes. You cannot make the outcomes totally shape the learning process, unless your purpose is conditioning to preconceived patterns of behaviour – indoctrination. How much of *what* people actually learn, let alone *how* they learn it, is really in the control of teachers? Do teachers need to perceive a much more modest role for themselves?

Unfortunately for the behaviourists, science just does not work as they thought. It tends to generate hypotheses, sometimes 'hunches', and look for evidence to support or invalidate the hypotheses. It starts from questions and/or guesses rather than from evidence: top down, not bottom up.

Sir Karl Popper in 1958, in *The Logic of Scientific Discovery*, proposed a new philosophy of science. Scientific method since Bacon had been thought of as demonstration of proofs, and research was concerned with proving the theory correct; scandals occurred when all contradictory evidence was suppressed. To be scientific for Popper a theory must be falsifiable, not verifiable. The proper business of science is the rejection of hypothesis. It starts with a conjectural hunch that often goes way beyond the available information; then the programme is set up to check the hypothesis against the world – does it explain the facts? will it predict what will happen if . . . ? A good theory will predict events under given circumstances. The test is whether or not the prediction is false.

Einstein's theory of gravity made very different predictions from Newton's. For example, he said light rays from distant stars would be bent if they passed close to the sun. This prediction was tested during an eclipse in 1919. Measurement was very difficult but it seemed to confirm Einstein against Newton. He was also correct in predicting that clocks would run slow in spacecraft. But Newton's equations are easier to use and more practical than Einstein's, so Newton is preferred in our everyday world.

Scientific theories, since Einstein and Heisenberg's Uncertainty Principle in relation to the structure of the atom, are no longer expected to demonstrate objective truth: it is enough that they work. So long as they will predict what will happen they are useful, and that is what is required. The great optimism about being able to explain everything has largely died.

Gagné's insistence on matching teaching to intended learning and analysis of 'how that is intended to happen' is extremely important. We must surely do the analysis. We must understand how to design a strategy of learning.

We must agree learning goals with students. They must be signposts rather than goalposts, since we cannot predict what will happen or how the goals will need to be redefined as the process evolves. And in any case a point of arrival is also the next point of departure. Nothing is once for all.

We also need to use feedback in a formative way. This is not to reinforce the learning in the behaviourist meaning and technique. That implies that we seek to shape the learning to teachers' predetermined models. Feedback is better seen as more in the nature of a mirror, to allow the students to match what they are doing against models and criteria that we have agreed with them and which they perceive. This will enable them to measure their progress and so to improve whatever they are setting out to learn – to set about learning consciously and intelligently, and so take responsibility for their own learning.

# 26 Insight Learning: Gestalt

Intellectual progress – psychology is no exception – takes place by challenge and defence. The school that arose in vehement opposition to the behaviourists was the Gestalt school.

Where Skinner spent many years studying rats, experimenters who wanted to challenge Watson and his school studied chimpanzees – our nearest cousins. I once had a very 'intelligent' cat who discovered how to get me out of bed in the middle of the night by rapping the knocker on the front door of my house: he climbed up the slats and lifted it with a paw. I certainly did not condition him to do it. How did he learn it?

Kohler (1887–1967) was interested in the ability of chimpanzees to solve problems (*The Mentality of Apes*, 1925). Since they could not tell experimenters their introspections, he observed their behaviour and created his own hypothesis to explain it. You may well have seen these experiments, since they were filmed. One was to give a chimpanzee the problem of getting bananas that were suspended out of the ape's reach. To solve this the animal placed boxes one on top of another.

How would you explain what the ape did? Surely not by stimulus–response chaining. Had the ape had experience before that had been developed through reinforcement to produce a capacity to make such inventive use of the environment? Or was it creative thinking of some kind? Was there a reorganisation in the brain or 'mind' of structures in the world? Did the ape perceive a different relationship of objects to make an 'artificial tree' that it could climb?

Another experiment used the ape's frustration at not being able to reach a bunch of fruit outside the cage. The ape apparently 'experimented'. Some jointed sticks had been provided, and after several attempts it succeeded in putting them together to reach the fruit. Studies of behaviour of similar kinds have been filmed in the wild, with various animals. What hypothesis could one put together to explain this? How would you explain problem-solving of this kind?

It was like my cat's 'experimenting' with the knocker on my front door. Kohler saw this behaviour as 'not connected with previous trial and error', not linked step-by-step into a chain, nor as reinforced patterning. In order for it to be stimulus–response bonding such links are necessary. Could it have been recall of past learning? and if so, of what kind of learning?

Kohler called it **insight learning**. It was, he thought, a restructuring in the mind to see how the whole thing might work: Eureka! I've got it. We have the experience ourselves quite frequently. It happens, in a **Gestalt**: when the structural essence of the total situation posed by the problem is perceived by the learner. You will have experiences like this with pets of your own, and similar personal experiences to reflect on.

We quite often use the phrase: 'Oh! I see it now!' This implies some kind of visualising of the problem in a new way. We see how the bits make sense together. For Gestaltists, 'the whole is greater than the sum of the parts'. It is 'seeing the whole' that makes sense of the parts.

What distinguishes insight learning for these theorists is that:

- the solution is a sudden leap, as if pieces were fitting together
- once it has been accomplished, it is easier to solve similar problems
- it leads to permanence in learning – it appears to become part of our way of dealing with the world – and we can transfer that learning to unfamiliar situations, in different contexts.

In other words, it appears to be about how we *subsequently* do things. It seems to improve our intellectual problem-solving skills and processes. The transferability is essential: cognitive skill becomes applicable to other contexts.

This suggests that if we want to improve people's skills we need to look at how people deal with things 'in the whole', and not try to improve skill by analysing it into constituent bits. It doesn't work that way. Gestaltists argued that a phenomenon like learning has to be studied as an organised, complex structure which changes as a whole by sudden leaps from one state of being to another. The pattern of activity that made this leap happen they called **insight**.

Certainly most things, from the simplest to the most complex such as human behaviour, are much more easily grasped and understood when we have a view of them as a whole. We cannot even begin to see what each bit does on its own; we can understand it only in relationship to the whole. There are multitudes of things of which the whole is not analysable into its constituent parts. For instance, a picture is perceived only as a whole. So is a piece of music, or tree. Analysis of constituents and processes helps you to appreciate it more, but to take it apart is to destroy it.

# Comment on Gestalt

The Gestaltists' explanation of how learning happens is important. They saw it as a dynamic process: not linking nor even associating with previous experience, but a creative restructuring that arises from thinking through problems. Challenge is part of learning. For them, the acquisition and retention of insight form the core of the learning process. Since this comes about through problem-solving, it will be most effective when learners are challenged by being given problems to find solutions for, questions rather than answers.

It demands a very different kind of learning programme from that proposed by Gagné's structural analysis. It must be dynamic and open in terms of any predicted learning. It is difficult to predict how a mind will restructure its experience. It involves productive thinking. A dynamic, creative process is involved. All decision-making will therefore be seen as a **creative response** to situations.

It is creative because it involves making a new structure of the problem in order to invent or discover a solution. The process is cumulative. This is contrasted with rote-learning, in which creativity is suppressed. It can be seen to happen when we are faced with a familiar object in an unfamiliar guise. We might have to rotate it in our mind's eye or picture it some new way to recognise it. It is a favourite game of local newspapers to present such picture puzzles to their readers: where is this?

Capacity for creative thinking will be present in most learners. This capacity is in the student, and is to be brought out; it is not in the teacher to be transferred to the learner by some techniques of knowledge transfer. How should the teacher attempt to bring it out, rather than to teach it or to put it in? Asking a question of this kind changes the perspective of teaching entirely.

Productive thinking involves learners grasping the essential relationships within a problem, grouping them into 'wholes' and restructuring the problem to find solutions. But we quite often might need to break down a problem into related stages in order to tackle it successfully. We may not be able to grasp the whole of something if it is too big.

## Teaching/learning strategies

Much of what makes a 'person' is a result of conditioning, whether it is consciously done by parents, teachers, employers, peer groups, churches, advertising companies and so forth, or just a series of pressures to conform, such as sex-role conditioning. It is helpful to understand the mechanism involved. Unlearning such reinforced behaviour is extremely difficult, particularly if it is accompanied by a mind-set of beliefs and attitudes.

Clearly, there is a place for rote-learning. It may be the quickest way to lay a 'sound' foundation of accepted knowledge. But again, there are real problems in overwhelming students with too much information at one time. And unless they use the new information it will remain 'in a memory box'. Indoctrination approaches to teaching clearly suppress creativity – are in fact intended to do so. Memory rote-learning has an important place in the laying of foundations, let's say in number work, but used as a major means of instruction it stifles the very learning we are trying to assist.

But it is fairly easy to test. Creativity is not testable. It relies too much on personal judgement, and is only indirectly observable as outcomes. It is obvious too that unless you have a sound basis of information to build your speculations on you will offer solutions that make no sense, no matter how creative you are.

As in science, the main criterion of feasibility in a theory is: does it explain the facts? It must make predictions that stand up to facts. It does not require insight learning to memorise facts. But that seems a poor reason to require *only* memorising of facts – or opinions masquerading as facts.

Problem-solving is a powerful tool of learning. It is creative, related to success as an organism in the world, to social behaviour as a social animal, to intellectual growth and development of skills and capacities – and through all this to self-esteem and independence. It has the additional advantage that we can use it to foster sharing and team-efforts, which are essential in our technological environment.

So in designing learning programmes, we must vary approaches to learning and fit them together to create successful learning strategies.

# Right answers

The major problem with the Gestalt approach, as it turns out, is that there is frequently too little information for the learners to have a view of the 'whole'. They have to make a leap with insufficient evidence (insufficiency of evidence hardly ever stops one, of course). Or the whole may be just too big a leap to make – we have to take smaller whole lumps, and hope to build them up into a greater whole later. I wonder if such a strategy would be acceptable as Gestalt?

One consequence is that we often end up with the wrong 'whole' – a delusion or a misconception of what it is we are about – which may lead us off in a totally unprofitable direction. Insight is fine when we leap to the 'right' answer. What do we do in such a description of the learning process if, as is often the case, the answer is wrong in whole or in part? Ensuring that students have the correct response is the intention of reinforcement. The transmission of 'non-false' information/knowledge is important if we are to avoid serious problems in later learning. It must be correct, if only because it is so hard to unlearn once it is established.

One of the great difficulties with discovery learning and problem-solving is this: at what point should the teacher intervene if it becomes obvious that the students are on the wrong track? How important is it that they do find the correct solution at the end of their effort? Obviously, wheels without an axle or bearings or gearing may well be ineffective for the purpose intended. The students need to have that pointed out.

The other great problem is that it can be very slow as well as very fast. Teachers (and students) easily become impatient. I remember well a student saying to me twenty-five years ago, 'Sir, why don't you just tell us the answer? It'll be so much quicker.'

The method is intended to accelerate the learning by a sudden leap in which the whole of the thing falls into place. This is how we often learn: we make a sudden leap beyond the evidence, and fill in the gap in retrospect between where we were and where we have arrived, with our knowledge of the 'whole' to guide us.

In support of the approach it is easy to show that a leap to a conclusion, and cutting out a great deal of rather tedious unit-building, is efficient as a methodology *as long as a student does fill in the gaps afterwards*. Frequently this last condition is unfulfilled, and gaps remain which later prove to be very inhibiting of future progress.

It may be very slow because students may not be very good at formulating or visualising the problem – discovering the questions or a method of looking for answers. They may go down blind alleys or run up against gaps in their knowledge or understanding that inhibit progress. If they are working in a group they may have conflicting Gestalts or paths of enquiry to follow.

Teachers will want to provide 'teacher's Gestalt' to hasten the process. A major problem may then be that the gap between where the learner is now and where the teacher is may be so wide as to make 'teacher's Gestalt' incomprehensible to the student. Teachers usually start from what *they* know, *their* picture of the world, and provide it as an insight for students. Or they may offer an author's 'picture of it all', a textbook solution.

This is the standard practice in complex subjects such as history, English literature, sociology and engineering science. The amount of detail is so huge that it is far too time-consuming a process to build up the students' 'picture of it all' by taking a tedious slow march through the details. In any case, from the practical point of learning, it is much easier to understand the detail and to know what you are looking for in the detail if you have a picture in the head of the whole thing. 'You can't see the wood for the trees.' It is a fact that too much information is confusing.

But we have to ensure that we do understand where the student is starting from: how he or she may 'make the leap' to the Gestalt, and what has to happen then in terms of 'filling in the gap'. And this is not easy to do if we have no view of what the gap consists of, or even that gaps exist.

This is part of what is wrong with providing teacher's or the textbook's 'right' answers. They may make perfect sense to the teacher and the author because they are restructuring information that is already possessed to make a new 'whole'. On the face of it, it looks like an efficient approach because it accelerates the students to a conclusion they might otherwise take a long time to reach, or which they might never reach at all because of lack of skill or information.

But the whole without the evidential information makes little sense – especially if students do not know *what* the questions are to which these are the 'right' answers. Textbooks rarely state the questions: too often, answers are to be learned as facts when they are truly one person's reconstruction of the world to make sense of facts. Teachers may be pleased with the efficiency of what they appear to have done but in Gestalt terms it is an illusion of knowledge, since the students have not actually made any leap at all.

They can only do that if they restructure their own 'picture of it all'. They must process information themselves; they must restructure their conceptual framework for it to become usable knowledge. To memorise and then to repeat accurately what they have memorised is not insight, although it is the way many examining systems work.

Enabling students to achieve insight learning provides a formidable challenge to teachers – which explains why it so infrequently occurs.

# 27 Cognitive Development: Concrete and Formal Thinking

Jean Piaget (1896–1980, for fifty years Professor at the University of Geneva and Director of the Rousseau Institute) studied hundreds of children, trying to understand how they learned. Like Gestaltists, he believed that all children are born with certain **innate mental structures** that determine the shape of their cognitive development. These structures provide their motivation to interact with the environment, and guide the growth of their knowledge about the world. But Piaget thought the **shape of the mind** was also affected by the environment in which the child grew up. Children construct grammar in their minds as they learn to talk, because their genes allow them to. He took a middle road in the prevailing 'nature–nurture' controversy.

Piaget concentrated his attention on the mind. He paid little attention to behaviour itself. It was the mental functioning controlling behaviour that interested him. 'The child is not shaped by the parents,' he said, 'the child is the teacher.' Your social environment merely provides the inputs; your mind interprets and reshapes these inputs to create the knowledge you presently have. He was much more impressed by similarities in all children than by individual differences. Intellectual development in every child, according to him, will proceed through four clearly defined stages. These occur in giant steps; they are not the slow and steady accumulation of knowledge and information. The four developmental stages of cognitive development are as follows:

1 the sensory–motor period: birth to 24 months
2 the pre-operational stage: two to seven years of age
3 the stage of concrete operations: eight to twelve years of age
4 the stage of formal operations: twelve years onwards.

Piaget maintained that the *average* age at which children attain each maturational level was about the same in all cultures. All infants explore and respond to their environment directly and rather automatically. Children explore the physical and maternal world up to around the age of eighteen months, when they truly begin to 'think': they thus build an internal representation of the external world, and learn to 'manipulate' objects in their minds.

Between the ages of two and seven children acquire sophisticated language which gives them the ability to deal with many aspects of the world in symbols, by talking and thinking about objects rather than having to manipulate them directly. They can remember past events and anticipate their happening again. But they exhibit only egocentric reasoning: they cannot differentiate between self and the environment.

By the time children reach six or seven they begin to acquire 'concepts' and see the objects 'out there', but only gradually perceive them in relationships. A new object (two halves of a ball, say) they believe to be new objects and so expect them to weigh more than the original whole ball. They *perceive* weight and number in a non-adult way. Counting is not the same as the concept of number. In infant and primary schools, for this reason, a great deal of effort goes into teaching number by concrete examples, by handling objects.

At about the age of twelve, Piaget believed for *all* children, a cognitive leap occurs. They begin to use abstractions to manipulate thinking about the world. People can then solve problems in their minds by isolating the important variables so as to manipulate them mentally or perceptually. Now at last individuals can draw meaningful conclusions from purely abstract or hypothetical data. They can now deal effectively with questions about how, what and why. Piaget identified this change as being able to reason 'formally', using abstractions, instead of seeing the world and themselves in 'concrete' or 'real out there' terms.

# Is it true?

The main problem is that Piaget did not conduct experimental research under the controlled conditions that present psychological research uses. Such research does not confirm his assertions. Many of his basic assumptions are suspect: in particular, that there are 'general structures of the mind'. There are also so many exceptions to his general rules.

But his are challenging ideas. I have found that many adults cannot deal with abstract conceptualisations; they see things in concrete terms, or even 'me and the world' terms. They can deal well with counting objects, but not with number concepts. Perhaps as many as eight out of twelve adults have failed to make this cognitive leap. Assumptions we make about ability to cope with learning goals and programmes that we teachers set up for them have to take account of such readiness; to recognise cognitive growth.

The recent change to the National Curriculum in Science in the United Kingdom has led to a crash training programme for science teachers: biologists have to relearn physics to integrate it into science teaching again. To do so, they have to explore new student-centred methods and projects. Thinking scientifically is impossible unless you can deal in abstractions, and can perceive variables and differentiate between them. To do a science experiment you must isolate one variable you wish to study and try to keep everything else unaltered, so as to measure change in that variable alone. This implies quite complex thought processes. The problem comes sharply back: so many students have not made the leap from concrete to formal thinking by the time they come to do GCSE (age sixteen), and they cannot deal with abstract ideas effectively.

The old input/output approach to memory training allowed teachers to get students through exams in science without real understanding of most of it. The new

GCSE will not allow that. Pupils have to conceptualise and design a method for investigating phenomena. You cannot do that without formal as against concrete thinking. Teachers therefore must tackle this cognitive change first.

The cognitive development problem exists, but not as Piaget envisaged; nor is the problem confined to science. *All* creative thinking involves the ability to conceptualise and use abstractions. It relates in fundamental ways to vocabulary – the ability to use words and symbols.

# 28 Perception

Common sense and my experience tell me that if I run headlong into a wall, I will do myself harm. But a nursing training officer once told me of patients she had known who had walked straight through walls without apparent harm to themselves; perhaps they did not perceive a wall to be an obstacle to them because of their 'insanity' at the time.

How far is what actually happens related to what we expect to happen? Does the learning come from experience – the way we investigate the world? or from inborn ways of visualising? from cultural beliefs? Why do some people have such a different view of the world from ours? How is it that people walk on hot coals without apparent harm, or put skewers through their faces without bleeding?

Creatures receive information about the world from sense organs, of which for humans the eyes are the most powerful. It was probably because they used sight in preference to the other senses that our ancestors took to walking upright: to get a better look at things. Dogs, by contrast, evolved the ability to differentiate smells, to which they are a thousand times more sensitive than we are. Sight is not so important to them. We may wonder what their picture of the world would be like. It would be fascinating if dogs could describe their 'view' of things.

Would we recognise any of it? Could we even have a common language when concepts for them would relate to smells we cannot smell, and concepts for us to colours they cannot see? It is encouraging to think that all humans seem to be able to use the same conceptual ideas – which suggests they have a similar experience of the world from which to derive them.

On the other hand, that common experience relates to physical capacity for sensing the world which excludes a great part of the available information. We are becoming familiar with very different pictures of the world because of television, probably the most powerful educational tool we have. There are images of galaxies and stars from radio telescopes, X-rays of the human skeleton, brain scanning using sound waves, and heat-imaging using infra-red light that appears to be used by snakes and other creatures. These are all converted into visual images we can deal with, using visible light. We cannot have direct sensory access to those images of the world. Similarly, we 'hear' sound-echoing used by bats and dolphins to picture their world or for navigation, but only by changing the frequencies to what our ears can actually hear. Are we in fact genetically programmed to have a particular perception and therefore knowledge of the world we live in?

We cling to our familiar picture of the world, brought to us only by visible light (the light we can see), as a true picture: the *only* picture. From a purely practical angle, what else can we do? But what has it to say about what the physical world is really like? Enormous parts of the information about even the most everyday aspects of our environment are not accessible to us through our senses. Or, if they are, we ignore them.

Clearly, our brains select from the experiences we have. Someone who loses the ability to see may become much more aware of the other senses: may hear things and smell things of which the sighted person is unaware. You can demonstrate this very easily to yourself. Make a tape-recording of an ordinary hour in a room while you are busy doing things there. Listen to it afterwards; you will hear so many things you did not notice at the time: clocks ticking, birds singing in the garden, the noise of footsteps or chairs moving, the sound of your own voice. Similar things can be learned by closing your eyes and exploring by touch only.

You normally filter nearly all of this out, presumably because there has to be a limit to the amount of information about your environment that your brain and nervous system can process. So much of what is there you do not 'see' or 'hear' or 'feel' or 'smell'. What you select is what you need at the time.

What do we do with the information, such as it is, when we get it? How do we see the world, for instance? Do we have direct access even by vision to an external reality? Vision was once thought of as the experience of a spectator, seated behind a screen, watching a perfectly formed image of the world. What is wrong with this idea? We are forced to ask: how does the spectator see what is on the screen? The same way I see – a 'spectator' looking at another screen in his eye? And then another 'spectator', another screen *ad infinitum*, an infinite regression? It cannot operate like that.

Jonathan Miller in *States of Mind* gives the example of someone driving along a wet road. He *sees* a three-dimensional scene of slippery tarmac. What he actually *sees*, the image in the eye, is neither slippery nor three-dimensional. This can only mean that the person is subjectively and actively creating it by conjuring up a 'model in the head' of what is there. I gave, in Part 1, another example of driving: of lights coming towards you at night. The amount of sensory information is very small indeed. Yet you usually have no problem with it. You build an image of a vehicle to which the lights belong and decide what you have to do, according to what you think that vehicle is and what it is going to do.

Without an image of it all in your head you could not deal with it. It is the same with a slippery road. You see it as 'wet' or 'slippery' because of your previous experience of such things. You may be wrong. It could be a mirage caused by heat on the road: I expect you have seen that too. But given alternative explanations, you normally go for the most common first. These are 'alternative perceptual fictions'. They are fictions because you have invented them as explanations of what you actually see. What your eye receives is light: directly received from the head-lights, received by reflection from the wet road. The eye makes an image on the retina.

What happens then? is the important question. An analogy may help. Think of how a telephone works on a principle of coding and decoding signals. Sound waves, coded as electrical impulses, are sent down a wire and decoded back into sound at the other end. Similarly, the optic nerves must take information coded as chemical messages from retinal cells. Nerves that run from the retina are part of the brain, not separate from it. They are the means by which the central nervous system receives this coded information. What kind of code? By a complicated chemistry, the light seems to trigger pulses of electrical energy that are transmitted along the nerves and have to be decoded in the brain. The brain does not decode them back into light! What does it do with them?

All sorts of interesting things, obviously. For one thing the retinal image must be upside down, since the lens works much like a camera lens. Look through a camera lens and you will see that. Why don't you see the world that way up? Then again, the image must be constantly changing. You cannot hold your eyes still – they flicker. What happens when you move your gaze around the world? Try starting at one end of a wall and letting your gaze travel along to the other end: does the wall appear to move? The image on the retina of your eyes is streaming past in reverse and upside down. How is it that you see a stationary wall?

How, in addition, do you see it as a solid wall, if all that the retina has to go on is light reflected from the surfaces? What a complicated business it must be! We see a three-dimensional world. Having two eyes makes it possible for us to see objects in perspective, but how does it work? If you put a patch over one eye, you still see the world as three-dimensional even if you find it hard to judge distances.

Your brain must in some way set up a constructed image of the world you are perceiving. It has to *know* somehow that the world is solid and motionless: it is your eyes that are moving across it. You will have experienced the confusion of not knowing whether it is you moving or the world when you were sitting in a train at a station and another train next to you appeared to move. After all, before Copernicus everyone thought the earth was motionless and the sun went around it. That was their hypothesis; his was different.

Your mind/brain interprets sense data to make them match the image it has constructed. If they fail to match, you become confused: you look for other information to help you. You look out of the other window of the train; you try various other models to see if they match. This seems to be what your brain does, without your thinking about it: it tests out alternative hypotheses, it generates explanations or assumptions about what is there.

What you actually do is to explore the world, set up hypotheses or models of what appears to be there and then test to see how well it all matches. For much of the time, too, the hypotheses are constructed from very inadequate information. Even when there is very little sense data – as with the lights coming towards us in the car at night – we still make hypotheses.

Look at the drawings made by young children. There is a pattern to the way all children make drawings of the world around them. Fascinating studies have been made of this. Why are the people in the drawings so similar? and the houses? Where do children get their images from? Are they representing some inbuilt, innate, models?

This is how Gestalt theorists explained it. Either all children see people and houses very differently from the way adults see them, or they deal with what they see differently. Are the 'models in the head' they use different from those of adults? If they are the same for all children, where do they come from? Or maybe it is physiological, something to do with their ability to co-ordinate hand muscles.

As we grow we accumulate experience: we appear to create more sophisticated models of reality to enable us to deal with the world and make sense of it. We certainly must have a larger and larger range of models to choose from, unless our experience is very restricted even in adult life. T. E. Lawrence in *The Seven Pillars of Wisdom* told how the tribesmen of the desert, who were brought up without representational images of people (it is taboo in Islam to make images of people) could not make any sense of a drawing he did of their Sheikh. The best guess one made was that it was a foot. They apparently could not 'see' it. Lawrence said that their ability to visualise people had atrophied.

Professor Richard Gregory of Bristol University worked with visual puzzles. He writes in *States of Mind*, 'It turns out that the generation of fictions is very important for seeing the richness of reality from the very limited amount of data, or information, which the senses can handle or have available to them. So generation of fiction is intimately bound up with generation of fact.' He identifies four kinds of illusion. Here are just two: ambiguity and fiction.

Try your own 'perceptual brain language' on the illustrations in Figure 10. The three boxes look like three-dimensional objects, but they are just lines on a flat piece of paper: how does that happen? Gregory wrote, 'Sometimes you find one face looks like the front and then suddenly it'll flip and become the back. You can make it happen when you blink, or when you move your eye about; it will also flip entirely spontaneously.' Try!

It is the ambiguity that we have problems with. We set up and test one of the possible alternative hypotheses of how this cube 'is', in a fictitious three-dimensional world we also create for it. We test out another, equally probable, hypothesis. We cannot come to a definite conclusion with the available evidence, so we try again . . . and again.

We do all this quite unconsciously too. It just keeps flipping from one to another. It is very difficult for us to control it. Try! This suggests that the part of the brain that is testing the hypotheses is not the same part we use to take conscious control, or even to think about what is happening and why. Is there a duality in the mind?

The 'Rubin vase' in Figure 11 shows two different kinds of object, the vase and a pair of faces, in profile. These are actually two different objects, and to get this to work, says Gregory, the objects must have roughly equal probabilities. The brain switches and tries out the two hypotheses.

*Fig. 10   Ambiguities*

*Fig. 11    The Rubin vase* (from *Synopleveda Figures*, S. Rubin, 1915)

Figure 12 was devised by an Italian psychologist, Gaetano Kanizsa. The central triangle in each of the figures is an illusion. Although we see the edges as sharp and clear, they are not there. There's no actual brightness difference across the edges: the triangle must be constructed by the observer, says Gregory. The lines seem to curve if you simply reduce the angles of white in the dark sectors: the visual system seems to join up an imaginary triangle with curved sides.

You actually *see* a white triangle, although all that there is on the paper is gaps in a black triangle and some little bits out of black circles. I have tried this with Japanese university students who have never seen it before: they also see the triangles, so it is not cultural conditioning. It seems to be a genetically determined trait in humans to make these hypotheses of 'the world out there'.

'If it's a figure that's got surprising gaps which are unlikely to occur by chance, it's more likely there's something getting in the way, producing gaps, than that

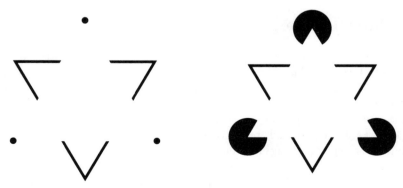

*Fig. 12    The Kanizsa figures* (from *Synopleveda Figures*, S. Rubin, 1915)

235

something is missing. This is the way the brain deals with experience. It is normally very useful to go on *seeing* parts of objects, or at least to believe that they're there, when they're hidden by something nearer,' says Gregory in *States of Mind*. Otherwise, we have to believe in bits of objects existing, like the Cheshire Cat's grin – impossible!

# Hypothesising

Professor Gregory has described many more visual experiments of this kind. The main conclusion he comes to is that **perceptions are predictive hypotheses**. The test of a scientific theory is whether it can successfully predict what will happen. We appear to behave in this fashion in perceiving our world: we make hypotheses and then test them out. As Gregory points out, in the Kanizsa figures it is *absence* of signals that makes us 'see' the overlying triangles. We hypothesise the existence of the triangles to explain the gaps. And this is not something over which we can take conscious control.

Even if we know something is wrong we cannot will ourselves to *not* see it. You cannot stop yourself from seeing the white triangles that are not there. It is as if knowledge of the world or objects is built into the brain somehow, together with the rules for making guesses and matching which we cannot have access to in our consciousness. We cannot observe inside our brains to watch ourselves think.

Gregory comments in *States of Mind* that the process of evolution has created brain structures, just as it has shaped our noses so that we do not drown when it rains. We have noses like roofs to keep out falling rain; why not brain structures that 'incorporate a more and more accurate model of the universe in which it lives'? The brain seems to have 'rule-observing processes which in brain language are more and more accurate pictures of the world'.

It exhibits pattern-making processes also. Are they the same? I suggested in Chapter 19 that the two hemispheres of the brain appear to have different functions or preferences related to pattern-making (images) and rule-making. Does this help to explain some of the enigmas of perception?

# Teaching/learning

It is essential that teachers know how people perceive the world if they are to help students to learn. A carpenter works with the grain of the wood in order to shape it successfully. We must work with the normal processes of learning if we are not to create problems for students rather than to help them learn.

Since our normal behaviour in learning is to explore, setting up and then testing hypotheses, we should recognise this in the strategies we devise in teaching/learning. Think, again, about the baby as it explores its world using all its senses; think too about the adults in Tony's class (Case Study 4).

People learn by testing hypotheses, but they have to want to. What drives them to put a great deal of effort into it is equally complex. No doubt a part is played by dissatisfaction: we modify hypotheses or models when they do not fit. If people are very happy in the conditions as they are (and with what the world is for them), they are not likely to change. It may or may not be a good thing for them to continue with their present models of the world and the way that affects their behaviour in it. It may be that the models they have are appropriate for their need. Needs change, however, and then there is a need for more appropriate models.

Teachers must remember that change is painful. There are costs in terms of self-image, adjustment, insecurity and so on. Students need our support as they deal with change. But since change is permanent, at least so long as we continue to evolve new technology, teachers will always be needed.

# 29 The Cognitive Revolution

'Most of the recently fashionable materialist conceptions of the mind – like behaviourism, functionalism or physicalism – end up denying, implicitly or explicitly, that there are such things as minds ... they deny that we do really *intrinsically* have subjective, conscious mental states.... If a scientific account of the world attempts to describe how things are, then one of the features of the account will be the subjectivity of mental states. My present state of consciousness is a feature of my brain.' John Searle *Minds, Brains and Science.*

We make progress in thinking about new ideas according to the kinds of analogies we have available to us: we compare our new ideas with things that are familiar. Searle is taking issue with those who believe the brain functions like a computer; that 'the mind' is an illusion created by the brain; and that we may be able to build a machine with 'artificial intelligence'. We use analogies all the time. In the seventeenth century, clocks offered an analogy for the workings of natural phenomena. Plato (429–347BC), the father of Western philosophy, showed the way; in order to make them accessible to people generally, his approach to problems in philosophy was to argue by analogies. His most famous comes from *The Republic* where he invites us to imagine prisoners who are inside a cavernous chamber underground, chained in such a way that they must face a wall, on to which a fire throws the shadows of all manner of objects, including figures of men and animals passing by; they hear only echoes of voices rebounding from the wall. Since they have no other experience to compare them with, they must take these shadows for 'reality'. What if someone were to go out of the cave into the light, to be dazzled by its brilliance and the colours of the 'real' world? What if he then came back and told them what he has seen? Clearly, they would reject him as deluded.

For Plato our world was merely shadows: 'ideas' existed in a 'real' (i.e. a permanent and unchanging) world accessible only to a disciplined intellect. Our world lacked permanence: everything was in constant flux. The concept of a permanent, 'real' other world of the mind is the basis of many great religions. It has provided a fertile ground for the mind–body controversy.

The revolution that occurred in psychology was the result of the invention of machines that appeared to behave intelligently. That made it possible to use taboo words like 'purpose' and 'goal-seeking', excluded from use in discussion of psychological behaviour since they were seen as mentalistic concepts – not demonstrable, objective, scientifically acceptable evidence.

Ever since Newton's time, it was thought that if you couldn't point to an object or some phenomenon, see an example of it in the physical world, you had better ignore it. You could not study it scientifically. Behaviourists said: introspection is all very well, but show me 'a goal' out there.

Once you have radar that locks on to a target, or an automatic pilot that is designed to keep you on a predetermined course, you can show that purpose and goal-seeking are eminently respectable 'out there' ideas that explain what happens. The new machines made it perfectly sensible to say: Look! it went for that target. The word 'target' is about the future. So is the future somehow controlling the present? In what sense do we talk of cause and effect if a cause is in the future?

Machine-talk has crept into thinking about our mental behaviour. The language of 'coding and decoding information' comes from information theory – intended to improve radio signalling, and applied to processing by computers. Some experimenters in teaching techniques, such as Edward de Bono, see the brain as largely a pattern-making instrument that works by encoding information into patterns which it can then store and retrieve in order to match with sense data as it arrives and is processed in the brain.

'The late twentieth century has witnessed an explosion in (our) ability to store knowledge in our culture rather than in our brains. We have invented a new phrase for such techniques: information technology. Information is treated as a commodity, something that can be bought and sold, measured in bits (binary digits, yes-or-no decisions). But information theory is a quantitative theory, whereas most things that are important to humans are qualitative ... those aspects of a message that matter to human beings, such as meaning and understanding, do not fit readily into a crude information-theory mould.' Cohen and Stewart *The Collapse of Chaos*. The analogy above is with a digital computer that uses electronic processors to 'encode' input as data and facilitate 'memory storage' of that coded information in 'data-base files' with a 'retrieval system'. Everything is 'systematised' in 'machine code' that only the machine can read. Since some of the functions of the brain appear to be describable in this kind of language, is the brain then a computer?

Searle says, 'Because we do not understand the brain very well we are constantly tempted to use the latest technology as a model for trying to understand it. In my childhood we were always assured that the brain was a telephone switchboard ("What else could it be?") ... or a telegraph system. Freud often compared the brain to hydraulic and electro-magnetic systems. Leibnitz compared it to a mill, and I am told that some of the ancient Greeks thought the brain functions like a catapult. At present the metaphor is the digital computer.' *Minds, Brains and Science*. Searle argues that those who believe they may build machines with 'artificial intelligence' are wrong. 'Minds have mental contents; specifically they have semantic contents.' (*ibid*). Computers do not 'think', they just follow programs: they manipulate symbols by computation, but they do not assign 'meanings' to the symbols; and they do not create 'internal, mental, models of reality'.

What is the process of encoding like? De Bono thinks of the brain as being responsive to patterns that become etched into the fabric of the brain in some way. His simile is of water that makes deeper and deeper channels in a substance. Where the channels go depends as much on the qualities of the substance (its resistance) as on the incidence of the water. Material that is soft will be channelled into more easily. The brain by analogy may be more receptive to establishing some patterns than to others.

In *Lateral Thinking*, he argues that the brain encodes into recognisable patterns. When new sense data is received there is a matching process with encoded patterns. Clearly, the least resistance will occur where the deepest channels have formed from previous experience. So we tend to have preferred ways of seeing the world. They are not innate but the result of experience, whereas the Gestalt theorists would have argued for innate brain structures that programme us to perceive the world in a particular way.

De Bono sees the activity of the brain as setting up hypotheses related to such pattern-matching behaviour. His view of creative thinking is totally different from that of the Gestalt school. It is not about the 'whole' at all, but about patterns that may build into wholes. The major problem he sees is that we will hypothesise the 'wrong' pattern, and that this will inhibit our making sense of things when new information arrives.

One effective way of avoiding this happening, since we are now aware of it, is to try to avoid setting up a hypothesis that an experience is of a specific pattern: what he calls **vertical thinking**. Once you have set yourself on a particular path by such a hypothesis you will block out all other possible patterns and so are very likely to miss another more useful pattern that makes better sense of the whole. You should aim to keep your options open, to allow your mind to generate numbers of different patterns out of the experience. It can then match against a range of possible coded patterns as additional sense data provide additional information. This he calls **lateral thinking**: it proceeds on a broad as against a narrow front.

Would he quarrel then with Professor Jerome Bruner? who comments in *States of Mind* that the most practical thing you can do is to have an hypothesis that you can reject on the basis of experience. This clearly echoes Popper's view of science.

Bruner (born in 1915, and Professor of Psychology at Harvard and Cambridge) argues that we 'perceive' the world by active selection from sensory information. It depends on setting up hypotheses and testing them out, as described by Richard Gregory. Previous experience is the key to what actually is perceived. And it is also strongly determined by the society in which the individual lives – by its culture.

So **knowledge is seen as a continuing process in the brain**, not a product. It cannot be packaged in 'lumps' to be put into some new brain in some way. It has to involve active processing on the part of the learner. The brain of any individual will be selective, according to such intangibles as needs, values and attitudes. Many of these are made part of a person by cultural factors in the society he or she grows up in.

Thus learning will depend on how far these attitudinal aspects of behaviour will affect what the individual does with the new information or new sensory data. There will be rejection of those parts that are found threatening or culturally difficult to deal with.

New studies on attention and alerting showed how the brain deals with the 'information–knowledge' process. 'Arousal of the nervous system with active scanning was seen to occur when the model of the world stored in the brain was violated in some way, i.e. when it was inconsistent with the incoming information,' wrote Gregory. How does the process work?

- There must be seeking of some kind.
- There is a selective mechanism.
- There is a means of reorganising the concepts already established to accommodate the new information to produce modified concepts – and from these 'internal models' of the external world.
- The process involves hypothesising to explain incoming information, and some testing of the new models/concepts to see how far they are meaningful when used to explain the world of experience.

Not patterns, but 'internal models of reality'. Bruner argues that physicists came to realise that 'the data of physics were related to the models in the physicist's head – the models he had constructed in order to build his theory of the physical world'. 'Post-war psychologists were into mentalistic matters such as the selective filtering of experience, the construction of selective representations of the world in memory, strategies for co-ordinating information. Its sum total amounted to "the Cognitive Revolution"' (R. Bruner in *States of Mind*). Bruner dates this from 1932, the year in which Heisenberg was awarded the Nobel prize for physics for his statement of the Uncertainty Principle: a revolution in the way scientists viewed the ability to observe the world, one outcome of which was to question whether the observer was in fact creating the phenomena he was attempting to study by the method he used for observing them.

As the science of computing began to grow, it was possible to see 'stimuli' as forms of 'input'. Their significance depended on how you coded the input, where you put it for storage, how you retrieved it and how you matched it with other coded inputs. You could store not only inputs in the memory of the computer, but instructions as well. Instructions were like thought processes.

Bruner has a very different view of **competence** from that being used at present in the United Kingdom. Competence, he believes, is what students should be learning, rather than particular performances: central to the attainment of that end is the acquisition of correct modes of thinking. In this, there is a central role for perception.

We live in an amazingly complex world. The brain can only deal with a limited amount of information at any one time – there is 'limited channel capacity'. An internal model of the world will make it possible to 'chunk' information into manageable packets, and to use this model to guide the search for, and processing of, information constantly arriving. If this is what is in fact happening in physics, clearly 'objective, out there' becomes more a matter of 'interaction between the observer and the environment'.

If perception involves actively exploring the world with our senses, there must be some mechanism in the brain which enables us to tell the difference between sensations which result from what *we* do – our own movement – and sensations that result from the world's movement. If we explore the world with our eyes, the world does not seem to move. We are constantly moving and so are our eyes, but we never get the impression of the world moving. 'Neurological mechanisms which anticipate the state of affairs which will result from a forthcoming action are called "feed-forward" mechanisms to distinguish them from "feed-back" mechanisms which provide information about the result of such movements. In fact, the comparison between feed-forward and feed-back represents one of the most important processes in the nervous system. The difference between what was intended and what actually occurred is what we process to correct the movement' (R. Bruner in *States of Mind*).

Learning behaviour relates to the learner's ability to create strategies: defining goals and ways of achieving them. This will involve feed-forward and feed-back. We might see Kohler's chimpanzees in this light. It also is necessary for learners to have a conceptual model to work towards. They must analyse available information and think about what is to happen. They must be prepared to take risks, to test out the hypotheses and so on – to come back from failure and try again – to explore and experiment.

This is essentially a creative process. Since what we are striving for are models which are transferable to enable us to deal with changing conditions and new situations, learners must be taught to see single instances in terms of principles and generalisations. They must develop the cognitive skills that enable them to grasp principles and to apply them to concrete instances in changing contexts: adaptability.

Learning is mainly cognitive: acquiring information, transforming it by the assimilation of it with previous knowledge, and checking how the knowledge structure now constituted works in relation to explaining new situations.

It is not very helpful to separate learning 'about' something from the process of learning to do it. It is better to learn physics by doing what physicists do. And it is the same with teaching: you learn to generalise about teaching by having experience of teaching. Realism and discovery come from actively doing what you are setting out to understand. So long as you do then reflect cognitively on the experience, matching what you expected to happen with what actually happened.

Telling the student about it in an expository way may be useful in terms of 'alerting and attention' (what I hope is happening now for you reading this book), but it will only become a part of your mental 'model of it all' through experience. Only then can it be transferred and become usable.

Bruner proposed a 'spiral curriculum'. By this he meant that learning had to be constantly revisited. If knowledge is a process, so is acquisition of skills, attitude formation, and so on. They are all part of growth. The most commonly occurring mathematical figure in nature, particularly in living organisms, is the spiral. This is because organisms grow by multiplying cells and that creates, mathematically, a spiral.

No learning is once for all. We have to revisit it constantly to reshape our skills and knowledge. Rudiments early, and Bruner insists that learners must proceed by mastering each learning task or skill. The concept of mastery is a dynamic one: it is related to growth and maturity. Although learning does not occur as a continuum, but by spurts and periods of consolidation, mastery at each point is essential. Gaps in learning can and must be overcome by revisiting. Development and redevelopment matter.

The model I have developed for this book attempts to interpret discoveries such as these about the human capacity to learn into practice in teaching.

# Appendices

# Appendix 1: More to Learn

Sir Karl Popper (1902–95) changed the way scientists were thought to go about their business of inventing and validating theories. 'The acceptance by science of a law or of a theory is *tentative* only; which is to say that all laws and theories are conjectures, or tentative *hypotheses*; and that we may reject a law or theory on the basis of new evidence, without necessarily discarding the old evidence which originally led us to accept it . . .' *Conjectures and Refutations*. In *Objective Knowledge: an Evolutionary Account* Popper argued that evolution is best understood in terms of 'trial solutions' to problems met by creatures in their environment. Each is a tentative adaptation to the world the individual lives in. So, animals and plants incorporated these tentative solutions into their anatomy and behaviour forming the bases for later solutions, equally tentative.

Theories and ideas develop in the same way. Each starts from what a previous theory had proposed and challenges it against evidence and new ways of perceiving what is actually going on. For Popper, achievement in all human affairs happens in the same way: in politics, economics and art, as well as in science and technology. Progress in all fields depends critically on changes taking place under the impetus of critical evaluation of predictions made by theories as against what actually happens. Recent history shows how much more successful dynamic, open societies can be than those in which leaders defend ineffective or unworkable ideologies.

Popper showed that any task must start from a problem: we have to ask why it is a problem, and define it clearly. The degree of success we have in tackling (solving) the problem is determined by how clearly we perceived and set out that problem. To understand also writers on any scientific or social topic such as education and learning we need to know what the problem was to which they tried to find a solution: what the questions were that they asked, and how they arrived at the answers they proposed. Then we need to evaluate those 'answers'.

Addressing questions of this kind at Level 4 of Questions (see Activity 13 on page 180) will ensure that problems are not only defined, but repeatedly redefined through a critical evaluation that compares an initial hypothesis, educated guess, with what actually occurs. In all human activity, especially in teaching, this is the way we learn and progress. It will be clear that all the Tasks set out in this book are best seen as problem-solving exercises. In tackling these, I have encouraged you throughout the book to set up tentative solutions to learning problems your students face, and then to use evaluation critically as feedback to redefine the problems and look for better, more effective solutions.

Your perception of what is going on in your environment, and for your students, will have changed through the process. So also will the way you approach your students and your preparation. I strongly advocate an integrated learning process, where learning is seen as cyclical, and where we progress by using feedback and evaluation as the major assessment procedure. Where no solution is seen to be final: we can always do better.

A major problem for doctors is keeping up to date with changes in drugs and treatments. New discoveries are made all the time. Drug companies spend billions of dollars trying to develop new drugs; and new techniques using new technology have revolutionised the treatment of diseases. But the diseases fight back and new diseases are constantly arising, because of the use made of new technology and chemicals or as a result of environmental changes we make, often unwittingly. A great deal of a doctor's time must be spent making sure he or she is up to date. One effect, naturally, is that all doctors become specialists in certain narrow fields and must refer patients to other doctors for diagnosis and treatment outside their field.

What is true for doctors is true for most people in employment. Ours is a rapidly changing world: new technology and economic forces not only change the rules of the game, constantly it seems, but they create new ball-parks and new kinds of games. There was a time when 'training' could prepare a person for a lifetime of employment. But now, many skills become obsolete and knowledge out of date. One of the biggest obstacles is 'attitude change'. Education and training should concentrate on preparing students so that they can cope with change, know how to learn and relearn to adapt rapidly to that change.

One purpose of the programme in this book has been to help you to learn how to learn, to appraise the tasks you and your students need to undertake, to evaluate what is achieved and to adapt the learning so that it is more effective in achieving its purpose. It was also intended to ensure that the learning is transferable to any new context.

You must keep up to date. Education, both institutions and methods of teaching and learning have been forced to change in order to keep pace with the world they serve. Many of those changes have perhaps been arbitrary, the result of ideological processes rather than pressures from society and employment. Nevertheless, there is no sign that changes will become less painful in the future.

---

### TASK 25: Keeping up to date

Your own field of expertise will be experiencing development and change along with everything else. It is essential you keep up with what is happening. Documents are produced by examining boards or other bodies providing guidance to teachers, tutors or senior staff who undertake training roles as new initiatives in education and training are introduced. How familiar are you with these? Where can you find them? Can you use them to make practical, workable schemes of teaching and learning programmes?

What other information is there? How can you discover that and use it to help you make sense of what you are setting out to do?

**First**, make a list or a collection of relevant documents – at least know where they are kept and how to get hold of them.

**Second**, try to identify what it is you need to find out and where to look for the information you need.

This will change with time. So you need to review your needs.

**Third**, at an appropriate time, which you must decide, undertake some research in depth into initiatives in your field as they affect what you as teacher or trainer need to do.

# Appendix 2: Effectiveness and the Curriculum

Welcome to the end of this part of your journey. What you have been exploring in this book is your role as teacher in a particular context. I hope that you have found plenty to stimulate and interest you along the way. What you have learned will depend on what you have done: how busy and active you have been in using the programme of Activities and Tasks in the book.

You have probably discovered a great deal about yourself. Whenever I have asked teachers to evaluate their learning on a programme such as the one set up here, they have always told me that they have learned most about themselves. They discovered strengths and talents and many things that surprised them. They learned how to cope with demands made by circumstances and other people. They learned how to take control of what they and others were doing.

I hope you also have gained insight and skills. You should have developed a new way of looking at things, be more observant, be able to distance yourself, to take a critical view. And you should have learned the skills of evaluation.

## Where to now?

Every arrival is a point of departure. We evaluate in order to decide what to do 'now'. We can always be better at what we do. Learning is for tomorrow, or next year. After all, we cannot change the past. There is really no point in learning something as complex as how to teach well so as to engage students actively in their own learning, unless you make it a matter of habit. Revisiting and consolidation are essential.

So far, you have been thinking about your own class or group of students: what they need to do in order to learn with your help. In most contexts, of course, students do not learn just with one teacher. They usually have a programme of studies of which your class forms part. What is the relationship between what they learn with you and what they learn with other teachers? How far are you aware of what other teachers teach? what they expect their students to do? what kind of learning behaviour they are looking for? How does what students learn in one part of their programme affect learning in other parts? It may be confusing for them to have contradictory messages from different teachers. In the past, it was usually left entirely to students to try to make links between different parts of their programme; and often enough there were no links – learning, or rather teaching, was divided into discrete 'boxes'.

Curriculum design is concerned to present an overview of the whole of a learning programme. The emphasis today is on teams of teachers working together; cooperating, too, with outside agencies, employers and others. Decisions by individual teachers have to be modified to take account of what others are doing. All should have a clear view of the intended outcomes of the learning overall.

---

### TASK 26:   Curriculum design

You have developed the necessary knowledge and skills to set about designing a learning programme with colleagues. So, working with a group of colleagues in your own context, design a programme of study, a curriculum that seeks to integrate all the learning activity for students in that context. Unless you share a perception of the overall learning that the programme is setting out to achieve, have an agreed sense of the curriculum design, you cannot contribute effectively to the overall achievement of your students.

The curriculum must motivate them and it should be designed to help them learn efficiently by using appropriate strategies of learning. The design should seek to integrate the disparate elements of syllabus content to provide effective learning experiences which are coherent overall.

---

# Effectiveness

A strategy is an overview, a model in the head if you like, which enables us to know what we are trying to do or how we perceive it happening. Although there are many strategies that may be used in the design of curriculum, some are more effective than others. In considering curriculum design for students at any level, it is helpful to have a view of the 'whole' as well as the parts. What is to change here? Surely, behaviour as a whole.

I have used the word 'competence' repeatedly throughout this book. You may still be a little vague as to what the word means. This may be because competence is a developing concept; the meaning and use of the term change with time and with who is using it and for what purpose. Most words tend to work like that. My own use of the word derives from a view I take of what is involved in demonstrating competence in a role. I designed a diagram (Figure 13, on page 251) to present visually an overview of it.

Competence can be viewed in a narrow sense – 'can do' statements related to specific, defined tasks – or in a broad sweep: 'able to take responsibility for ...'. I choose to use the latter mainly for the reason that training in specific tasks is highly contextual and does not allow for transferability to new contexts. Nor does it address the problem of 'Can do ... intelligently'. Whereas if we consider roles that people occupy, we can design training that is generic and will be transferable from one context and responsibility to another.

The role of 'teacher' embraces many other 'roles' and skills that a teacher must be prepared to learn. Some training programmes identify up to 12 roles and seek to develop those independently, but in parallel. For example, they may identify the role of 'tutor', or at some levels that of 'counsellor'; the role of 'assessor' may also become a major one. As you make progress in your career, you will find yourself undertaking many roles, but it is important to avoid isolating those roles from the major role of 'teacher'.

It is the level of responsibility that determines 'roles'. In designing the learning in this book, I assumed that you first have responsibility at the level of a class. The second part assumed greater responsibility: for a programme of learning activity with a group of students over, say, an academic year. Implied in that was a change in the way your role as teacher was defined as well as deeper understanding and increased levels of skill. You were asked to consider tutoring, for example.

Analysis is fairly easy to do. We can break down behaviour into constituent parts. Identifying criteria does just that. We can, if we wish, train parts and test them. What is more difficult to do is to put the parts back together, to synthesise them into the behaviour as a whole that we really are trying to achieve.

The language used in discussion of competence shifts. There is much more emphasis now on 'effectiveness in a role'. This is to recognise that tasks do not make sense in a vacuum – they relate to context and role. It is the role that integrates the parts.

But there is much more to effectiveness in a role than technical skill in achieving specified tasks. To identify what is required a person needs a conceptual framework – that is, to be able to grasp what the role is about, to understand what purpose it serves and what are the essential qualities and attitudes that a person needs in order to fulfil the role successfully. Insight into the way this role fits with roles of other people is essential; so is an understanding of the theory as well as the practice, the underpinning knowledge that enables him or her to use skills and expertise intelligently: to think through problems, set targets, design action plans, get properly organised.

1 Let's look at an example. If I say the words 'personal assistant', you will immediately have a view of what the person is likely to be doing; there is a concept that you understand. Anyone who is to undertake such a role has to work with this concept. But there are so many more concepts, understanding, insights that he or she will be expected to grasp to become effective in the role. Training must develop this conceptual grasp/framework.

2 There is no such thing as 'personal assistant', an abstract concept; there are only particular people who are engaged in specific contexts. Their role depends critically on the role of others, especially the person they assist.

Without full understanding of the context, and the demands that are made in the context and by others, we cannot design any training programme related to tasks, as we do not know what the trainee will be expected to do or at what level of competence. Will the trainee be required to keep accounts? use a wordprocessor or a fax machine? What skills will need to be developed? It depends on what the context requires. So much training has had to guess and provide for general possibilities that it often happens that the skills someone really needs are not included while others are practised that are never used – or the context demands things are done quite another way.

So, the concept of someone's role is modified to take account of the context they are actually working in. In designing training, we must attempt to develop tasks that are generic and transferable (and develop insight and skills that are equally transferable), but that require learners to interpret them in their own context to make sense of them.

3 This cannot be all, however. We appoint people, not personal assistants. The person in the role makes it what it is. If that person is to be effective, he or she has to develop those personal qualities that the role demands. These require growth that results from experience by using experience intelligently. A training course must concentrate on self-assessment, taking responsibility for one's own learning. It cannot be set up so that external assessors test task competence.

4 Once we have a mechanism for developing the framework for a design that will deliver effectiveness in role, we can then analyse what tasks and technical skills the role requires. We can set about developing them, ensuring if we can that learning is transferable to other contexts.

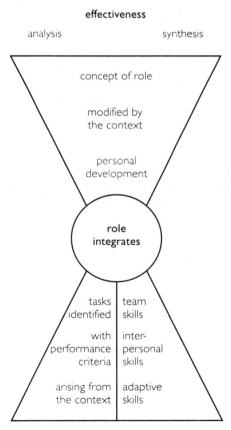

Fig. 13   An overview of effectiveness in any role

We can also apply quite demanding performance criteria. But we should ensure that the criteria identify good practice in fulfilling aspects of the role. The tasks have to become habitual: the skills are a means to an end – to do the job.

5 At low levels of responsibility, that may be enough. There is clearly an absolute necessity that people do have sufficient insight and skill to do the job properly.

But it is rare for people to be isolated, working on their own. The great majority work as part of a team. A personal assistant can only be as good as the boss. Together, they may form a good team (or not). In terms of effectiveness, it is essential that they do.

At all levels beyond that of no responsibility at all, there is a pressing demand for the development of interpersonal skills. How they work depends again on the context. Training programmes must, however, concentrate on those learning activities that will develop these skills.

6 But no amount of good practice and skill is much use if, when circumstances change or new challenges arise, they become outdated and an obstacle rather than a help. Dinosaurs were among the most successful creatures ever to evolve. Why did they become extinct? It seems that they could not adapt to the catastrophic changes that happened in their environment.

This has happened so frequently in the past decades in our highly technological and rapidly changing world. Dinosaurs die: adaptable mammals thrive. Training in tasks may make for highly proficient skilled workers so long as things stay the same. Adaptability requires problem-solving skills, and the ability to design and take control of what you do. Training programmes have to make sure learners are able to adapt.

I hope it is clear that the design of the programme in this book for teachers exhibits the logic of the above argument. Competent teachers have to be effective in the roles they undertake.

**How far will the curriculum you design with your colleagues help students to become competent and effective in the roles they occupy?**

# Suggestions for Further Reading

Annett, J. *Feedback and Human Behaviour*, Penguin (Harmondsworth), 1969

Ardrey, R. *The Social Contract*, Fontana (London), 1971

Ausubel, D. *Educational Psychology: A Cognitive View*, Holt, Rinehart and Winston (New York), 1968

Belbin, R. M. *Management Teams: Why they Succeed or Fail*, Heinemann (London), 1981

Berelson, B. and Steiner, G. *Human Behaviour: Inventory of Scientific Findings*, Harcourt Brace Jovanovich (New York), 1964

Berne, E. *Games People Play: Psychology of Human Relationships*, Grove Press (New York), 1964; Penguin (Harmondsworth), 1970

Bligh, D. *What's the Use of Lectures?*, D. A. Bligh (London), 1971; Penguin (Harmondsworth), 1972

Block, J. H. *Mastery Learning: Theory and Practice*, Holt, Rinehart and Winston (New York), 1971

Boud, D. *Enhancing Learning Through Self Assessment*, Kogan Page (London), 1995

Boud, D., Keogh, R. and Walker, D. *Reflection; Turning Experience into Learning*, Kogan Page (London), 1985

Bourner, T. and Race, P. *How to Win as a Part Time Student*, Kogan Page (London), 1991

Brady, M. *What's Worth Teaching?*, SUNY Press (New York), 1989

Bruner, J. S. *The Process of Education*, John Wiley (New York), 1977
*Actual Minds, Possible Worlds*, John Wiley (New York), 1986

Buzan, T. *Use Your Head*, BBC Books (London), 4th edn, 1995

Castling, A. *Competence-based Teaching and Training*, Macmillan (London), 1996

Chapman, A. H. *Put Offs and Come Ons*, Putnam Berkley (New York), 1968

Coating, B. F. *Science and Human Behaviour*, Macmillan (London), 1953

Daines, J., Daines, C. and Graham, B. *Adult Learning Adult Teaching*, University of Nottingham, 3rd edn, 1993

Davies, I. K. *The Management of Learning*, McGraw-Hill (New York), 1971

de Bono, E. *Lateral Thinking: a Textbook of Creativity*, Penguin (Harmondsworth), 1990

Ebel, R. L. *Essentials of Educational Measurement*, Prentice-Hall (New Jersey), 1972

Edney, P. *A Systems Analysis of Training*, Pitman (London), 1972

Egan, G. *The Skilled Helper*, Brooks/Cole (London), 2nd edn, 1995

FEU *Managing the Delivery of Guidance in Colleges*, FEU (London), 1994

Gagné, R. M. *The Conditions of Learning*, Holt, Rinehart and Winston (New York), 4th edn, 1985

Gelb, M. *Present Yourself*, Guild Publishing (London), 1988

Goldner, B. *The Strategy of Creative Thinking*, Prentice-Hall (New Jersey), 1963

Gregory, R. L. *Eye and Brain*, Weidenfeld & Nicolson (London), 1977
*The Intelligent Eye*, Weidenfeld & Nicolson (London), 1970

Hall, E. T. *Silent Language*, Fawcett, Premier Books (New York), 1959

Handy, C. *The Gods of Management*, Pan Books (London), 1979

Herzberg, F. *Work and the Nature of Man*, World (New York), 1966

Hilgard, E. and Bower, G. *Theories of Learning*, Appleton-Century-Crofts (New York), 1966

Hills, P. *Teaching and Learning as a Communication Process*, Croom Helm (London), 1979

Hoffman, B. *The Tyranny of Testing*, Crowell-Collier Press (New York), 1962

Hollander, E. P. *Leadership Dynamics*, The Free Press (New York), 1978

Hoyle, F. *The Intelligent Universe*, Joseph (London), 1983

Hudson, B. (ed.) *Assessment Techniques*, Methuen (London), 1973

Jacques, D. *Learning in Groups*, Kogan Page (London), 2nd edn, 1991

Jarvis, P. *Adult and Continuing Education Theory and Practice*, Routledge (London), 2nd edn, 1995.

Jessup, G. *Outcomes: NVQs and the Emerging Model of Education and Training*, The Falmer Press (London), 1991.

Kohler, W. *The Mentality of Apes*, Harcourt Brace Jovanovich (New York), 1925

Kounin, J. S. 'An analysis of teachers' managerial techniques' in Morrison, A. and McIntyre, D. (eds) *The Social Psychology of Teaching*, Penguin (London), 1992

Magee, B. *Popper*, Fontana (London), 2nd edn, 1985

Marland, M. *The Tutor and the Tutor Group*, Longman (London), 1989

Maslow, A. *Motivation and Personality*, Harper and Row (New York), 1954; Addison Wesley Longman (New York and London), 1987

Mason, R. *Using Communication Media in Open and Flexible Learning*, Kogan Page (London), 1994

McConnell, J. V. *Understanding Human Behaviour*, Holt, Rinehart and Winston (New York), 1983

Miller, G. A. *Psychology: The Science of Mental Life*, Harper and Row (New York), 1962; Penguin (Harmondsworth), 1966

Miller, J. *States of Mind, Conversations with Psychological Investigators*, BBC Books (London), 1983

Morris, D. *Manwatching*, Panther Books (London), 1978

Moseley, D. *Helping With Learning Difficulties*, Open University Press (Milton Keynes), 1976

Nash, R. *Classrooms Observed*, Routledge & Kegan Paul (London), 1972

Nierenberg, G. I. *The Complete Negotiator*, Souvenir Press (London), 1987

Oborne, D. J. *Ergonomics of Work*, John Wiley (New York), 1982

Peng, T. H. *Fun With Chinese Characters:* Straits Times Collection, Federal Publications (Singapore), 1980

Piaget, J. *Language and Thought in the Child*, Routledge & Kegan Paul (London), 1926
*Behaviour and Evolution*, Routledge & Kegan Paul (London), 1979

Popper, K. *The Logic of Scientific Discovery*, Hutchinson (London), 1972
*Objective Knowledge: an Evolutionary Approach*, Oxford University Press (Oxford), 1981

Rackham, N., Honey, P. and Colbert, M. J. *Developing Interactive Skills*, Wellens Publishing (Northampton), 1971

Reeves, F. *The Modernity of Further Education*, Bilston College Publications and *Education Now* (Bilston), 1995

Reynolds, V. *The Biology of Human Action*, Freeman (Oxford), 1980

Rowntree, D. *Assessing Students: How Shall we Know Them?*, Harper and Row (London), 1977; Kogan Page (London), 2nd edn, 1987

Satterly, D. *Assessment in Schools*, Blackwell (Oxford), 1981

Shannon, C. and Weaver, W. *The Mathematical Theory of Communication*, University of Illinois Press (Illinois), 1949

Shostrom, E. *Man – the Manipulator*, Bantam (London), 1967

Skinner, B. F. *The Technology of Teaching*, Appleton-Century-Crofts (New York), 1968

Sotto, E. *When Teaching Becomes Learning: a theory and practice of teaching*, Cassell (London), 1994

Sperry, L. *Learning Performance and Individual Differences: Essays and Readings*, Scot Foresman (Glenview III.), 1972

Sutcliffe, J. *Adults with Learning Difficulties; Education for choice and empowerment*, NIACE/Open University Press, 1990.

Watson, J. B. *Behaviourism*, J. B. Lippincott (Philadelphia), 1924

Wertheimer, M. *Productive Thinking*, Harper (New York), 1959

Whitehead, A. N. *The Aims of Education and Other Essays*, Williams and Norgate (London), 1950

Willmott, A. S. and Fowles, D. E. *The Objective Interpretation of Test Performance*, NFER Publishing (Windsor), 1974

Wisker, G. and Brown, S. (eds) *Enabling Student Learning: Systems and Strategies*, Kogan Page (London), 1996

Woodcock, M. *Team Development Manual*, Gower Press (Farnborough), 1979

# Index